The Brian Epstein Story

The Brian Epstein Story

compiled and written by Deborah Geller
edited by Anthony Wall

ff

faber and faber

First published in Great Britain in 1999
by Faber and Faber Limited
3 Queen Square London WC1N 3AU
This paperback edition first published in 2000

Photoset by Parker Typesetting Service, Leicester
Printed in England by Mackays of Chatham plc, Chatham, Kent

A CIP record for this book
is available from the British Library

ISBN 0-571-20156-3

2 4 6 8 10 9 7 5 3 1

This is for Nigel Finch
who should have been here

Contents

Acknowledgements

Just as films are collaborative efforts, so books depend on the kindness and hard work of others. So there are many others I need to thank for the help and sympathy in helping the book of the film to see the light of day.

Alison Willett really shouldn't be thanked. Somehow there should be a way to include her on the title page. Her dazzling efficiency, reliability, good humour, inexhaustive energy, proofreading skills (notice all the commas), computer savvy and visual intuition made it possible to complete this book. *The Brian Epstein Story* is partially hers.

Thanks to Matthew Evans and Clare Reihill at Faber and Faber for their enthusiasm and patience.

In New York, Mark McDonald gave me the time and more understanding than he should in allowing me to neglect some major responsibilities to complete this project. Damian Fowler helped out on some early editorial work and always manages to appear enthusiastic about the obsessions of an older generation. Jon Savage came up with the idea for an *Arena* on Brian Epstein in the first place and has gone on to be one of the best telephone pals in the world. Diana Mansfield, beyond her work on the film, offered arcane and priceless information on where they are now.

I also have to thank my friends and neighbours Karen Denker, Rob Marx and Paul Bertaccini and my father Arthur Geller for the meal breaks which couldn't have been much fun for them. Those friendly voices on the phone, Wayne King, Francis Liscio, my sister Ruth Athan and mother Annette Mac-Nair also provided much needed diversion and encouragement.

Dilly Barlow's generosity during the final push was way beyond the call of duty. When the production combine took over her home, she did nothing but make conditions comfortable, from providing delicious meals to turning on the central heating in the middle of the day to letting us kidnap her computer. I can't imagine anyone being more gracious.

In the Arts and Classic Music Department of the BBC, Erica Banks was once again the unit manager made in heaven.

Some others who made life infinitely easier: Jessica Taylor at the *Arena* office, Bob Spitz, Malu Halasa and my Macintosh Powerbook Duo 2300cs that performed with distinction on both sides of the Atlantic.

Finally, if you're uniquely fortunate, there are a handful of friends in your life without whom your life is unimaginable. Ever since we distinctly did not hit it off at a party at the ICA more than a hundred years ago, Anthony Wall has been one of those friends. For the chance to do this book, work on the film, for all he has taught me and all that I know as a result of knowing him, for the opportunities he has given me, I wish I knew how to thank him adequately. I just know that without his friendship, I would have no stories to tell at all and I hope he realizes how much I treasure that.

DEBORAH GELLER, NEW YORK & LONDON, MARCH 1999

I'd like to thank Jon Savage for suggesting a film about Brian Epstein in the first place and for his advice and insight; Diana Mansfield, particularly for her acute understanding of life in Britain in the '50s and early '60s and how it feels to be a fan; film editors Roy Deverell and Guy Crossman for their skill and patience; cameraman Luke Cardiff, his assistant Louis Caulfield & sound recordist Godfrey Kirby for all their support during filming; Michael Dobson in BBC Co-productions for never taking no for an answer.

Thank you to Reggie Nadelson for starting the ball rolling and to Matthew Evans for making it happen.

Above all I want to thank all the contributors and Henry Epstein whose help throughout was invaluable. Finally thanks to the late Derek Taylor. Derek inspired us to see the project through.

ANTHONY WALL
LONDON, MARCH 1999

Quotations from *A Cellarful of Noise* by Brian Epstein by kind permission of Souvenir Press Ltd.

We are grateful to the following for permission to reproduce photographs 1, 2, 3, 4 and 15 courtesy of the Epstein family; photograph 5, Redfern Library; photographs 6, 8, 9 and 10, Apple; photograph 7, Rex Features; photographs 11, 12 and 13, Bob Whitaker; photograph 14, Hulton Getty.

Prologue

JOHN LENNON: He was just a beautiful fella . . .
BBC REPORTER: What are your plans now?
JOHN LENNON: I don't know – we haven't made any.
We've only just heard.
.BBC TV NEWS, 27 AUGUST 1967

Peter Brown, friend and colleague: He'd driven to London, we don't know what happened after that. The next day, the houseman called me to say he was still in his room and he was concerned there was no sign of life.

Lonnie Trimble, former houseman/cook: It was Sunday, 27 August 1967, I turned on the television and it was announced that he was dead and I cried – like other people cried.

Paul McCartney: My feeling is that he would wake up in the middle of the night and wonder, 'Why am I not sleeping? I haven't had my sleeping pills –' in a drowsy state and take a couple more. Since then, of course, there've been millions of rumours – was he killed? Did he kill himself, or what?

Nat Weiss, US attorney: He was certainly in a very positive frame of mind. He'd made plans for the future, I'd spoken to him two days before and he was anything but suicidal.

Bryan Barrett, chauffeur: There were two strange expressions he used prior to his death, one was 'Beware the Ides of March' – this must have been about three weeks to a month before he actually died – and also, 'I feel I'm Svengali that's created a monster.'

Simon Napier-Bell, friend and rock manager: I felt like I'd opened up a newspaper, seen a riveting headline and had it snatched out of my hands before I could read the details. I wanted to spend more time with him. There was the whole story of the Beatles in his head and now he'd deprived me of it.

Joanne Petersen, personal assistant: Dr John Galway told me to wait outside the room. My immediate feeling was just real shock, shock and disbelief that this could happen. I didn't know if it was suicide, I didn't know if it was an accident.

Gerry Marsden, of Gerry and the Pacemakers: The last year of his life was very hard for Brian. He'd get very depressed and at times the whole thing just got to him – but it wasn't suicide. It was too much stuff. He was taking too much stuff.

Alistair Taylor, General Manager of NEMS Enterprises, Epstein's firm: Joanne opened the door to the house and just pointed upstairs and as I was halfway up, I heard splintering wood as they broke the door down. I was right behind the doctor – he was looking at Brian and Brian just looked like he was asleep.

Marianne Faithfull (with the Beatles and the Maharishi in Bangor): It was agony to be with the Beatles when there was nobody else there. Normally there were loads of minders around and there was no one. I mean they just didn't know what to do; it was the most terrible thing.

> When Brian died, I thought, 'We've fucking had it now.'
> JOHN LENNON, ROLLING STONE, 1970

Foreword

My father said, with great justification and dwindling patience, 'I just don't know what we are going to do with you.'

Nor did I, and it was another fifteen years before I showed any promise. I must surely be one of the latest developers of all time, for not until my mid-twenties did any pattern or purpose emerge in my life. If Keats had waited as long as I did to get going, he wouldn't have written more than a couple of poems before his death.

My parents despaired many times over the years, and I don't blame them, for throughout my school days I was one of those out-of-sorts boys who never quite fit. Who are ragged, nagged and bullied and beloved of neither boys nor masters.

At the age of ten I had already been to three schools and had liked none of them. I am an elder son – a hallowed position in a Jewish family – and much was to be expected of me.

BRIAN EPSTEIN

So begins *A Cellarful of Noise*, Brian Epstein's own account of his life, published in November 1964. The guardedness and frankness, the self-confidence and self-effacement of that passage are indicative of a character defined by contradictions. He was a one-off. There he was, being asked to write his autobiography at the age of thirty – three years later he would be dead.

He is remembered only for managing the Beatles, and for his mysterious death. When the writer Jon Savage came to me and suggested making a film on Brian Epstein, I was reluctant at first – we'd made so many films about the sixties on *Arena*, plus I thought that everyone knew enough about him and the Beatles already. However, the more I thought about it, the more I realized how little I knew about him. I began to remember just how famous he was, how, when the Beatles were mentioned, he was invariably mentioned in the same breath. He looked so different from them and yet in endless newspaper reports, newsreels of boarding and disembarking from planes, and in all the photographs, he and they looked oddly harmonious, like a flower among its leaves.

There had never been a manager like this before: suave, urbane, soft-spoken, utterly non-showbiz. Epstein wrote the primer that all his successors would depend on, learning through his mistakes as much as his triumphs. And while the mistakes can be dissected, analysed and understood, the triumphs have retained their mystery. No one has been able to repeat them since.

This is the story of an individual who had a hand in changing the world and whose credit has quietly evaporated. His was a picaresque journey, full of incident, twists and turns of fortune and passion. It might well be called 'The Tragical History of Brian Epstein'. For although he was always with the Beatles, he could never become one of them.

The speed with which he travelled from Liverpool shopkeeper to one of the most glamorous figures in the world puts him at the heart of the social changes of the sixties. Neil Aspinall, who was with the Beatles from the start, remarked to me, 'All of them, Elvis, Brian and the Beatles, went somewhere no one had ever been before, but the Beatles had each other. Brian was more like Elvis; he was out there by himself.'

The book that follows is woven out of the testimony of people who knew him, worked for him, loved him and disliked him. All of these witnesses were there in his life. There's no one in this book who wasn't there. Most of all, it's a collection of their memories.

We asked everyone to remember events of thirty, forty, fifty, even sixty years ago. The best observation I know about memory was written by the great surrealist film-maker, Luis Buñuel. At the beginning of *his* account of his life, *My Last Breath*, he wrote:

> Memory is what makes our lives. Life without memory is no life at all. Our memory is our coherence, our reason, our feeling, even our action. Without it we are nothing.
>
> As time goes by, we don't give a second thought to all the memories we so unconsciously accumulate until suddenly one day we can't think of the name of a good friend or relation – it's simply gone, we've forgotten it. In vain we search furiously to think of a commonplace work – it's on the tip of our tongues but refuses to go any further. Once this happens, this and other lapses, only then do we understand the importance of memory. Our imagination and our dreams are forever intruding in our memory. And since we're all out to believe in the reality of our fantasies, we end up transforming our lies into truths.

The truth of the book that follows is as self-evident as any story made up of recollections and impressions. It's a montage of the life and world of Brian Epstein, then, and now, as he exists in the memories of those who knew him.

ANTHONY WALL, EDITOR, *ARENA*, 1999

Cast

Joe Ankrah was the leader and oldest member of the Chants, a black a capella group, another of Brian Epstein's earliest signings. They left Epstein's management after a year as a result of his complete indifference to them. Joe stayed in music while his younger brother Ed Ankrah is now a graphic designer living in London.

Bryan Barrett was Brian Epstein's chauffeur and stayed on to drive for the Epstein family. He's now retired, but his interest in horses, going back to his Royal Guardsman days, helps him get work as a horseman in films and in re-creations of historic military battles.

Lionel Bart is best known for writing *Oliver!*, one of the most successful musicals of all time. He died of cancer on 3 April 1999.

Sid Bernstein: the Beatles concert at Carnegie Hall was Sid Bernstein's first independent production. He then went on to form the Sid Bernstein Organization, which presented most of the bands of the sixties British invasion. He became notorious during the seventies for his invitations to the Beatles to re-form, offering them up to a million dollars to do so. He is still involved in Liverpool cultural projects.

Peter Brown was one of Brian Epstein's closest friends and associates. He worked closely with the Beatles, running their day-to-day business until the end of Apple. He went on to work for Robert Stigwood and now has his own PR firm whose clients include the Prince of Wales.

Vera Brown was a friend of the Beatles in their early days and remains a dyed-in-the-wool Liverpudlian.

Stella Canter is Brian Epstein's paternal aunt. She lives with her husband MEIER, a retired lawyer, in a comfortable flat in Southport, and remains a homemaker *par excellence.*

Geoffrey Ellis was one of Brian Epstein's oldest friends and the CEO of NEMS. His legal and financial skills were later put to use by Elton John's management. He is now retired with a *pied-à-terre* off Eaton Square and a house in the South of France.

Marianne Faithfull lives in New York and Ireland. One of the great icons of the sixties, she continues to perform in a variety of musical genres, writes and acts on stage and in movies.

Yankel Feather began his art career in Liverpool and owned a club to make ends meet. He makes his living as a working painter and has recently moved to London from Cornwall.

Joe Flannery, Brian Epstein's childhood friend, had a variety of vocations before entering the music business. He went on to run the Star Club in Hamburg and now lives in Liverpool, where he makes cameo appearances in *Brookside*.

Johnny Gustafson was the guitarist for the Big Three, the second band Brian Epstein signed after the Beatles. He is still a musician.

Billy J. Kramer is alive and well on the oldies circuit along with the Dakotas. He now lives in New York State.

Helen Lindsay remains a working actress, making television and occasional West End appearances.

Alan Livingston was president of Capitol Records in New York. He is now retired and living in Los Angeles.

Paul McCartney has had a successful solo career after the break-up of the Beatles. The interview for this project was conducted at Carnegie Hall on the day of the American première of his most recent classical work, 'Standing Stone'.

Rex Makin was the Epstein family lawyer and neighbour on Queens Drive, Liverpool. He is one of the city's best-known lawyers and maintains a large suite of offices in the building that was once NEMS Whitechapel headquarters. He also writes a weekly column for the *Liverpool Echo*, 'Makin His Point'.

Gerry Marsden broke up with the Pacemakers in 1966. He has since appeared in the West End as well as touring in his own musical, *Ferry 'Cross the Mersey*, which includes a tribute to Brian Epstein. He has never lived anywhere other than Merseyside.

George Martin, the Beatles' producer, is now officially known as Sir George. Until his recent retirement, he was always regarded as one of pop music's best record producers.

Albert Maysles's reputation as a documentary film-maker is almost mythical.

He and his brother David made *Gimme Shelter*, as well as many other influential documentaries, like *Grey Gardens*. Their film about the Beatles for Granada was the inspiration for *A Hard Day's Night*. He continues to work in New York.

Simon Napier-Bell managed groups from the Yardbirds to Wham! He is also a writer, contributing to magazines and newspapers. He is the author of perhaps the funniest and most insightful book ever written about pop music, *You Don't Have to Say You Love Me* (first published 1982; 2nd edn, Ebury Press, 1998).

Ken Partridge designed Brian Epstein's house at Chapel Street, as well as John Lennon's in Weybridge. He is still a well-known interior designer.

Joanne Petersen, née Newfield, was Brian Epstein's personal assistant for the last two and a half years of his life. She later married Colin Petersen, the Bee Gees' drummer, and moved to Australia, where she has had a long and successful career as a record and music publishing executive.

Robert Stigwood, a manager and briefly Brian Epstein's business partner, became one of the biggest players in records and films. His relationship with his discovery, the Bee Gees, produced one of the largest-selling records of all time, *Saturday Night Fever*. He lives in retirement on the Isle of Wight.

Alistair Taylor was Brian Epstein's first personal assistant in the Liverpool family store. He then went to London with NEMS to become the organization's general manager, and stayed there until Brian's death. For a while, he personally managed the Silkie, one of NEMS's later signings. He is now a welcome fixture at Beatle conventions around the world.

Derek Taylor was the NEMS press officer. He became the most beloved public relations man in the entire music business. Among his clients were the Beach Boys, the Byrds, Captain Beefheart and Apple.

Lonnie Trimble, Brian Epstein's first 'houseman', is originally from Atlanta, Georgia. He now lives in Putney, London. He went into private catering for the likes of Ava Gardner but is now retired and planning his memoirs.

Nat Weiss was Brian Epstein's American business partner and co-founder of their record company, Nemperor. He remains a well-known music attorney in New York. His clients have included Cat Stevens, James Taylor and Bonnie Raitt.

Publisher's Note

All unattributed extracts are from Brian Epstein's own unpublished diaries and writings.

1. Could Try Harder

Stella Canter: My father Isaac was born in Lithuania in a village called Hodan. He arrived in England when he was probably about eighteen or nineteen, somewhere round there. He came to Liverpool and eventually met my mother, who lived in Manchester with her parents. I think my mother was born there but her parents came from abroad also. I think they were from Poland. My mother and father moved to Liverpool when they got married and they had six children. I came very late on, eleven years after my next sister. Harry was the third eldest. I think he was about sixteen years older than me. I had a sister older than him and another brother and then two more sisters between him and me. So I came as rather a shock.

My father was in the furniture trade. He had a furniture shop and he worked very hard. He used to go in exceedingly early and work all the hours that God gave him because in those days, I suppose, that was the only way to make a living and he had six children to support. It was very hard work.

Eventually he bought another shop, which was next to the furniture shop and which he called NEMS. It was a music store and the word NEMS actually stood for North End Music Stores. He made a way through the two shops so that you could get from one to the other. Eventually, they had another shop and two more shops in town also called NEMS.

Rex Makin: Brian's grandfather started the business that was a furniture store. They certainly didn't have much in the way of musical instruments but I suppose they had an odd twang or two.

Harry was born in England. The family lived in Anfield, which was by the football grounds, as a number of families did, and that is why his business was near by in Walton or County Road, the north end of the city.

I think that you might describe the store as very enterprising from someone who recently arrived here and had aspirations for a business progression.

Aunt Stella: Queenie came from Sheffield. She was eighteen and she may have met Harry in Bournemouth on holiday – I'm not absolutely sure. Maybe they met at a dance. I do know that he was absolutely nutty about her; she was very pretty and they were very much in love. Then they got engaged and eventually married.

I know that Queenie was eighteen when they got married in 1933. So Harry must have been twenty-eight, twenty-seven, because I have a picture in my mind of my brother at twenty-seven. For me he was always twenty-seven.

Rex Makin: The route from the City upwardly was from the centre. You started off with the gentry living in Sefton Park and from Sefton Park people moved up to Colderstones, Childwall and Mossley Hill.

Harry and Queenie definitely moved up in the world when they moved to Queens Drive. They lived at 197. I later moved next door at 199. The particular stretch of Queens Drive that we lived in might be described as the Bishops Avenue of Liverpool. Prestigious people lived here and the houses were somewhat above the normal standard for the age. It grew from the late twenties onwards and you can see by the architecture how it developed. We lived in the better, if I may call it the swisher part.

The dual carriageway wasn't always here. When I came to live here forty years ago there was a single carriageway. There were two lines of what appeared to be forest trees. When the city chopped all the trees down and they made a dual carriageway, the whole character was changed.

Aunt Stella: They built their home for themselves. They lived on Queens Drive. It was a detached house with five bedrooms and plenty of living rooms and so forth. It was very nice indeed. A lovely garden.

I thought it was a beautiful house and I suppose they did too. In those days that house was not as it is now. Queens Drive is now a very built-up area but it wasn't when they first built the house. There wasn't very much around there at all really when they first moved there. It was pretty open. I think their house was probably the last house along the road there. Now there's a big pub on the corner and there are other houses and shops very close by, but they weren't there then.

Uncle Meier: Harry and Queenie took continental holidays – that was highly unusual. I didn't see the South of France or, should I say, the Mediterranean until I was in the forces. We couldn't afford holidays in the South of France in those days but I think Harry and Queenie probably could because at that time Harry was in business with his father and his elder brother, Leslie. Of course they had quite a business in Liverpool and probably could afford a holiday in the South of France where we lesser mortals couldn't.

Rex Makin: They were very well known and very well respected and took their part in the local community. Harry was involved with Green Bank Drive

Synagogue where he was a regular worshipper. He was also one of the founders of the Old Age Home and became a treasurer.

Aunt Stella: Brian was born a year after Harry and Queenie were married and actually he was born on Yom Kippur, which is the holiest day in the Jewish calendar. That was 19 September. I presume it was in 1934. Then two years later Clive came along and they were a very happy family. It looked in those days that the Epsteins were a golden family, quite like a fairy story. Unfortunately, later on things became very sad.

Joe Flannery: Brian's father was in the retail furniture business. My father made furniture for Brian's father's business and of course that's how we knew each other. Two young lads, their fathers in the business and we came together.

I would be taken to Brian's house in Anfield Road. He had a nursery, of course, which I didn't. He had nice toys. I only had wooden toys that my father would make from scrap.

Brian had an advanced copy, I should think it was, of the Coronation coach that would be coming out for the forthcoming Coronation of our present-day Queen's mother and father. I fell in love with this coach because it was made of tin. It would have been about seven or eight inches long but it had six white horses, this beautiful little copy of the Coronation coach, and I liked it very much.

Of course, children like to take things home with them or borrow them, or, as we said, have a lend. I said, 'Can I lend this?' The answer was definitely not. You could feel the tension, or probably Brian's mother could feel the tension between us because she did ask, 'What's the matter?' and I said, 'Well, I want to lend Brian's Coronation coach.' She said, 'Lend it to Joseph. It can't come to any harm.' But it immediately did come to harm because he put a stop to it. His foot went right onto the coach part and trampled it.

Aunt Stella: I would think he was quite an old-fashioned little boy really. Both Clive and Brian were exceedingly well brought up. They were very polite. Perhaps they were little rascals at home but certainly when they were out they were very well behaved when they used to come to my parents' home, or anyone else's home for that matter. I think people used to say, 'They're lovely little boys.' They were always very nice.

I remember once chatting to him. I think I was baby-sitting and he was on his bed. He must have only been about seven or eight and he said, 'Tell me, Auntie, how is Mrs so and so?' He sounded like a little old man. I thought it was very funny.

BRIAN EPSTEIN'S SCHOOLS

- Prestatyn Nursery School, North Wales
- Beechenhurst College, Liverpool
- Southport College, Liverpool
- Croxton Preparatory School, Liverpool
- Liverpool College, Liverpool
- Wellesley School, Liverpool
- Beaconsfield Jewish School, Sussex
- Claysmore School, Somerset
- Wrekin College, Shropshire

Evacuation to various parts of Wales and the North of England during the war years caused my education to be disastrously broken.

In 1944 I returned with my family to our home in Liverpool and I started out at my fifth school, Liverpool College. It was planned that I should complete my entire education here, passing from the lower to upper school. After approximately a year I was expelled for being a lazy pupil, unwilling to pay attention and concentrate in the classroom.

A design for a theatrical programme which I had drawn in a mathematics period was produced as evidence. When my mother, distressed and weeping, pleaded with the headmaster that I should be given another term, he replied, 'Madam, we have no room here for your problem child.' It was known that anti-Semitism was an important factor.

At that time I feel sure I could not have worried greatly on my own behalf but I have no doubt that I felt the effect of my family's distress.

Much later, in a course of psychoanalysis I discovered that it was at this school, following my expulsion, that I can first remember my feeling for other male persons and a longing for a close and intimate friend on an entirely platonic and emotional level.

BRIAN EPSTEIN, A MEMOIR

Uncle Meier: At Brian's bar mitzvah, which was held at Green Bank Drive Synagogue, I found he knew his party piece, and his performance was very able and very competent. He was obviously well educated in Hebrew and Hebrew liturgy. Later on at the reception I also got the strong impression that he had a degree of refinement and culture which was unusual in a boy of his age and he had a good deal of self-assurance. It did occur to me that he was going places, even then. I felt that he was going to make a mark somewhere, even at the day of his bar mitzvah.

He appeared different and he was different in the sense that he'd acquired a sort of style about him which was absent in other people in their young years. I can't exactly say exactly what it was, how it came out, but he certainly spoke beautifully. He had a great deal of charm.

I was next sent to a Jewish Preparatory School in the South of England. Here I spent an occasionally happy and normal period although I was considered somewhat backward in my studies. The matter of always attaining low marks, being bottom of the class and receiving poor reports and other factors contributed to my thinking of myself even then as a failure, dullard and inferior person.

As I could not pass the examination for a major public school, I was finally accepted at a minor public school in the south-west. The school was a singularly fortunate choice in that I found the progressive and new ideas of the school (a greater degree of freedom was one of these) very suitable.

Naturally my first term at a public school was slightly marred by the ragging – being a Jew and not showing a great keenness for sport, the boys had good enough reason for my persecution. However, even amidst all this I found myself taking a serious interest in painting and thus deriving great pleasure. I was keen and encouraged. My work was considered extremely promising. To my delight a number of my works were bought by members of the staff.

In my second term, my academic studies showed signs of improvement. This, I think, came from a new-born confidence I found in myself. I even began to play games and tasted the delights of congratulation from friends after a successful sprint or a game of football. By my third term, I had acquired respect from both friends and teachers. For the first time in my life (and the last) I was not made to feel ashamed of being. I began to think for myself. The first half of that third term was, I think, perhaps the only content period in my life.

BRIAN EPSTEIN

Rex Makin: The Jewish community in Liverpool is a very old community. It's the oldest outside London and has a very rich tradition. Liverpool is a cosmopolitan city and not particularly anti-Semitic. We have the terrible sectarian business between the Catholics and the Protestants but it didn't really matter so far as Jews were concerned whether you were a Catholic Jew or a Protestant Jew.

Derek Taylor: The stratification of Liverpool society was plain to see and everybody knew it. You'd hear phrases like 'Jew Boy' from people of my father's generation who had a Victorian to Edwardian childhood. Anti-Semitism had always been there, but it wasn't that bad.

There were an awful lot of Jews in Liverpool at various levels, showbusiness and trade, and they were perfectly assimilated. It was always cosmopolitan. There wasn't a lot of racism either. There were a lot of people who were treasured because they were different. The Chinese were treasured because they brought a lot of colour into Liverpool life. There were a lot of Chinese restaurants, opium dens and things that seemed exciting.

In those days it was still such a big port, much in decline, but there were still a lot of liners coming in and going out.

Rex Makin: Brian's feelings about his Jewishness were ambivalent. His second name was Samuel but he rather disliked that, although today it's very fashionable to have a biblical name. He did not have an affinity with Jewish matters, whatever the cause was. I believe it was because he was the subject of anti-Semitism at school and perhaps other places as well. It gave him a kind of inferiority complex.

He went to a minor public school and I think there was endemic anti-Semitism there, as was the fashion, and misfortune perhaps, of that age.

At half term, my parents, who suspected with dislike both the school and the artistic element around me, phoned to say they had managed to have me accepted at Wrekin College, a wonderfully modern and clean public school nearer home in the north. Recently referring to a diary which I kept at the time, in a preface to the year 1949, I found I had written in reference to the forthcoming term at another, my ninth, school, 'I go only for my parents' pleasure.' Even then I realized how wrong this arrangement was and I regret that those words have a malicious sound. But I do not condemn or blame my parents for this or for anything else encouraging my upbringing. Their wrongdoings were committed unknowingly and with the best intentions and with love and devotion. And whilst the result, myself today, says little for the good of my upbringing, who can say with certainty that I was not born with a disability unfit for society to tolerate?

My wonderful new school proved to be fair enough. Lack of encouragement lessened the time spent at my easel. Games were the rule of the day. I enjoyed these at times and played with a fair degree of success. I disliked the fact that, as I then thought, my time for painting, acting and listening to music should be wasted in such frippery. Loneliness and lack of friends (which are two different things) entered my life to stick. I can remember endless turmoil and debate in my mind that I should need to 'walk to tea alone' whilst the other boys passed by laughing and joking in twos and fours. And later, on the not so infrequent occasions I was with another boy, I invented stories to prove my non-existent popularity.

After the first three weeks of my sixth term, I wrote a long letter to my father telling him that I had decided to become an actor and that I wished to train in London. I added that I hoped he would understand and that I was sorry to disappoint him by not going into the family business. A week later he came to tell me this was impossible and that it would be stupid to give up going into the business and security. I was furious and in a rage of temper demanded that I should leave school at the end of the term. As I was only being educated for business life I saw no purpose suffering any longer at school. My parents argued with me and asked me to stay on but I was stubborn and left at the end of term.

BRIAN EPSTEIN

Joe Flannery: Brian and I were of different faiths so naturally we were friends through the businesses but we didn't meet socially or through school or anything like that. So there was a big time lapse between when we first met with the Coronation coach and Brian going to public school and things like that. We didn't meet for quite a long time but then I took a shop on a road further along from the Epstein shop. It would have been about half a mile away and I got a bit curious, because now I'm a young a man and I've got my own business, and I went along to see the Epsteins. Mr Epstein said to me, 'You remember Brian, don't you?' I said, 'Oh yes.' I didn't forget my young adolescent days.

Going back a little bit further, I was working in the Adelphi Hotel as a commis waiter in the French restaurant there. I wanted to go away to sea like the rest of my mother's family did and I had to have some experience in silver-service waiting. One night, I was delighted to re-meet with Brian who was out with his mum, dad and his brother Clive having Friday night dinner. I was allowed to wait on them with bread rolls.

I wasn't allowed to do any silver service because I was only learning but Brian said to me 'Please don't stand at the table talking to me because my mother doesn't like it,' which I was too young or naïve to protest. I would probably say to myself today: servants or waiters can't stand talking to the élite, because that's what they were. They were like nobility to me and I really liked to watch them and mix with them. For him to say to me, 'Don't stand talking to me,' didn't upset me. I just immediately said, 'Oh, I'm sorry, I won't do that.'

Aunt Stella: The family expected Brian to go into the business, follow on in his father's footsteps as Harry had done, but that wasn't to be at first because Brian was not interested in that sort of thing. He would have liked to have been a dress designer. I found this out much later because I think that Harry and Queenie must have gone up the pole. This wasn't their scene at all.

Epstein: When I left school I went directly into my father's business and began to study all the various aspects of retail furnishing. I took a keen interest in display work and interior decoration. I worked well and had some new ideas. It is possible that even then I may have been able to settle down after all that had happened, remaining, as I did, unaware of my latent homosexuality, had I not been due for National Service.

In November 1952 I enlisted at Aldershot in the RASC, and within the first few weeks I met all sorts of young men who little by little revealed the strange homosexual life in London. Later, when I was stationed in Regent's Park, I never went near the notorious bars and clubs of which I had been told. But I became aware of other homosexuals everywhere I went.

In my free evenings I went to concerts, the more serious theatre and cinema, attended a course dealing with the making of furniture and began to read a great deal. Although I was nearly always alone, I never whilst I was in the army had a physical relationship with anyone. No one explained anything to me and I knew nobody to approach. (Indeed no one had explained to me the facts of life.) My mind was confused and my nervous system weakened.

I venomously hated nearly everything about the army and suffered at the merciless hands of the RSM. I remember one night travelling from Liverpool after a weekend at home on the midnight train; I was unable to sit quietly in my compartment and paced the corridors throughout the night. Several of my valuables were stolen from my luggage while I was away.

BRIAN EPSTEIN

Epstein applied for the RAF but was sent to the Royal Army Service Corps. One night, he returned to the Regent's Park Barracks in a large car. He marched in wearing a bowler hat, pinstripe suit and an umbrella over his arm. He drew suitably respectful salutes from the sentries and the guard commander, but was apprehended by the orderly officer, who charged him with impersonating an officer. He was confined to barracks and referred to four separate psychiatrists. He was discharged. His papers generously describe him as 'a conscientious and hard-working clerk of smart appearance and sober habits. At all times he is utterly trustworthy.'

I was not told what was wrong with me and not allowed to see a report of my medical discharge.

BRIAN EPSTEIN

Rex Makin: I first met Brian when he came out of the army and, of course, I knew who he was. The families knew one another and at that time I used to see him around town. They used to pop out at the Adelphi from behind a column, when my wife and I were going out together before we were married, with a rather big theatrical expression. I would also see him at concerts and the theatre. He took to asking my advice with regard to his unhappy career and he had certain problems which he discussed with me.

We discussed his personal problems. He was enthusiastic about a lot of things and very pessimistic about a lot of things. He was pessimistic about himself. He felt himself a square peg in a round hole for a long, long period and wanted to escape the background in which he'd been brought up.

In March 1954 I returned to business. It was after I left the army that I found out about the existence of the various rendezvous and homosexual 'life'. My life became a succession of mental illnesses and sordid, unhappy events bringing great sorrow to my family. My loneliness throughout has been acute. I found myself unable to concentrate on my work and unable to live in peace with my family. I tried psychoanalysis with a psychiatrist but I was so embarrassed by the arrangement that every time I visited him (two or three times a week) I had to go to my father and request three guineas to pay him. I could not proceed for very long.

BRIAN EPSTEIN

Rex Makin: He certainly wasn't conventional and he certainly wasn't usual. It was as if he was trying to break out of himself and take an uplift. He had enthusiasm and sudden bursts of flights of fancy but he wasn't really very stable. So he was rather like a butterfly, and of course butterflies are very colourful as well as floating and don't settle for very long at any one object.

I used to pour water over his enthusiasm but it never seemed to dampen him or have any adverse effect, so I suppose he must be said to have had strength to resist me in that way. He had strength and stubbornness.

THE LAST WILL AND TESTAMENT OF THE
WRITER BRIAN SAMUEL EPSTEIN

1 *Within this drawer lie all my most personal possessions and I desire that they be disposed of by my father and brother as they feel it right.*

2 *I desire that all my possessions and estate be left for my immediate family or issue except – that my clothing be sent direct and immediately to the State of Israel; that the main part of all my artistic possessions including my collection of records, magazines, theatrical programmes etc. be left to my dear and great friend, Brendan H. Garry, excepting those few items which my family desire for themselves.*

3 *I desire that no 'Kaddish' should be performed in my memory and that mourning should not last longer than seven days.*

4 *I desire that my mother, father and brother know of my eternal love for them.*

Signed by the writer,

Brian Epstein
21 February 1956

2. A Magic World

I have a middle-class background, perhaps a little better – shop, you know, retail stores, old established. It was started by my grand-father, principally in furniture. When I left school, about the age of sixteen, I had ambitions to be a dress designer, and also to be an actor, but my family weren't very keen on this and I allowed myself to be swayed into going into the business. I think I was more anxious to leave school than anything else, which I didn't enjoy very much.

That was Wrekin College, Shropshire, a minor public school. I went into the family business and I did an apprenticeship for a furniture company outside of ours for about six months and then found myself back in the family business and interested myself in the display and advertising side. In fact, we opened a store specifically for me to work in and develop interior decoration, which I was rather interested in. But by the time I got to twenty-one I was still feeling this sort of bug about acting and the stage.

BRIAN EPSTEIN, BBC HOME SERVICE, 7 MARCH 1964

Joe Flannery: Growing up, we went through many discussions about our private lives. Brian and I would discuss how our feelings were different to other young people. First of all you notice that you don't discuss girls so much and you discuss leading players in plays and shows and cinema, things like that. You realize you're more attracted to a star.

You've got to be as honest as possible but at the same time the people you don't want to hurt are your parents, particularly our mothers because they're the people that are the guiding light in your life. They've brought you up to be the person you are sitting with a friend in the back of my shop in Kirkdale Road discussing your feelings and finding out what you were.

In those days it was a terrible description. You were a queer and it wasn't a very nice thing to hear about yourself because you know that you're not queer in your head. It's probably like when you're a young person being asked if you're gay, you resent it and you try and fight what you're being called.

We knew of people who were taken away to a place called Rain Hill which

11

is about ten miles outside Liverpool. It was a loony bin, a lunatic asylum and there was no way I was going there. There was no way I wanted Brian to go there.

Helen Lindsay: I probably met Brian towards the end of September 1955. I think I was playing in an American comedy, because I remember I had rather a sort of brittle, witty part. And to my astonishment this very nice little note arrived in my dressing room one night from a young man saying that he very much enjoyed my performance and could he possibly take me out for a drink. Since fans usually didn't write and immediately ask you out for a drink, I thought it was slightly intriguing, and I went down into the Green Room and there he was waiting for me.

My first impression was that he was very sweet looking, impeccably dressed in a very expensive suit, not a gushing fan at all, very courteous and very gentleman, sort of old-fashioned in a way. So I didn't think I was going to be whirled off and raped or anything like that. I thought, 'Yes, I'll go with him for a drink,' and we retired to the Basnett Bar, which was the favourite watering hole for the company at that time. It was a very nice little bar, just near the stage door. We started to talk and Brian wanted to know a lot about the performances that I had given in the previous season, which he had obviously seen before he had written this note and asked to meet me.

Yankel Feather: There was a pub next door to the Playhouse. It was called the Old Royal and it was run by a woman called Mrs Taylor. On one side there was a bar and that was where all the gays went. On the other side was where the sailors and slack-arsed trimmers would stand. All these effeminate type of boys were all the passive ones and the butch-looking people were all the active ones. I was rather surprised when somebody explained how it all worked. Further on there was a place called the Magic Clock. That was facing the Royal Court. The Magic Clock was slightly more hysterical than the other places. I think that was full of more ambitious people. Whereas the Old Royal was full of working-class boys and working-class people who knew what they were and were satisfied with the sort of life they lived, people like Brian Epstein and his cohorts would go to the Magic Clock. It was a little bit more uppity – you know, more progressive – and people had better clothes and talked with posher accents. It catered for a better class of client.

There was a marvellous bar next to the St George's Hall. It was called the Old Victoria. It was a hotel and it was a pub that was frequently mostly by prostitutes and homosexuals, and the people who frequented them knew exactly why they went there. I don't know how these things come about but I suppose a lot depends on the proprietors. If you've got to make a living, who can pick and choose? I mean, there was a recession before the war. People found it very hard to make a living. They didn't have the government subsidies like they have now, so I suppose they were glad of any clientele, homosexual or otherwise.

Helen Lindsay: He was very conversant with all the plays of the previous season and wanted to talk about them, particularly the *Twelfth Night* we'd done and *The Confidential Clerk*, the T.S. Eliot play. I thought, 'Well, he's not at all a stage-door Johnny. He's not a besotted fan and he doesn't ask how I learn all my lines and he hasn't fallen over the furniture.' So when he said, 'Could I possibly meet you again?' I agreed to meet him for tea or something.

We went to tea and he wanted to know about the part that I was then rehearsing, which would have been the next play, which was Sean O'Casey's *The Plough and the Stars*. He was very intrigued about the fact that we were all having to do Irish accents, because in those days it was a resident company and all the actors at the Playhouse company would have signed a year's contract. There was no such thing as different actors coming in for different plays. We were a resident company of about twelve or fourteen actors so it was very easy for him to follow our progress. We were very definitely there for a year and he came to all the plays. We used to change the plays once every three weeks and frequently I would go out to tea with Brian and he would want to know all about the rehearsal schedule and how we were approaching our parts.

I remember we were doing *Othello* before Christmas, and he was very intrigued with that. It was an imperfect production, if I may say so, and he wanted to know about how I thought it should have been done, or how it could have been improved. He wanted to take the whole thing apart.

There was a sort of wistfulness about him. He wanted to belong to what he perceived was a charmed circle. He was obviously bored to death with the furniture business and he thought we were terribly lucky people, that we inhabited a magic world, which he wanted to become a part of.

It looks like an urban wasteland in the late nineties, but in the fifties, the Liverpool town centre was teeming with bars, meeting places and drinking dens. The Basnett Bar was around the corner from the Liverpool Playhouse and was the chief haunt of the repertory company and other visiting stars like John Gielgud and Michael Redgrave.

The Playhouse was a centre of Liverpool's cultural life. During this period, it was home to a new group of young actors, notably Helen Lindsay and Brian

Bedford. Bedford's acting was in the same style as Albert Finney's, to whom he was often compared – working class, Northern and direct.

Helen Lindsay: After I'd known him for quite a long time, and this was probably during the time when he was very, very keen on Brian Bedford's performance in *Ring around the Moon*, he suddenly asked us very shyly, and with this very disarming smile, if we possibly would consider helping him. It so happened that he was thinking about becoming an actor, and would like to audition for RADA. Brian Bedford said that he couldn't possibly coach him, that it wasn't his thing at all. But I think Brian Bedford probably said, 'Well, you could do it, darling. You'd be quite good at it because you're bossy.'

LETTER TO RADA

Dear Sir,   *August 31st, 1956*

Earlier this year I applied for your prospectus and entrance form which I now have in my possession.

Due to difficulties of a domestic nature, I have not been able to train for the stage previously. It is only recently that my family have agreed to my training to be an actor.

Thanking you in anticipation of your consideration and a possible favourable reply.

Yours faithfully,

Brian Epstein

Helen Lindsay: I think that Epstein wanted to go to RADA because he always wanted what he perceived to be the best. He had a great feeling for quality. It was reflected in his clothes and in his manners and in his general style. There was something very correct about him, and I think he would have thought that RADA would be the place to go. He had a maturity beyond his years, and he had a tremendous sort of natural dignity. There was something very correct about him. He wanted to be beautifully dressed, to be nicely spoken, which are some of the reasons why I thought he wasn't an actor. I didn't feel at all that he had an actor's temperament.

I think he was definitely stage-struck and I didn't want to pour cold water on this idea of going to RADA. He was so determined that was what he wanted to do. He wanted to send in an application form straight away. I think he was also dying to escape from the family business.

At this time Epstein was working in the family store in Walton, helping out in the new small record department. He was earning more than five pounds a week. He had use of a car, having passed his driving test at the fourth attempt. He was living with his parents and had, to all intents and purposes, settled into the family business.

Yankel Feather: He was a very secretive person and he wouldn't have let me know what he really thought because I wasn't a particular friend of his. I don't think he even liked me any more than I liked him, but I respected him because he was good to look at. He was a nice Jewish boy and I felt at least I owed him the respect of listening to him and being pleasant to him, even though he was very hard to be nice to because he didn't particularly want me in his company. He wanted to mix with the darling people – you know, the people at the Playhouse Theatre: Helen Lindsay and Brian Bedford and all these people who got to be big stars.

> Once more unto the breach, dear friends, once more;
> Or close the wall up with our English dead!
> HENRY V, ACT II, SCENE III

Helen Lindsay: I said that we would help him, that we'd work on things. Then, if he felt comfortable with whatever piece he'd chosen, he'd be in a better position to judge whether he wanted to go ahead with the application. Anyway, he was very determined and took it very seriously.

I had a large, sunny living room in the flat that I rented in a lovely position overlooking the Anglican Cathedral in Liverpool. It was a lovely great big room and we could push the furniture back and make quite a big acting area. He used to come on Sunday afternoons for about three hours after lunch. To begin with, he wanted to pay me for lessons and I said, 'Oh good God, Brian, I couldn't bear it. No. I'm a chum. We'll work together and we'll see. It'll be very good for me also.'

I remember he then said something that he'd never said before. He said, 'When I first met you, or when I enter a room, do you notice that I'm Jewish?' And I said, 'No, it didn't strike me at all when I first met you. Now that I've got to know you and I've known you for several months, I know you're Jewish and I've met your parents. But why, Brian? Is it important? Are you worried about the fact that people might think you're Jewish?' He said, 'Well, you see, I think I'd like to do possibly Henry V and will they think I should never choose Henry V because I'm Jewish?'

I said, 'At the RADA audition, there will probably be three boys who do 'once more unto the breach, dear friends', and you want to choose something more unusual. Also, you must choose something which is right for you physically.

'You must choose something that is near you physically and near your temperament. I simply do not see you as a man of action. I don't see you as a soldier, and Henry V is a soldier. And I think you should keep away from heroic parts.'

He then asked if he should perform Prince Hal. I said the same thing. 'You don't want to play a soldier. You don't want to do Julius Caesar.' Then he wanted to do Mark Antony. I said, 'I'm a bit worried about that because I think that you need a colossal amount of power for that speech. We could certainly work on it and see.'

> Friends, Romans, countrymen, lend me your ears;
> I come to bury Caesar, not to praise him.
> JULIUS CAESAR, ACT III, SCENE II

I think we did work on Mark Antony for a while and it became crystal clear that he didn't have the power for it. I thought his most endearing qualities were this sort of slight soulfulness about him, the fact that he did convey a maturity beyond his years and he had colossal dignity. I thought that he knew *Henry V* so well so he should do the Duke of Burgundy in the final scene of *Henry V*. He's the great statesman of France who has this beautiful speech at the end, after the battle and discussing peace and reconciling the two kingdoms. It's very diplomatic and it's very beautiful. It's very still.

> . . . And my speech entreats,
> That I may know the let, why gentle Peace
> Should not expel these inconveniences,
> And bless us with her former qualities.
> HENRY V, ACT V, SCENE II

That was important, because one of the things that became extremely evident as soon as we started working was that Brian was not a natural mover. He had no flow in his movements. His movement was completely unrelated to his speech. He'd learn the piece and work on it intelligently and try and keep the flow of the rhythm. We'd discuss what the speech meant. Then he'd get up to do the speech and he'd tack on a few gestures and I thought – when his arms, which are usually screwed to his side, would move from the elbow – it was like a mechanical soldier or like a tailor's dummy. He couldn't move. So I said, 'We'll have to do some relaxation exercises and we'll have to move about quite a lot and touch your toes, walk about, swing your arms.'

Brian still finds it difficult to cope with his physique as an 'instrument' – mostly due to tension. Must work technically for relaxation and suppleness.

RADA END-OF-TERM REPORT, AUTUMN 1956

Helen Lindsay: We did a few movement exercises and things but he still persisted. So I said that the trick with the Duke of Burgundy is that you don't have to move at all. It's a great advantage in an audition. He wouldn't be cantering around the stage by himself, which is quite difficult anyway. If you don't move naturally, you don't have to move at all when you're the Duke of Burgundy.

Brian was worried that the Duke of Burgundy was not an important part. I said, 'I think, actually, it's a very important part. What better position in the play can you have? You come on at the last scene where you have the King of England on one side of the stage and the King of France on the other and you're in the middle making the Peace Treaty.'

That cheered him up a lot. But I still felt that he did not have an actor's instinct. I think he had a completely unrealistic idea of what preparation to become an actor would be.

Rex Makin: I think he was rebelling against everything in his background. I mean, so far as he was concerned he wanted to be in the flamboyant, artistic, show-off world.

He was elegant, fastidiously so, and he had a very great presence. He was good-looking, pleasant, well mannered. He was temperamental, volatile. He could be very effusive or he could be very taciturn.

He always seemed natural to me because he was always the same to me. After all, he always had theatrical aspirations, which unfortunately weren't fulfilled. He was a dramatic person. I don't think he was really a success as a businessman. I think he had a shrewd outlook but I don't think he was really up to the vast money-making machine that he ultimately helped to create and was responsible for.

During his time at RADA, Epstein played the following roles:

Proteus	*The Two Gentlemen of Verona*
The Narrator	*The Dynasts*
Constantin	*The Seagull*
Posthumus	*Cymbeline*
Lucentio	*The Taming of the Shrew*
Orlando	*As You Like It*
Sir Toby Belch	*Twelfth Night*

Hard work at Voice Projection and Movement are vital at the moment, to give Brian's very pleasant personality full scope.

RADA END-OF-TERM REPORT, SPRING 1957

Helen Lindsay: I was very surprised that he made it to RADA because all the indications did not look good. I had sneaked him on to the stage at the Playhouse, just shortly before his audition, probably after lunch on a Saturday. I was desperate to get him not to do traffic-warden acting. But I thought he understood the speech and got the stress in the right places. He got the musical shape of the speech and he had a great kind of quiet dignity. In spite of everything, I thought he might just pull it off.

An interesting and rewarding term's work of great variety. There are glimpses of latent power and breadth, which augur well. A sensitive intelligence and understanding are expressed with control and a sense of direction and form. His characterization is subtle and deep. A really promising student.

RADA END-OF-TERM REPORT, SPRING 1957

Brian began his first term at RADA in September 1956. He left less than a year later.

Living alone in London I have felt again acute frustration and loneliness. But efforts at school have been fruitful and my last report was excellent and full of promise for the future. I had begun to grow away from sexual inclinations which I sublimated in my work. Life had a purpose and direction. I began to feel I had overcome a great deal. Work and study, an appetite for knowledge (although I now realize I possess both intellectual and intelligent capacities, my general lack of knowledge caused by my retarded development at school is of persistent annoyance to me) have taken precedence in importance over a non-existent sex life.

The Easter term ended on March 30th. I arranged to work in a book shop during the vacation. On Sunday, April 14th, last, I went home for a week so that I might please my family by being home during Passover.

I returned to London on Easter Monday evening. Wednesday evening after work I saw a play at the Arts Theatre Club, and after a quiet coffee after the play I took the tube home to Swiss Cottage. When leaving the tube at Swiss Cottage tube station I walked hurriedly to the lavatory in the station to urinate. When I came out of the lavatory I saw a young man staring hard at me.

Being an artist and not an unobservant person I have learnt to recognize a homosexual. How a homosexual recognizes another is a somewhat indefinable thing but I presume it is the same, to a lesser degree, the way in which a male recognizes a girl of likely easy virtue (I do not mean a prostitute.) From the point of view of appearance and behaviour the young man fitted my ideas of a homosexual. When I saw this man (who I will refer to as X) staring at me my mind was almost blank and all my past fears (which I thought had gone for ever) returned.

I walked around the arcade surrounding and within the station. For five minutes I tried to think straight and sensibly, during which time I was aware that I was being looked at by X. Then I saw X go into the lavatory. I looked straight in front of me, my eyes downcast.

Whilst there I did not move from that position. After approximately one minute, I knew he turned his face to glance at me and then walked out and waited outside. I followed. He loitered. I loitered. After several minutes passed, I took a hold of myself and decided that what I was doing was very dangerous and stupid and I walked away towards home.

When I walked across the road at the entrance to the station, at the corner of Belsize Road and Finchley Road, I turned to look back and see that he was not following me. He was standing quite still in the entrance staring directly at me when I turned and looked at him. After a further 45 seconds he nodded again and raised his eyebrows. Then I walked back a little; I saw his reflection still on the opposite side of the road (Belsize) in a shop window. All this time I knew he was watching me. I then walked further down the road and stopped approximately 100 yards on at the corner of Harben Road and Belsize Road. He followed.

On reaching me at the corner he nodded slightly again. I made no return. He crossed the road to the opposite slightly away from the view of the main road and stood looking pathetically at me. I crossed to him.

'Hi!' I said.

'Hello,' he said

'What are you doing out so late?' I asked.

'Nothing much. You?'

'Nothing.'

Long silence.

'Know anywhere to go?' I asked.

'No. Do you?'

'There is an open field along the road.'

'Along there?'

'Yes.'

'You show me.'

Silence

Then we crossed the road to the other corner. We stopped and he said. 'Along there?' he asked, pointing.

Silence.

'It is rather dangerous. I have to be home early,' I said.

'All right,' he said.

I left him and walked hurriedly away along Harban Road and turned right up Fairfax Road and right again at Finchley Road. My mind was in great fear and turmoil. I looked in the shop windows, trying to relax myself after the nerve-racking experience. I looked back and saw X with another man following me on the other side of the road. I walked on quickly, forgetting where I was going. Then I stopped still to look in a chemist's window, determined to let them pass me. After a few minutes they arrested me for 'PERSISTENTLY IMPORTUNING'. As far as I can remember I was too stunned to say anything immediately but as I walked with them on either side of me, X holding my arm stiffly, I pointed with my free arm at this and asked the other man, 'Is this necessary?' He replied, 'Yes . . .'

When I eventually arrived at the police station the sergeant asked the detective for a brief description of the charges.

'For persistently importuning various men for immoral purposes, etc.,' he answered. The sergeant wrote this down, but I could not hear completely what was written down nor had I been told the full charge before I questioned all this. The sergeant read out to me what he had written down. 'For persistently importuning several men, etc.' I questioned the discrepancy of several and various. 'How many men was it?' the sergeant asked the detective. 'Four,' replied the detective.

In Marylebone Magistrates' Court the next morning, I pleaded guilty because the detective advised it. 'If you plead not guilty your history will be taken in court and it will take a long time,' he said. He gave me every incentive to plead guilty. In fact he asked, whilst we were waiting, whether I had money on me to pay a fine, he was so sure that I would be fined or conditionally discharged.

When he gave evidence after I pleaded guilty in court he included 'persistently importuning seven men'.

I do not think I am an abnormally weak-willed person – the effort and determination with which I have rebuilt my life these last few months have, I assure you, been no mean effort. I believed that my own will-power was the best thing with which to overcome my homosexuality. And I believe my life may have become contented and I may even have attained a public success.

I was determined to go through the horror of this world. I feel deeply for I have always felt deeply for the persecuted, for the Jews, the coloured people, for the old and society's misfits. When I made money I planned to devote, and give what I made to these people.

I am not sorry for myself. My worst times and punishments are over. Now, through the wreckage of my life by society, my being will stain and bring the deepest *distress to all my devoted family and few friends. The damage, the lying criminal methods of the police in importuning me and consequently capturing me leaves me cold, stunned and finished.*

If I am remanded or given a prison sentence, please telephone my father Harry Epstein at Liverpool North 3221 (if he is not there, that is the number of his main office and the staff should tell you where he is or what time he will return).

I must apologize for my writing which I realize is difficult to read. I was unable to procure a typewriter and my hand is nervous.

BRIAN EPSTEIN

Geoffrey Ellis: I met Brian Epstein in Liverpool in the mid-fifties, I think. He was then in his early twenties. I was three or four years older. We met through mutual friends and struck up a friendship then.

I always knew that Brian was homosexual. You couldn't help knowing that he was homosexual, partly from the choice of some of his friends and associates, partly because in his private life he made no secret of it at all. As to the extent to which it affected his personality and his life, I think it had a very deep effect, a very profound effect upon him. Originally, when he lived with his family, he had wanted to present the image of a normal person. It didn't really work because he always knew – and I believe that his family knew from very early days – that he was homosexual.

When he lived in London – and perhaps particularly when he visited America and he was fascinated by the American homosexual scene in the sixties – he behaved sometimes in a way which was very dangerous, and he was conscious of this. In some ways he sought out danger. It gave him a thrill, but of course led him into many very awkward situations from time to time. I think deep down he didn't want to be homosexual but paradoxically he enjoyed his homosexual experiences very much indeed.

LETTER TO RADA

197 Queens Drive
Childwall
Liverpool 15

Telephone Childwall 3106

3/10/57

Dear Mr Fernald,*

It is with regret that I must write you that I have finally decided not to embark upon a career as an actor. I hope you will understand that although this is not the place to analyse my decision I have thought the matter over very carefully for some considerable time.

On the circumstances I feel it would be wrong from all our points of view to continue with my course at RADA.

I would like you to know that as far as I'm concerned my time at RADA has proved an invaluable experience and given me a real insight to a great craft. Certainly my appreciation and support of the theatre is unlikely ever to cease.

Yours sincerely,

Brian Epstein

Helen Lindsay: He left and went down to RADA at the end of '56 and I stayed on for another season, and I did see him again because we went together to see Vivien Leigh in a play. He was besotted with Vivien Leigh; she was incredibly beautiful. But I never saw him again after that because I left and went to London. But I was very, very touched in 1964, when I received this copy of *A Cellarful of Noise* with an enchanting little inscription in it. That was quite a few years later, you see.

Aunt Stella: He'd said that he'd like to go to RADA, so Harry and Queenie said, 'If you can get in, well good luck to you.' And he did get in. But I'm afraid that his time at RADA was quite short and he didn't really enjoy it in the end. So he decided he would come back and go into the business, which he did.

* Director of RADA at the time.

3. Prodigal Son

When I left RADA I was determined to throw myself into the family business and make an increasing and lifelong success of it. It was 1957 – I was twenty-three and full of resolve to do well for my own and my parents' sake. My brother Clive had now joined the firm and my father hoped for great expansion.

BRIAN EPSTEIN, A CELLARFUL OF NOISE

Peter Brown: His parents had to have something for him to do. So they expanded from the suburban store that they had out in Walton to the little store in the development in the centre of Liverpool, and resurrected the name NEMS. The store that Brian's grandfather had started was a furniture shop. The new one was essentially an electrical appliance store – washing machines, televisions, radios – and that accounted for two-thirds of the store. Brian was given the rest of the store in which to run a record department.

And he did it so well and so efficiently that they needed more space and more space and more space till very soon it took over probably about three-quarters of the shop. It was not a very big shop but it was all the ground floor and half of the upstairs. That was the start of his role as far as music was concerned.

The first Epstein family store – which consisted of two separate shops knocked together – was in Walton, far from the Liverpool city centre. After two generations of success, Harry expanded NEMS in 1957 when he opened a store in Charlotte Street, downtown Liverpool. This store had a larger record department than the Walton store and was opened by Ann Shelton, a popular singer whose biggest hit, 'Lay Down Your Arms', was produced by the legendary Joe Meek. Brian was put in charge of the record section and was given an assistant to help him. In Walton, NEMS had been fortunate to make seventy pounds a week in record sales; it took in twenty pounds on the very first morning in Charlotte Street.

Joe Flannery: Brian was always proud that he had an original copy of *My Fair Lady*. This was our type of music. We liked stage shows, musicals and musical films. This is the music we enjoyed.

Brian adored and liked Peggy Lee and he always listened to her. Another female artist he liked – I think she was a one-hit wonder – was Caterina Valente and the title was 'The Breeze and I'. He loved that record and he played it over and over again.

We went to see *A Streetcar Named Desire*, which is prominent in my memory, starring Vivien Leigh. We booked to go and see that show for a full week, night after night. On the Friday night Brian wasn't able to attend because of his Jewish faith. I went, of course, as usual, but I didn't replace anybody so the seat was empty next to me. Vivien Leigh took the trouble of putting her foot through the floodlights and leaned straight over to me, 'cause I was only in the second row from the front, and said, 'Where's your friend tonight?'

Geoffrey Ellis: I found Brian very agreeable, very personable, a very nice chap to be with, and we shared some mutual interests such as going out to dinner together. There weren't very many places of interest to eat round about Merseyside in those days, and we used to drive out to places in the country to have meals together. I think occasionally we went to concerts together. By concerts I mean it was classical concerts in those days, and a friendship developed between us.

Brian was a bit different to many friends because he did have this slightly curious background. He'd been an unhappy child at school, he'd had an unhappy period in the army, which he'd left rather prematurely to the relief of both sides, and he was really still trying to find his feet at that time. I had been to university myself and I was starting on what appeared to be a fairly conventional career in insurance and he at that time didn't really seem to know what he wanted to do. He had no horizons at the time other than his family business. He had experienced a period at RADA, the dramatic arts school in London, which hadn't worked for him successfully, and I'm not sure if he was resigned or not but he certainly wasn't wholly contented with his lot at that time.

Yankel Feather: Somebody brought him to my house to look at my work. I had a house in Upper Parliament Street and I used the ground floor as a studio. I wasn't painting full time at the time. I was just hoping to be a painter. I was a member of the Liverpool Academy and I talked to him about that once or twice and he said he'd like to see my work.

He didn't know anything about painting but I didn't know anything about music, even though I used to buy records from him. Gradually I got to know him quite well through going into the shop, and he'd choose very good things for me, all sorts of good artists. I wasn't terribly interested in music but I liked good music. I liked dancing and I liked running the club and it was a great help having him to advise me. Obviously he was a good businessman because he used to buy good records, which I bought from him, so a good time was had by all.

He was sort of fickle, I would think. He wasn't the sort of person I enjoyed being with but I thought at that time he was the sort of person I should get to know because he was rich, he was attractive and he wanted to go places. I never ever thought he would go anywhere but it's obvious he had ideas that I didn't know anything about.

Wherever homosexuals were they had to be secretive. There's lots of beliefs amongst tough men that so-called poofs or pansies and people like that have a harder time. There were slack-arsed trimmers, as the Liverpudlians called them, around the clubs and the odd sailor would come in, but it wasn't always the poofs who were the passive ones and it wasn't always the sailors and the slack-arsed trimmers who were the tough ones.

Joe Flannery: I'm not saying he was a Jekyll and Hyde character but in those days he had to be two people. He had to be the beautiful Brian, the well-dressed Brian, but then he had to be somebody else. I'm sure he had a fight in his nature. It must have been a great fight for him.

First and foremost we didn't want our family to be upset. When we went into the city, we were getting to like theatre, we were going into pubs and things like that. We were two good-looking young men. In the early stages we became known as the Untouchables because we'd stand there and take no notice. We didn't fall for anyone's charms or their approach or anything like that.

After a certain time at night he became somebody else. The Brian that I was with at the theatre or the cinema or going out for a drive wasn't the same person that could find himself in these tight squeezes. I thought he was very vulnerable in who he met or who he would come in contact with, and I think he liked the rough element. He was happy with that and he took his chances.

Now I could never work out why Brian liked that element. He was precise in his ways and full of charisma and all that sort of thing. I would always try and advise him not to do things, but nevertheless he sailed into it and that drifted apart a little bit. I loved his company and Brian and I had some great times, but then I had to put this wall between us whenever he was going off. Then I wouldn't join him but I would also say to him, 'Now you be careful,' because in those days Brian and I realized that we were breaking the law to be gay.

I think he took too many risks. I tried to tell him that he could have love in his life without endangering his life.

One night, he'd left my house about ten o'clock for wherever he was going. By about a quarter to midnight he was back on my doorstep. He left my house in a beautiful white shirt. I don't know if they're still in business, but he always wore a Peter England shirt. It was a beautiful white when he left my house and when he came back on my doorstep it was a brilliant red. He'd been knocked about so much that he didn't even come back in his car that night, which I could never fathom out or work out why.

The person had left him in this state. I bathed him. I got him right. He stayed the night and went back home or wherever he went the next morning looking reasonably good. He lost quite a lot of blood that night.

This episode had traumatic consequences. Not content with beating him and stealing his car, Brian's assailant contacted the Epsteins demanding money to keep the story quiet. The family brought in the Liverpool police, who arranged for Brian to go along with the blackmail scenario in an effort to capture the man. The blackmailer was arrested during the transaction and later sent to prison.

Peter Brown: The whole blackmail situation happened just before I knew him, so I could see the effect of it. It was something that wasn't talked about and I didn't know about it for a little while until he felt comfortable enough to let me into this very, very embarrassing secret. Actually, I think it was pretty well contained as a secret within Liverpool. But obviously there were some people that knew about it and the gossip got pretty nasty. He explained it to me. This whole episode was a horrendous experience, not only the physical beating but the humiliation of his family having to go to court and his being Mr X. It scarred him dreadfully psychologically, apart from the fear of the man coming out of jail sooner or later.

I first met Brian at a twenty-first birthday of a friend of Clive's and mine. I was a contemporary of Clive and I'd got into this group of Jewish guys who lived in Liverpool through a friend of mine called Alistair Berman, who I worked with at Lewis's department store, where I was running the record department. I was introduced to Brian by David Bergson who was a contemporary of Brian's. We met that first night because I think David had a feeling that we would get on well together and we did. We instantly became friends and remained the closest of friends until he died.

At the time I was running the record department at Lewis's, which was the biggest department store in the city.

There was a little group of gay men in Liverpool who were professional men all about the same age, and we would go to each other's houses although we never really went as a group anywhere. Brian and I did a lot of going out to restaurants on our own. There were not that many choices in Liverpool itself so we would often drive quite a long way into the country – Cheshire, Wirral and the outskirts of Manchester – to go to these kind of quaint rural restaurants which were attached to hotels or pubs, small hotels or pubs which were very common in those days.

All the time that I knew him I don't think that one could ever say that he had any proper long-term emotional relationship. The people he was attracted to were not the kind of people you settle down with. They were just not interested or he wouldn't have wanted to be with them for more than a short period of time.

It could have been as a result of his being deeply unhappy about being gay. He wasn't comfortable about the fact that he was gay and therefore that led to a situation when he couldn't have a successful homosexual relationship. That inability came from the fact that being gay was not his ideal way of living his life, subconscious as that may have been. I don't think that was unusual for the time.

Up until just before Brian died, it was actually illegal to have a homosexual relationship for men in England and this pervaded the whole life of a gay man. I can think of very few successful homosexual relationships in those days. There were very few long-term ones.

Liverpool was a provincial city with a largely uneducated attitude towards that kind of thing and it wasn't acceptable. In those circumstances you went to a particular gay bar in the centre of Liverpool which was pretty seedy but you had no choice. There was a particular element of risk just going there for Brian because he came from an affluent family.

Yankel Feather: I don't think he was unhappy. I think he was very sure of himself, a cocky sort of sureness, sort of: 'I'm Brian Epstein, I'm rich, there aren't very many people in Liverpool, if anybody, like me. I know things that nobody else knows. I come from a wealthy family. I'm powerful. I can do things.' He proved his point later on, but at that time I didn't care for him very much because I didn't know where he was going. I knew who I was already and I knew what I wanted to do.

In 1959, NEMS expanded further and opened a bigger store in nearby White-chapel, the heart of Liverpool's shopping district. This time, the opening ceremony was performed by Anthony Newley, whose popularity was so great that this appearance stopped traffic in the centre of Liverpool the way a Cup-winning football team might.

Alistair Taylor: The advert in the *Liverpool Echo* went something like *'Young man wanted for sales assistant in city-centre record shop. Apply in writing, Brian Epstein, NEMS Limited, Whitechapel.'* That was perfect for me because (a) I wanted to get back into retailing and (b) I'd been a record buyer all my life and I thought if I could get into retailing and in records that would be great. What a combination. So I sat down and I wrote to Brian and got an interview which went on for about two hours.

We just gelled immediately. We got on very well and then he got into his head this idea that he really couldn't pay me enough as an assistant. I would be an assistant when necessary on the counter but basically he'd been toying with the idea of having a personal assistant. So I nearly pulled his arm off. I jumped at the chance.

As I was leaving the office, he said, 'Oh and by the way there's some posters on the window ledge there. Can you get them framed for me?' That should have given me a clue as to what life was going to be like for the next nine years. They were bullfighting posters. He was a bullfighting fanatic, actually, and in fact that Christmas he gave me one as a present and I still have it. It's the one thing that I treasure.

I would say it was unusual for someone in Liverpool to be so interested in bullfighting. I certainly got interested in it but I think Brian was the only person I knew that was into bullfighting and he used to go off to all the major corridas through the bullfight season.

I never saw anything but marvellous times between Harry and Queenie and Brian. They were happy because, according to them, he'd suddenly settled down. He'd been a bit of a wayward lad. He always wanted to do something different and here he was very successfully running an honest-to-God business in the High Street, which pleased Harry no end.

We had fridges, televisions, radiograms, or what today is called white goods, which of course a lot of people would love to have bought but there wasn't that kind of money around then. They were expensive. Brian and I weren't really involved in that side. That was run by his brother, Clive Epstein, who sadly is not with us any more.

We had the finest collection of jazz records. I think we were probably one of the first shops in England to stock the whole of the Blue Note catalogue, which was quite something for Liverpool. People used to come from miles around just to get the records here.

Students, teachers, older people also came in to buy the classical records, and very often it would be the conductor of the Royal Philharmonic Orchestra where Brian used to go a lot. He was a friend of Brian's. The store had a very good reputation and the ceiling was wonderful because Brian had LP sleeves all over it.

Derek Taylor: All the people in NEMS, in the retail end, had to call him Mr Brian. People had to know their place. He didn't like over-familiarity and I found that quite a Liverpool middle-class characteristic.

Peter Brown: It was the dark ages in those days, I mean the class structure and all that kind of thing. They were the shop owners and it was Mr and Mrs Epstein and the people in the shop who were the sales people called them Mr Brian and Mr Clive. Having worked at Lewis's, I already knew what I was doing. That was one of the reasons Brian asked me to join NEMS in the first place.

He'd already established his shop as the place you went to if you were getting a hot record or an early record or if you were interested in music at all. There was a lot of interest in Liverpool in music because there was a very substantial part of the working-class population that were seamen. They would travel a lot, particularly to the United States.

They would know about rhythm and blues, rock and roll, country and western and were very on the cutting edge of what was happening musically in the United States. So we endeavoured to keep up with them and they in fact kept us on our toes about what was happening. Brian's credential was the fact that we would have every record that was issued, and if we were out of stock of it our boast was we would get it for you within twenty-four hours.

Alistair Taylor: Brian's claim was that if a record was available anywhere in the world he would get it. It might take six months, it might take a year, but if it was available Brian would get it. And I don't remember him ever failing to do that.

He was quite a taskmaster and we never got away on time. He and I used to do the ordering and it was jackets off when deliveries came. We'd get a whole vanload of records all in, but it was great fun and he was terribly generous. He would very often say, 'Right, let's go and have dinner,' or 'Let's go and have a drink before you go home.'

Brian followed his nose when it came to stock. He was an amazing talent. He would put on a demo and say, 'Right, we'll have 500 of that,' which was an awful lot of records for two shops in Liverpool. When Brian ordered like that the major record companies – Decca, EMI, Pye – would just get on the phone to the factory and say, 'Right, up the pressing order. Brian Epstein's ordered them.' Then other times he'd say, 'All right, I'll just have two, one in each shop.'

Peter Brown: The records were all listed by numbers, not by names. We all more or less had to remember all the numbers. The records were categorized by numbers on a card. Each record had a string on it with a paperclip. This paperclip was attached to the card. When a record was sold the paperclip was detached from the card and it would hang, so you could immediately see at a glance what had been sold.

Therefore, when you went to a card, you could see how many records had been sold and then make a decision to buy more. On the card it said when the record was ordered, how many were ordered and when it was reordered. It sounds a bit Heath Robinsonish but it actually worked very well and it certainly worked from the point of view that we quickly became the most successful record retailer in that part of the country.

Alistair Taylor: He didn't just put record sleeves in the window. When you walked down Whitechapel, from the outside it was like looking at a film set or a theatre set. There was a particular time coming up to Christmas when cocktail music was really popular, all that tinkly pianos and stuff. So Brian dressed the window like it was a night-club, if you like. He put in a little table with a white cloth on it and glasses and a bottle of wine and chairs and the record sleeves would be lying around. He always did this, which he loved. Having been to RADA, he was very theatrical in everything he did.

Paul McCartney: I only knew about NEMS as a record shop. My initial impression was that it was just a shop we went into to gaze and to admire all the beautiful record covers and occasionally buy a record. I never realized till much later that NEMS stood for North End Music Stores and that Brian's dad, Harry, had once sold a piano to my dad, which I still have. So there was a family connection before I even met Brian. So for people who like to think things are fated, there we are.

Alistair Taylor: Saturday afternoon is when all the kids used to come in and it would be packed. We had turntables behind the counter where we would play records and there was a row of booths, which I don't think you get any more. Brian used to tolerate this. A lot of them never bought anything, including the Beatles, though we didn't know who they were then. They were always in there. But it was just wonderful. It was fun and Brian didn't mind. In fact he loved it. You know, he loved young people but the weird thing is that he spent most of his time down there and he didn't like pop music at all or jazz.

Gerry Marsden: We used to go into Brian's shop and ask for records from America, not British ones, because at the time Cliff was in the charts and Adam

Faith. Great lads, but we didn't play their type of music. We wanted stuff from America by Fats Domino, Jerry Lee Lewis, Ray Charles. And Brian would say, 'Why do you want these strange records?' We said, 'Well, this is the stuff we play down the Cavern.'

Vera Brown: It was just like a store, but then there would always be a couple of friends there you'd meet. So it was like a meeting place. It was just a big room really. There was a counter at one end. There was booths along the left-hand side. If you wanted to hear a particular record you could go in there and put the earphones on and listen to it, mainly Jerry Lee Lewis, Fats Domino, Little Richard, Elvis, and anything that was going at the time. You'd ask for a certain record to come on and we'd all sort of move about to the music and then, as more people came, somebody from the shop would come out and say, 'Come on, buy a record or leave,' but we just wanted to listen to the music. If one person bought a record out of about ten, the shop was lucky. I suppose other people bought records but the people I was with didn't. I didn't see much of Brian. It was his store but usually you saw a woman or his assistants. Sometimes you saw Brian walk through. He didn't spend much time with the people.

I'm not sure if there was an office at the back. There must have been because Brian could appear and disappear. Brian was then sort of an authority figure. He wasn't one of the crowd. He was different. He was very distinguished. He had money. He always looked in charge of everything. You knew he was confident and my friends were just stupid, really – you know, just standing around. We were there to meet friends rather than buy a record and Brian knew this. So he would say, 'Well, come on, enough.' But he seemed a lot older than he was at the time. Brian was someone you'd look up to – somebody important.

Alistair Taylor: The main thing was that he had this nose for finding hit pop tunes. He didn't like pop music and yet he could just listen to a promo copy and say, 'That's going to be number one.' The one that we used to joke about, almost to the day he died, was released in 1960 or '61, before we'd found the Beatles. Ray Charles brought out 'Georgia on My Mind'. I'm a great Ray Charles fan and jazz fan so when I heard it I said, 'Right, Brian, let's just have a couple in each shop because I want one.' And he listened to it and said, 'Right, that is going to be a number one round the world.'

That was the first time we ever had a bet about a record. I said, 'I'm sorry Brian, I love it but it's a jazz record. That's not commercial.' And he said, 'I'll bet you a gin and tonic that's number one.' And that was the first time, and that became a bit of a habit. Whenever I argued with him if I thought I was right, he'd always just say, 'Alistair, you've forgotten Ray Charles.'

One day Brian said, 'Do you ever watch a programme called *Compact?*' which was a show about a magazine. And I said, 'Well, I don't but Lesley [my wife] does.' So Brian said, 'Well, will you watch it because I've got this press blurb here and there's a guy called John Leyton who's singing at the Christmas party. He's going to be singing this song.' So I watched the show that night and thought the song he sang was absolutely diabolical.

The next morning when Brian asked me if I had watched the programme, I said, 'Yes, Brian. Forget that record. One copy in each shop, that's all.' Well, I think it was the next day that the record company rep came into the shop and said, 'Oh, by the way, this is the record by John Leyton.' So Brian says, 'Oh well, Alistair's heard it and he thinks it's terrible but let me put it on. I'd like to hear it.'

Brian just stood there and he said, 'Right, we'll have 250, 300.' I just looked at him. I said, 'Brian, you're joking.' It was called 'Johnny, Remember Me', and of course it roared away. We were the only shop in the north-west to have copies of it, thanks to him.

Yankel Feather: I had a club that was down a dark passage. We kept it dark because we didn't want everybody to know where it was. It took five years before the police found it. It was here for about ten years, and once a week Brian would come in. At my club I had some very attractive young men coming in. There were lots of waiters who worked at the Adelphi Hotel, and I bought most of the music from Brian and the music was good. I had some very attractive people so naturally he would come and mix. It wasn't a gay club. I had all sorts of people there. Brian was very presentable and he mixed in very well. I thought he was a man of celebrity at the time, even before the Beatles.

He always hesitated by the door, came in like a sort of startled bird. I don't know whether he expected people to look at him, but he would hesitate and stop as though he was waiting to be looked at. Once he'd made his mind up which bar he wanted to go to he would approach it and strike a pose, and he always stood back from people and was always better dressed than everybody round him. If he didn't have appointments to meet people he would watch.

He never spoke to strangers; he would only speak to people he knew. I don't think he had the ability to go up to somebody. I don't think he would talk to anybody just for the sake of talking. If there was nothing in it for him he wouldn't bother and so he would drink on his own. If he met people he would relax with them. He wasn't a warm person. I don't think he was in the slightest degree interested in world affairs or what was happening to anybody; he was only interested in what was happening to him – what was going on in his own immediate circle.

Alistair Taylor: He was tunnel vision into Beethoven and Mozart and that kind of music. I can remember one day he came into the office and he said, 'Alistair, have you ever heard of Thelonius Monk and Art Blakey and the Jazz Messengers?' And I said, 'Just a bit. They're are just about the best.' He said, 'Well, they're playing the Philharmonic Hall. I'm going to get us a box. We'll go.'

So I took him to his first ever jazz concert at the Liverpool Royal Philharmonic Hall to watch Thelonius Monk and Art Blakey, and then we went to see Kenny Ball and his Jazzmen at the Empire. He didn't understand it but he enjoyed himself. I mean he had a very open mind. He wasn't narrow-minded and bigoted. It was just that he'd never been over that side of the road before, and that's where I added to his life a little bit.

Yankel Feather: He sold me records by Mary Wells, the Shirelles and Sam Cooke, Sarah Vaughan and lots of the American rhythm and blues things that were prevalent at the time. People used to talk over my head about music and I would listen. All I did was run a club and supply it with music. I wasn't terribly interested in the music but I did enjoy it and eventually I got a very good collection of records from him. The last record I think I bought from him was that Frenchman Sacha Distel. Brian was mad about Sacha Distel. That's as far as he'd got at that time.

Lionel Bart: He was not ostentatious. I'd spoken to this person on the phone way before I met him. He was a fan, I really have to say. There was this young Liverpool person calling me with a posh accent really. He said, 'I'm from Liverpool,' and he worked in the record section of his father's family department store. He was up on what was going down in the charts and in those days it was me a lot. I'd just had an immense hit with Cliff Richard doing my song 'Living Doll', and it had broken all records in his little shop there.

So he said he'd love to come down and meet me. We corresponded for a year or two until eventually he did appear and he looked the same then as he always did: immaculate – the suit, the very highly polished shoes, the tie, the cuff links, terribly correct, more British than I think he needed to be. But he kept this thing up and it wasn't an image. That was what he presented to the world. He blushed easily. He couldn't take compliments.

Yankel Feather: I was buying records off him one day. I think he was one of those people who could do two things at once, so while he was serving me it wasn't unusual for him to look over my shoulder and see what was going on behind me.

This day he seemed to be looking out the window. I said, 'What are you looking at, Brian?' and he pointed to a boy standing on the corner. I asked, 'Who's that?' and he said, 'That's the boy who's just come out of jail.' I think he said he'd just done four years for beating him up – he'd beaten Brian up with a milk bottle.

The boy had turned up and Brian had made an appointment to meet him on the corner. I said, 'You're not going to see him after he's beaten you up?' He said, 'Well, I've got to go and see him because he needs help and I want to help him.' That was Brian, that was another side of Brian.

4. Love Me Do

To write at all I found it very necessary to consume five whiskies
before putting pen to paper. Of course, I'd planned writing for a
long time. This was the big let out – the only way to rid myself of
humdrum, dreary, god-forsaken suburbia. The thing is to get away.
Away from it all! What a worn-out, meaningless phrase it is – but
it isn't all that meaningless because everybody wants to – but who
does? I fancy Rome – I want to live in luxury, learn the language,
live Italian and just add myself to that very attractive, utterly
ridiculous little group that calls itself – or, at least, is named by
newspaper hickeys as – the International Set.

BRIAN EPSTEIN, JOURNAL, 1960

Alistair Taylor: The legend has it that a lad named Raymond Jones walked into
the shop and asked for 'My Bonnie' by the Beatles and that Brian put his name
in the book and that's how we found the Beatles. What in fact happened was
that I got fed up with youngsters coming in asking for the Beatles record. So I
put a name, Raymond Jones, in the order book. I just made it up. Otherwise
Brian wouldn't have paid any attention. Our pledge was that anyone who
ordered a record would get it. Once a name was in the book, we would have to
order twenty-five. That was the minimum.

As it happens, we had to import it from Germany, since the record had
never been released in England. I bought one copy myself to cover the
Raymond Jones order and I don't even think Brian ever found out there never
was a Raymond Jones.

Anyway, salesman that he was, Brian did a handwritten notice in the
window which said BEATLES RECORD AVAILABLE HERE. Within an hour or so
it had sold out. All the rest, the other twenty-four, had gone. So we ordered
another twenty-five. The same thing. Bang. Gone.

It just built and built and built. Then Brian came in one morning and told
me he'd seen this poster at the bottom of Mathews Street advertising the
Beatles direct from Hamburg, and of course Mathews Street is where the
Cavern Club was. He said, 'I'm intrigued because we've sold so many records
of this, if you remember it.' So I said, 'Yes, of course I do.' He said, 'I'm just

intrigued to go and see how come they have sold so many records.' This was unheard of as far as we were concerned. So we decided to go see them during our lunch hour.

We've been accused that we surely must have known they were from Liverpool. Well, we didn't. We weren't interested in pop music. And on the poster it just said DIRECT FROM HAMBURG THE BEATLES, and the label on 'My Bonnie' was all in German. It was only later that we suddenly thought, 'We've seen them before in the shop and they were from Merseyside, from Liverpool.' We certainly didn't realize that they were Liverpool's favourite group.

The name on the label of the record in question was Tony Sheridan and the Beat Brothers. Tony Sheridan was a Liverpool singer then living in Hamburg. The Beat Brothers were the Beatles, which was common knowledge to young people in Liverpool. Like many other Liverpool groups, the Beatles had been playing in Hamburg off and on for the last year and a half and had been signed to German Polydor by Bert Kaempfert, the bandleader who was then Polydor's A&R man. But all he did was assign them to provide backing for Tony Sheridan on a set of recordings.

Paul McCartney: He came to see us famously at the Cavern. It was announced that Mr Brian Epstein of NEMS record store was in the audience. He came to say hello and that was basically it.

Alistair Taylor: It was an awful club. There was condensation running down the walls. It smelt because it used to be a vegetable warehouse and when it got hot it was even worse. This was lunch time, this wasn't an evening session, and all the groovers with their beehive hairstyles and the lads trying to look cool made the place very hot and very sticky.

There were these four guys onstage in black leather, wearing what we call bomber jackets today, black trousers, black T-shirts, and they were so loud. There was smoking onstage and they were joking with the girls in the audience and it was just like, 'Oh my God, what are we sitting here watching?' I mean we were in suits. I always had to wear a suit when everybody else was freaking out. So here were these two straight guys who liked classical music sitting in the back two seats of this smelly, sweaty club. And these guys were just so awful. They really were. It was quite appalling, really.

The Cavern had opened in January 1957 as a venue for traditional jazz and occasional visitors from America. Big Bill Broonzy and Sonny Terry and Brownie McGhee had all played there.

Soon afterwards it provided a venue for bands of the skiffle craze, which in turn gave way to the Liverpool beat scene.

By the time Epstein went there with Alistair Taylor, the lunch-time sessions had been pretty much taken over by the Beatles, one of the most popular of the 300 or so beat groups playing in the city.

Alistair Taylor: It took about half an hour after Brian saw the Beatles to decide to manage them. We went for lunch and he asked me my opinion first, and I said I thought they were awful but there was something there. He said, 'They *are* awful but I think they're fabulous.' And then he suddenly said, 'What do you think about me managing them?' And it was as quick as that. It was just overwhelming. That was 9 November 1961.

It's been said for years and years that the reason he signed them was because he fell in love with John instantly. That is a load of rubbish. That's another Beatle myth that somebody thought up and wrote and so everybody copies it and it suddenly becomes fact. Well, that wasn't the reason for signing them. The reason he wanted to manage the Beatles was because they were just incredible.

Paul McCartney: He was completely different from anyone in the Liverpool music scene. Having gone to RADA, which we found out later, that's quite unusual in Liverpool. You don't get that.

The big impressive thing about Brian was his car. He had a bigger car than anyone we knew. He had a big Zephyr Zodiac and we were really impressed. We knew people in Ford Populars. I had a Ford Classic but Brian had a big Zodiac so that was obvious wealth there. So he was quite different from anybody else.

We had been playing together a little while and we were starting to feel that we were getting good, but there comes a point in everybody's career when you think you need a little bit more than just being good. We needed someone to manage that goodness and push and give us a few clues as to how we might go a bit further.

It became obvious that Brian was that person. He had a theatrical flair. Having gone to RADA he was interested in the theatre. He knew a lot of people. So it became clear that he would be very good for us. We really just had to argue about how much we would give him. Do managers take ten per cent or fifteen or what? We had no idea.

My dad, when he heard about Brian wanting to manage us, said, 'This could be a very good thing.' He thought Jewish people were very good with money. This was the common wisdom. Dad thought Brian would be very good for us. He thought Brian was very sensible, very charming, and he was right.

Dear Mr White, 8th December, 1961

As I'm somewhat disappointed at not having heard from you with regard to the matter we discussed last week, I thought I'd write and attempt to impress you once again with my enthusiasm for, and belief in, the potential success of 'The Beatles'. If I didn't mention that they were so much better in reality than on the disc it was because I may have assumed that 'you'd heard it all before'.

Next week the Group will be seen by A&R men from Decca. I mention this because (as you may appreciate), if we could choose it would certainly be EMI. These four boys, who are superb instrumentalists, also produce some exciting and pulsating vocals. They play mostly their own compositions and one of the boys has written a song which I really believe to be the hottest material since 'Living Doll'. This is a Group of exceptional talents and appealing personalities.

I look forward to hearing from you.

Yours sincerely,

Brian Epstein

Alistair Taylor: It was downstairs at the store that the boys signed the first contract with Brian. There are only five signatures on that contract. The fifth signature was mine because Brian never signed that contract. He always said at that time that he didn't want the boys to feel bound to him. They could walk away from the contract any time they liked and he couldn't hold them if he didn't sign it.

So in a way the agreement was one-sided. In other words, if he didn't sign it and they weren't happy with what he was doing, they could walk out. If the contract was signed by him he could hold them to it. So I witnessed his non-signature because he said, 'I'll sign it later, Alistair. Witness mine as well.' So I'm down in history as witnessing a non-signature.

There was a second contract later, which he did sign. Anyway, I think probably Rex Makin told him that it was about time he signed a contract with the Beatles. In the very beginning you've got to remember that neither of us knew the first thing about management. We just ran a few record stores, that's all, and furniture shops. We were on one hell of a learning curve, frankly.

Derek Taylor: When he signed them up, when he had them in that office in Whitechapel, he told them, 'I think I can help you.' He actually believed he could and he was prepared to sit it out with them, with all their cheek and impudence. In a way they had a lot in common, just the vernacular was different.

The access he gave them to another side of Liverpool must have been important to them, the sense that they were on the move. He had a great style and a good car and once he got his confidence and got his bearings he was very funny, very comical and upbeat and witty. When he'd had a few drinks in him, in a gambling club or anywhere he was comfortable, he was very funny. He laughed easily and said amusing things.

Paul McCartney: We were just Liverpool guys so the word was queer not gay. We didn't really have a problem with it. It was just something you made fun of. That's the way it was. We actually didn't know anybody gay. Well, we probably did but we didn't even talk about. So it was, 'Oh, he's queer,' just like, 'Oh, she's a prostitute.' It was just sort of a strange term you used then. The word was out that Brian was gay amongst people.

The great thing for us was that it didn't really affect us in any way. I think we suspected that he might hit on one of us. So I think in the early days we were slightly wondering whether that was his interest in us. But in my personal knowledge that wasn't his interest.

Peter Brown: The Epsteins were a very close family. It was the father and mother and two sons. They ran the family business and they were very, very tight. So I don't quite know their initial reaction to Brian's managing the Beatles. I mean, they were always very supportive of Brian and so, to the outside world even somebody like me who was sort of inside, I was never privy to what went on around the family dinner table on a Friday night.

Alistair Taylor: They couldn't quite understand what this son of theirs, who used to go to the Philharmonic Hall and listen to Mozart and Beethoven, is suddenly talking about. And actually managing four leather-clad rockers from the Cavern Club – I mean, this is like hitting Harry over the head with a mallet really. They ended up incredibly proud of him for what he did. The marvellous thing from their point of view was that he made a success. Having been a success in the shops he then moved on and became a success in the pop-music business. So they had a lot to be proud of.

Aunt Stella: I really can't tell you whether Queenie and Harry bothered very much when Brian wanted to manage the Beatles. They were probably amazed but they let him carry on.

Rex Makin: I saw the boys coming to him on a Sunday morning when I was in my garden. They came and they looked what we term in Liverpool a set of scallywags – untidily dressed and all the rest of it and not quite the thing for the genteel atmosphere of the part of Queens Drive where we lived.

Vera Brown: We'd been to the Knotty Ash Club for my sister's engagement. The Beatles had played there, as did Rory [Storm] and a few other groups. Afterwards, as usual, we all went back to the house and Brian came along.

If you saw the Beatles in my mother's they were just a scruffy bunch of boys. And who'd look at them? I wouldn't bother with them but then Brian stood out and Brian looked like the real thing. He was handsome. He was tall. He was immaculate. That's why I let Brian get behind the bar with me and help me serve the drinks. He was the best of the bunch.

So we were just behind the bar when Elvis came on, 'Heartbreak Hotel'. He loved it, I loved it, and we started dancing. There wasn't much room. You know, you could go two steps forward, three steps back and that was it. So we sort of got a bit close and everyone was laughing at us, saying, like, 'What's going on?' But if you moved sideways you fell over the crates. There were crates of beer in there and everybody's coats. We ended up on top of the coats or on top of the crates if we just moved the wrong way. And we got pretty close but I wasn't surprised by the way he was acting towards me.

We were dancing and kissing at the same time. He was probably one of the sexiest fellas I had ever met. People say, 'Oh well, Brian was gay,' but he wasn't very gay with me. He was just like any other man and more. He was very easy-going and casual and funny. He'd make you laugh and he could dance. You know he could move. He said to me, 'I've seen you in different places and I thought you were stuck up.' And I said, 'Well, I thought you were stuck up because I remember being in your shop and you were like the big boss.'

I think he was pretty fresh. In a house where people are looking at you it's not like a club with all the lights out and people tend to be aware of others but Brian wasn't that bothered. He was interested and he showed it. Maybe he'd had a bit too much to drink. I don't know. But I can't say that because I met Brian afterwards and he was still interested.

The next day he called round to the house. I wasn't there so he talked to my mother about poetry. I don't know how they got talking about poems but Brian came the following day with a book of poems for my mother with a little letter. He also gave her a letter thanking her for having the party because everyone had made such a terrible mess of the house. It was full of eggs and rubbish and bottles everywhere and he apologized for the actions of everybody else at the party.

Well, my mother just thought he was the most wonderful person in the world. At last a gentleman has come through this door and not Teddy boys and hooligans and all the rest of it. In the first letter he said he'd enjoyed meeting her, loved coming to the house, felt so welcome and would she mind if he came around again to see me. I said to my mum, 'Well, that's impossible. How can I see him? You know I can't go out with Brian.' She said, 'You will have to.'

My mother was in love with Brian: 'He's beautiful. He's wonderful.' So she sort of arranged it. I didn't want him to come and pick me up at the house because I didn't want people to see us going out. I arranged to meet him in a little café in Bold Street. We had a coffee and a chat and then I can't really remember where we went. We went somewhere for a drink around Bold Street where there were all these little dives at the time. But I had to be back for nine o'clock. Another time I met him in the Tower and we had a little chat. We met in the back office and had a talk.

I liked Brian as a man and I think Brian liked me. But then he suggested if we were to go out we'd have to go to Southport or Manchester – anywhere out of Liverpool because he didn't want to walk into my husband in Liverpool. We were separated at the time but it was a little bit awkward, you know.

It's hard for me to believe Brian was gay. I think if I had been free and if I'd seen more of Brian I think we could have got serious. I think he was all man. I just can't accept that he was gay.

In the shop Brian seemed like a man, like your dad shouting at you and superior. He had an attitude of superiority. But later on I discovered he was just like any other man. I thought he was a very passionate, loving person. He was like two different people. So if there's a third person involved – this gay person – I just say he's one hell of a man to be able to please everybody. You know, he was just unique. That's all I can say.

Paul McCartney: Brian suggested we get into suits. We'd come back from Hamburg and we'd bought leather jackets, being guys on the loose in Hamburg, with leather trousers, leather boots and hats and stuff. We were four little Gene Vincents really. I think Brian was actually attracted to that image, as it turned out later, but in actual fact he said, 'It might get in the way of you getting jobs.' A different image would open the door for a lot of the good-paying jobs, which was actually what we were trying to get: fame and fortune. There was no philanthropic edge to it at all, then.

Peter Brown: I think that maybe the way, in the early days, he directed the Beatles and told them what to wear and how to present themselves and helped choose the music – all that was part of him being the performer, but he was really more presenting them and being the director.

On a personal and intellectual basis he probably identified especially with John, and I think that they in return respected him for being Mr Epstein with the very successful and groovy record store. And then he talked to them about music, which he clearly knew something about, and was able to really seriously contribute to their material and their development as creators as well as their presentation.

The balance in the Beatles was affected enormously by Brian. I always believed that initially when Brian asked to manage them back in '61, one of the reasons it went through was that John Lennon saw himself as the band leader. He realized that Brian identified more with him than any of the other three and that he could control the situation and continue to control the situation through his influence over Brian. And this continued all the way through.

Billy J. Kramer: I always thought the Beatles could be stars. The first time I saw them at Lytham Town Hall I thought, 'They've got something different and they're very special.' Funnily enough, when Brian came along and started managing the Beatles and putting them into suits, I thought, 'This guy's going to do things for the Beatles. He's going to make something of them.'

Nat Weiss: I don't think what the Beatles needed was a great businessman. They needed a person who would inspire them, whose neurosis was sufficient for him to identify with them. And for Brian the Beatles were an alter ego. Brian was on the stage with those Beatles emotionally and he devoted his life to them.

Derek Taylor: All the things he did were right for them. There was a lot of posthumous, wise-after-the-event stuff like John saying he shouldn't have put them in suits, that it was a big sell-out, etc. They didn't mind at the time. They were making more money that way and they were starting to think that the leather was rather foolish anyway.

Paul McCartney: A lot of the good-paying jobs were cabaret-type things, slightly posher jobs. There was a place in Liverpool called the Cabaret Club, and they obviously wouldn't take us with leather. So when Brian suggested that we get suits, and even though the myth is that we all hated it and have said we would rather stay with the leather, in actual fact my memory is that we didn't mind at all.

It was just a change of image and, because none of us had suits before, it was quite cool. We went over to Birkenhead, 'over the water' as we say in Liverpool, to a place that had been recommended to us. We picked out some very groovy mohair suits, which were OK. If we wanted to go leather, we could go leather. If we wanted to do the mohair thing, we could do that. It was a good thing. It did open doors for us. He was right. It meant that people who wouldn't accept the leather look could have us looking a bit more seemly.

Alistair Taylor: He smartened them up. He taught them stage discipline. They were told in writing that they must stop swearing onstage, they must stop joking with the girls, they must stop smoking onstage or carrying cans of Coke onstage. He tidied their hair up and he put them into smart suits. His great thing was his projection of the talent that he realized. Brian could see what could happen with this band and he channelled it in exactly the right direction, which no one else has ever done, if you think about it.

His parents were rather worried by all this, particularly Harry, because Brian used to go down to London a lot. He was pounding the pavements, trying to get somebody in this world to listen to this wonderful group that he'd found in Liverpool. So Harry would come into the shop and I daren't say anything to him because sometimes Brian would say, 'Don't tell Daddy.' He always called them Mummy and Daddy. 'If he comes in the shop don't tell him where I've gone.' And he'd be down in London and I used to think of all sorts of excuses to explain where Brian was. I might say he was late back from lunch or he'd got another business meeting somewhere but Harry wasn't silly. He'd begun to cotton on that Brian was away a bit too often. But I think they were worried rather than annoyed.

Peter Brown: It was difficult for Brian because he was still running the record store, and it was successful, and he was making these trips to the record companies pitching the Beatles. It seemed like an awful long time that he was doing this and coming back dejected for having been rejected. But it was all right because it was a challenge to him and he was not going to give up.

The amphetamine time started around then. My personal recollection of it is of having to do more and more because I was running my own shop and helping with Brian's shop when he was not there. I was going to London with Brian being there a lot of the time and it was great fun for me. I was travelling backwards and forwards and there was a lot of lost sleep.

I was encouraged to take amphetamines and I did. Fortunately, my personality was such that they didn't get me. There's no question that Brian had much more stress than I did, and he was doing it much more and his personality wasn't the same.

He was introduced to these amphetamines by the Beatles and other groups who had played in Hamburg where they needed stimulants to keep going. So I'm sure there was an element of being cool. It was a cool thing to do. He wanted to be part of the little group – I mean, part of the Beatles. I guess he wanted to show that he was cool and hip. I'm sure that was part of the whole idea initially, and also it did help when he was travelling so much.

Paul McCartney: Brian's mum had been a pill taker. I don't know whether it was for slimming or what. It was probably for anything – slimming, sleeping. His mum Queenie was a very nice lady, always really friendly to us, but I suspect that's where Brian got the pill thing. So Brian would take a pill if he needed to get up, like people who take coffee.

Geoffrey Ellis: Brian always had a very good relationship with his parents, particularly with his mother, to whom he was very close. His mother, I think, was only about nineteen when he was born, and she was exceptionally close to him. I think more so, in point of fact, than she was to her younger son, Clive. As far as I knew, he had a good relationship with his father, too.

His father was indulgent with him when he was setting up as manager of the Beatles. I think Harry did get a little bit impatient at the amount of time that Brian was taking to try to sell the Beatles and get them a recording contract, because at that time he was still employed by his father's business. But I never heard and certainly never saw any indications of any hostility between Brian and his father.

Paul McCartney: John and I used to wait at Lime Street Station in a little coffee bar called the Punch and Judy. We used to wait for Brian arriving back from London, and when he'd come off the train we'd take a look at his face to see if it was good news or bad, and it was bad. It was always bad. He'd be, like, 'Sorry.' We'd go, 'Oh,' and we'd have a cup of coffee and discuss what had happened. He would just say, 'You know people aren't generally interested. You know it's going to be a hard sell.'

George Martin: There's no question of them employing him. No, he was in charge and they did what he said. I mean, he was their only hope. They'd done a pretty hard grind all over the place. They were convinced they were going to get to the top but they found it hard. Even in Germany they were booked as a backing group and Bert Kaempfert saw them as a foil for Tony Sheridan.

They'd had a tough time, so they were prepared to go along with Brian if he could bring them results. So they did listen to him. When he told them to tidy up their appearance and do their hair in a different way and put on different suits later on, they obeyed. They did what he said.

Nat Weiss: Brian fused everything. The Beatles were together before they met Brian and they had the talent. But it was Brian who was the emotional and psychological catalyst. He had the vision to say the Beatles would be bigger than Elvis in 1961. When all the record companies told him to go back to his record store and forget about it he refused to give up.

He always told me that he really believed that he was a man of destiny. He knew that the Beatles would be bigger than anything and he never gave up on that. Every other word out of his mouth was that they are too important even when they were nothing. It would be like me taking a group down a basement and saying they are too important to be paid in coins. He used those phrases and he always stared up at the sky when he said these things.

George Martin: Brian was full of confidence for the Beatles. He was the first time I met him. This was before he introduced me to other artists, and he had this unswerving devotion and faith in them, that they were brilliant and they were going to conquer the world. And looking back on it this was all the more remarkable because he'd been completely rejected by everybody. Absolutely everybody in this country had turned him down. And he still had that blind faith: 'They're gonna make it, I don't care what happens, they're gonna make it.'

To begin with, Brian needed another demonstration record to play to people. He'd exhausted all of his demos with all the people that he'd been rejected by. So he went into the HMV shop in Oxford Street with a tape that he had of the Decca recordings. He asked the man to transfer it to disc, because in those days you didn't have cassettes, you either had discs which you played on a record player or loop-to-loop tape which was very cumbersome. So he had them transferred. The engineer thought it was very interesting and asked who the group was and whether they had a contract. Brian said, 'No. I've been trying everywhere and everyone.'

The engineer introduced him to a man upstairs who was the music publisher for EMI, a chap called Sid Coleman. He went through the story again, and Sid asked if he had been to EMI. Brian said, 'I've tried EMI and I was told no go.' So Sid asked Brian if he had gone to George Martin at EMI. Brian asked, 'Who's he?' Sid said, 'Well, he runs Parlophone.' It was a kind of jazz/comedy label at the time so Brian groaned inwardly and realized he'd hit rock bottom.

Sid told me he'd have to talk to me and that he would arrange the whole thing. And that was how Brian walked into my office with these discs. He gave me his spiel, and although I was sort of a little bit cynical I was quite impressed with his devotion and his zeal for this group, which made me want to see them. I hadn't got a great deal to lose.

Of course, when I met them and saw them, worked with them, I got the same kind of feeling that he'd got. It was a kind of falling-in-love business because they had this tremendous charisma, which nobody else seemed to have recognized, and I was puzzled by it. But there we are.

He certainly wasn't cast in the mould of the hardened professional. He seemed to be a little bit ingenuous but for that reason he was fresh. I liked him. I thought he was good and I was persuaded by his enthusiasm. Anyway, I don't believe that you have to be a hardened criminal to be in the music business.

Yankel Feather: I don't think Brian had a clue who he was. I don't think he liked being who he was and I think he had every intention of altering that, although I think he found it easier to create the Beatles than he did to reinvent himself. He was a homosexual and it's not easy being a homosexual, but there's homosexuals and homosexuals; some are simple, some are clever, some are brilliant.

He wasn't at all happy as a homosexual even though I don't think he wanted to be what one would call normal. He was quite happy being different. Obviously it was part of his plan that this difference would eventually pay off, even though he was not a happy person.

But then it would take an unhappy person who was sure of himself, it would take somebody as mad as Brian, to have dreams that he had to accomplish what he did accomplish in the end. I mean, an ordinary person couldn't do it. If he had been a young married man with two children, would his wife let him out to spend his time with four unruly boys? No, it couldn't have happened. For the Beatles to make it, they had to have somebody as strange as him.

Simon Napier-Bell: When Brian met the Beatles, something about them energized him. It may have been to do with his protected middle-class background and feeling he was not a part of anything. It may have been to do with homosexuality, but one way or another he was excited by them to a point where he just devoted himself to them.

The luck was that the excitement and the way he devoted himself to them and the music they were playing and their personality all gelled into something which happened. You can see it was luck by the number of times he was turned down. Still, he thought, 'Just one more trip and one more trip.' If he had been turned down on that one last trip to London, it wouldn't have happened. It was just by the skin of the teeth that the thing came through. After he was turned down by Decca, he went back to Liverpool and almost didn't try again.

Lionel Bart: Right from the very early days, when Brian was trying to promote the Beatles in London and get them record deals, he said, 'Well, they're going to be bigger than Elvis.' And of course everybody laughed at him. I did too, really, but it wasn't sort of cynical laughter. I said, 'Come on, Brian, give us a break.' But he was totally dedicated and this dedication, together with the suit and the gentlemanly appearance which he had and his demeanour, may well have been a key to allowing him into the American great razzmatazz and the great pressure of the business.

George Martin: I initiated the thing about Pete Best, but I learned later that I wasn't the only one who had reservations about him. On that first recording I was aware that I needed a stronger and more steady and more powerful drum beat than I was getting. Drums are terribly important in this kind of music and, although the drummer was a very good-looking lad, he didn't have the overt personality of the other three. Certainly on sound alone I knew that I had to have a change.

So I said to Brian, 'On the next recording I'm going to book a different drummer. From your point of view it needn't make any difference but we will have in the studio a professional drummer.' So I booked Andy White, who was the top drummer of the day. It was then that I found out that the group had independently been wanting to get rid of Pete and this was a good excuse. So they fired him.

They just said that he wasn't the strong member of the group and that they needed a good drummer. They were fortunate in getting Ringo. I mean they actually pursued Ringo, because Ringo was a bit of a star then. He was the drummer with Rory Storm and that alone was like he was a big cheese.

Brian didn't say it was difficult, but he regretted it because he liked Pete. He realized, though, that it was inevitable and he had to do something about it. It made me realize that he knew what to do with the boys. He didn't like being ruthless but he knew he had to do it, and for the good of the band he did it.

If anything, Pete Best was probably the most popular Beatle among Liverpool fans and his firing caused a prolonged and angry backlash. Demonstrations outside the Cavern Club got so rowdy and feeling ran so high that Brian actually feared for his safety for weeks after he forced Best to leave.

With the addition of Ringo Starr, it was easy to complete the new image of the Beatles, mainly because Ringo's hair fell naturally into the 'Beatle cut' while Pete Best never gave up his quiff.

Aunt Stella: When I first heard 'Love Me Do' I was sitting at Harry and Queenie's house. It was New Year, Rosh Hashanah, and the family were all gathered there. I was there with my children and Brian made an announcement that he'd like us to hear this group that he had. I think it was a demo disc and he put 'Love Me Do' on. I must admit that I wasn't used to this type of music. I had heard the Shadows and people like this but I couldn't say that it was my favourite record. I love the Beatles music, a lot of it, but that one not particularly. However, I was asked, 'What do you think of it, Auntie Stella?' And I said, 'Well, Brian, I'm a Frank Sinatra fan.'

Peter Brown: Once the record deal had been done and once the records were coming out and there were tours to look after and the success started to build, there was more stress, and Brian decided to give up all the responsibility for anything in Liverpool and just concentrate on the Beatles management.

Simon Napier-Bell: If you think of the Beatles, you think of four faces, because their imagery became so much stronger than their playing. This is rather an insult to the Beatles because they were such fantastic musicians and made amazing records, but you tend to think of the imagery dominating the music and I think that's what's happened ever since, that the imagery of a boy group has become more important than its music.

There's no question Brian created the image because of his own middle-class ethic. He discovered these boys who he found tremendously exciting. What he would have liked was to become a working-class boy with them. That's what he really wanted. He knew he couldn't do that so he had to turn them into something presentable he could take home to his mother for tea or something.

So he turned them into pretty, cleaned-up boys who would become part of his middle-class life. A lot of people said to me that he put them into the image of what he fancied. I doubt that. He probably liked them rough and ready as they come but he wanted to introduce them to his aunts and uncles.

Brian got the image right and he's 100 per cent responsible for that. I bet they went to the hairdresser he chose and had the hairstyle he chose and he chose the jackets. I'm absolutely certain that everything came from Brian in terms of the image.

Derek Taylor: The Beatles trusted Brian completely. It was a wonderful thing that happened to the boys. Everyone knows that these are not easy people to please; they picked up on everything. They were in their own little tiny world that had always been there since school. Ringo joined because he fitted just that tad or two more more than Pete. So for Brian's acceptance to be so total, being such a different type of bloke, and just sufficiently older to be too old, he had to be completely trusted with almost everything. He was, apart from any of the famous stories about unwelcome comments about somebody singing flat or songs not being suitable.

Paul McCartney: If anyone was the fifth Beatle it was Brian. People talked about George Martin as being the fifth Beatle because of his musical involvement but, particularly in the early days, Brian was very much part of the group. He wasn't musically. We generally wouldn't listen to him musically unless it was down to choosing a single. We would offer him some songs and he'd say, 'I like that one best,' and we'd usually go with it. But it was theatrical management that we'd listen to Brian about.

One of the biggest things he ever told us to do was to bow, this sort of Beatle bow from the waist. He said this would be very good. The great thing was that I think it is always very helpful having someone theatrical out front.

If you're in a theatrical endeavour the only way you can tell if you're doing good is if you have someone out there who says, 'That was really good. When you moved over, they lost you. Don't do that next time.' He was a director. That's really what he was.

5. The World Comes to Liverpool

MICHAEL CHARLTON: *How ruthless does Epstein find the business underneath?*
BRIAN EPSTEIN: It depends. In certain parts it is – in the agenting, the buy and selling side of things. I wouldn't say it was ruthless but I'd say the competition was very keen.

CHARLTON: *Well, you've toyed with the idea of saying it's ruthless. How ruthless do you think you have to be?*
EPSTEIN: Not very. It may be a fault of mine in the business that I'm not ruthless enough.

CHARLTON: *Do you feel you exploit teenage talent?*
EPSTEIN: No. Talent? No. I think I develop teenage talent rather than exploit it.

CHARLTON: *What about teenage emotion? Does the business exploit teenage emotion?*
EPSTEIN: No, because you don't make a record and set out to make scenes in theatres. This just happens. You don't really think about what's happening in a theatre as unhealthy. You never think of it as unhealthy. You think of it as being good. I know it sounds funny but if there are a lot of screams in the theatre and there's an enormous amount of noise going on, you think, 'It was good tonight. It was a great show.'

CHARLTON: *Because your people are so young, do you think we could accuse you of exercising excessive control over them?*
EPSTEIN: I don't think it's true that I exercise undue pressure. Actually I've been very fortunate. Every artist has bettered themselves as a result of having signed an agreement with me. I'm not going to say that I could do it with everyone but it's turned out well in all cases.

CHARLTON: *But when you signed and launched the Beatles, did you know or suspect that they might gross, as we believe they have, £5 million in twelve months?*
EPSTEIN: I wouldn't have said that because I didn't think in terms of money, really. But I would have said they would have been one of the biggest, if not the biggest, theatrical attractions in the world.

PANORAMA, BBC, 30 MARCH 1964

Gerry Marsden: Liverpool groups didn't have managers. My dad looked after us, which meant he'd be on the phone to take the bookings down and tell the clubs how much we wanted. There might have been a couple of small-time managers, but not managers as we know them now.

When Brian came on the scene as a manager we realized what a manager meant because Brian then took the bookings, sorted out the money, got us a few quid, sorted out the tax, sorted out the publicity. We'd never had that before. Before that you did your own. If you had a manager he drove you to the gig, collected your money and paid out. He didn't think of publicity. So Brian was the first big-time manager on Merseyside.

Before Brian came I never considered making a record. We started in about '57ish and Brian started in '62 so we were five years, six years before Brian actually signed us. He signed the Beatles and we went to Hamburg, and when we came back from Hamburg he wanted to sign me and I thought, 'Brian, you certainly can, my son.' He'd just told me he'd got a record deal for the Beatles and I thought, 'If Brian can get us a few more quid and maybe a record deal, well, that would be the big time for us.'

We thought, 'He's crazy but, OK, let's make a record. At least we can tell our kids we made a record and maybe that record can get us a few more quid, a few more jobs,' never thinking for one second that we would become famous or that the Beatles would become the biggest thing since sliced bread. It was just Brian's great foresight. We didn't know. The Beatles didn't even know, nor did London. London didn't know about Liverpool. They didn't know what was going to happen.

Brian made us wear shirts, stop smoking non-filtered cigarettes. I was fed up wearing old shirts on stage and old sweaters and Brian made you feel smart. You put a suit on. You looked good. You felt good. You smoked the right cigarettes. You didn't smoke these woodies or roll them. Brian made you feel good. He tried to stop us talking badly. He said, 'Gerry, nobody will understand what you're saying.' So we had to try and change and be a bit more cosmopolitan in our accent, which I think we did.

When Brian became our manager he realized we needed publicity. We were the first agency in Liverpool to get a PR guy in to do the publicity. Brian also realized we needed television, we needed radio. We'd never thought of doing radio and television. We didn't have a PR guy. We didn't care about that. Brian was the first one to bring that in and he realized just how important it was. He had the Beatles doing their own radio show for the BBC in Manchester long before they'd done 'Love Me Do'. I think we actually did the show with them when they we were on television from Manchester with little diddy David Hamilton.

Joe Ankrah: I first met Brian Epstein just after we'd done our first engagement on stage at the Cavern. It was an afternoon session and there was a lot of fuss about how good we were. Brian asked me to come to his office over at NEMS because he said he wanted to put us under contract. He didn't ask me. He just said, 'I'd like to put you boys under contract.'

My overriding impression was that he was somebody that I just couldn't approach. The thought of him actually being a manager was, 'Great. We're under management. We have a contract, you know, you can't book us 'cause we've got a contract. You have to see our manager.' We used to enjoy saying to people, 'You'll have to speak to our manager about that.' We used to love to say that. It was great.

He always seemed to look like someone you'd expect to be in charge of something, and being the manager of NEMS alone was good enough. If Brian was with us and we wanted something you'd ask Brian if he could do it for you. He commanded respect. He never used to order us about or anything like that. He just used to suggest things.

We did a few more shows with the Beatles as sort of guests. Then not long after that they recorded their first record, which was 'Love Me Do', and then we didn't see Brian for almost a year.

Johnny Gustafson: I was in the Big Three and Brian approached us. I think it was at a gig in Southport. We were supporting the Beatles that night and I think John Lennon had spoken to him. I've got a feeling that Lennon said we were his favourite group at the time and he put a word in. Brian came to see us a few times and he obviously liked what he saw and he thought he'd add us to his little stable of artistes.

First of all we thought it was actually amazing. Well, it was amazing to be managed by somebody like Brian, who was doing reasonably well for the Beatles. For instance, at the Cavern we were getting six pounds for an evening session and he bumped it up to nine quid immediately after he took us over. So we straight away thought it was great guns to have him as our manager.

It was fine at first but Brian had other ideas. His idea was based on, I suppose, his background and his style of dress and everything else. I presume that's where it came from. He wanted us to be suited up in the best finery money could buy but we didn't really think very much of that idea. I remember one time he gave us some money to go and buy suits. It was eighty pounds, I think. We ran across to C & A over the road and bought these suits for three quid each with odd trousers and things and the rest of the money we spent in various pubs around Liverpool. Of course, when he found out there was hell to pay and he cracked down after that and took us to a real tailor's and kitted us out in mohair suits. Just what he wanted, really.

Rex Makin: I knew every move, step by step. In the intervals between trying to sell me things he used to come in to tell me of his progress in the rock world. He'd tell me about his visits to the Cavern and how he discovered the group and what he thought was to be done with them and how he had discovered Priscilla White and how he'd discovered the boy who called himself Billy Kramer and other people too. And he went on and on and on about this. I found it rather boring at the time because I had two young children and I wasn't really very interested and I thought it was one of his usual enthusiasms which would peter out. Then I really had very little faith in the stability of the pop music world or the entertainment world as a whole.

Billy J. Kramer: After he signed Gerry Marsden and the Big Three, he then approached me and showed that he had an interest in my talent and believed that I could be somebody. Obviously I did think I could do something.

I was playing in a band with local friends of mine and just doing the same circuit as everybody else. I worked with the Beatles and things like that. There was a popularity poll in *Mersey Beat* and Brian Epstein gave a prize for whoever came highest, non-professionally. At the time I was working for the British Railways as an apprentice fitter and turner. I came in third in the poll. The Beatles came first and Lee Curtis came second. Brian saw me performing at the award ceremony at the Majestic Ballroom in Birkenhead and shortly after that he approached me.

I had been given an ultimatum by my boss at work either to find accommodation in Crewe for a year or leave my job. So I met Brian at the Grapes, the pub opposite the Cavern, and told him the situation.

Then the man I had as a manager at the time, a guy called Ted Nibbs, said to me one Saturday, 'Do you fancy coming into Liverpool for the afternoon?' We went to a restaurant. Brian was there and Ted said, 'You know, it's very simple. I don't want to beat around the bush but I've done all I can for your career, and Brian would like to handle your career if you're interested.' I was aghast. I thought at the time that Brian was very influential in a local way and people really respected him, and for him to be interested in me was, like, *wow*.

He changed my band. He put me with the Dakotas, who were from Manchester. They were very professional, very good musicians, and Brian thought they would be the ideal band to back me. We had a rehearsal at the

Cavern and I didn't think they were that keen on doing it. I think they thought I was this guy from Liverpool who wore all these flamboyant clothes and was a bit crazy.

But we got on very well and agreed we would set out on a career in show business together. Then Brian told me that he didn't like the way I dressed because I used to wear lamé jackets and lamé suits. He took me down to Dougie Millings in London and I started wearing black mohair suits and being very smart. I thought, 'This will last for a short while and then I'll go back to all the wackiness.' But I didn't mind because I thought Brian knew what he was doing.

George Martin: The Beatles were number one in Brian's life always – as they became my number one. Then he brought along another act, which was Gerry and the Pacemakers. He was very sold on Gerry as a person. I quickly realized that Gerry did have talent, but I also realized that the band behind him weren't as good as he was. But nevertheless we thought we could make some records together. But the Pacemakers weren't number one to Brian and they could never be number one.

The first record that we made with Gerry was one that John Lennon rejected. I'd found a song for the Beatles that I thought was great. I thought it was a hit in any case. This was 'How Do You Do It?' We actually recorded it with the Beatles with John singing the lead, but I'd already listened to a song that they'd given me called 'Please Please Me', which I liked but thought was much too dreary. 'Please Please Me' originally was a kind of Roy Orbison ballad, very slow and dreary. I suggested they double the speed and they might have something. Well, when we recorded 'How Do You Do It?', which is very upbeat, with John, he said, 'We've just done "Please Please Me",' and that he didn't want to do another upbeat record like that. So I agreed to drop 'How Do You Do It?' as a song for the Beatles. So I had this good song when Gerry and the Pacemakers came along. I said to Brian, 'Let's do "How Do You Do It?" with Gerry.' And it gave him his first number one, and Gerry actually had a hat trick – his first three records were all number one, which was amazing for a completely unknown act.

Alistair Taylor: He was an absolute stickler for information, for clarification. From day one in management all our artists had to have gig sheets which told them the date of a gig, where the band were playing, who the contact was, what equipment was being supplied, how many electric points there were, what time they were supposed to be there, which hotel they were staying in, and so on.

That was one of my main jobs. I'd book all hotels. They were billed to us so because Brian's attitude was that an artist should only have to worry about his performance on stage. Everything else we took care of and that was unique. It was a completely new form of management because normally other bands would just be told, 'Right, you're playing Glasgow tomorrow night.' 'Well, I've got no petrol.' 'Tough. Get some petrol.' Not Brian, and he kept that up to the day he died. That's where he was so unique in management. He created a whole new form of management.

Johnny Gustafson: We weren't allowed to record what we wanted. The first single we released, 'Some Other Guy', was actually a demo for Decca we had recorded the day after we got back from Hamburg, where we'd been for four or five weeks. So being in the studios four hours a night every night without much of a break shot our voices to pieces. It wasn't very good. We didn't sing. It was awful, we thought.

We were actually in Hamburg again at some point when Epstein sent us a telegram to say that we'd passed the recording test and everything was going fine. When we got back to Liverpool again and went to his office, he said, 'Congratulations, boys. Your single's out very soon.' We said, 'What single?' And he said, 'Well, "Some Other Guy", of course.' We were astounded because we expected to rerecord that song but he and Decca were quite happy to release this substandard material and it went on from there. We were shunted on to these pop songs that Gerry did, songs by Mitch Murray. We were never allowed to choose our own material. We did one B-side, 'Cavern Stomp', which was as near as we ever got to doing what we really wanted to do, which was a shame really. But that's the way things were, then.

George Martin: After Gerry, Billy J. Kramer was brought to me, and we started a similar kind of system – finding the songs, recording them and hitting oil. We were striking pay dirt. Everything that I recorded with them seemed to be accepted by everybody.

Billy J. Kramer: My first song was 'Do You Want to Know a Secret?', which Brian gave me to me. We did the song for a couple of record companies and in Hamburg and all over Great Britain and nobody liked it. Nobody clapped and nobody went crazy. Then we did a recording test for George Martin and George decided to release 'Do You Want to Know a Secret?', and nobody was more amazed than me when it turned out to be a big hit.

I always though that somebody who speaks as well as what Brian did and dressed the way he did has got to be a snob. I was from a different side of the tracks. Let's face it, if you are just a working-class kid from Liverpool and you become associated with somebody who speaks very well and wears Savile Row clothes and Turnbull & Asser ties and handmade shirts, it's a bit intimidating. I never forgot myself with Brian. I respected him too much.

People told me he was gay. But if you're from Liverpool and you meet somebody who dresses that way and talks that way, right away you think that they're gay whether they are or not. It never bothered me at all. I know Brian had this thing and I had my thing in life. I always just hoped that he'd be happy because there were times that I sensed a certain sadness about him.

Peter Brown: There was a point just before the Beatles explosion where he got himself a small apartment in the centre of Liverpool not far from me. It was explained to his mother that he was keeping funny hours because of the tours and everything so he should have this pad. I suppose there's a rationalization in his own mind, but essentially I think it was also a knocking shop but I don't know for sure. It was never a place where he was thinking of living because it wasn't furnished. I mean if Brian was going to live there he would have done a whole job on it. Of course, John Lennon married Cynthia and she was pregnant or had Julian, and Brian gave it to them to live.

Essentially he was living at home until he moved to London.

In April 1963 Brian took John Lennon on a twelve-day holiday to Barcelona. This trip has been the source of endless speculation.

Paul McCartney: I don't actually know the truth of the John rumour. I suspected that the John trip to Barcelona was a power play on John's part because John was a very political animal. I think John went away on that Spanish holiday because nobody went on holiday. I would have gone, anyone would have gone. A free holiday? You're kidding. I'm there. Number two, I'm sure John took Brian aside and said, 'Hey, you want to deal with this group, I'm the guy you deal with, OK.' John was that kind of guy. He was a very sensible, very pragmatic guy. So I'm sure that was the main reason John went there. As to whether there was any sort of gay dalliance or whatever, I don't know.

All I can ever say about it is that I slept with John a lot because you had to, you didn't have more than one bed – and to my knowledge John was never gay.

Brian was very straightforward with me about being gay. We could talk about it quite openly, particularly once we got to know each other.

He never hit on me at all. There was never any question of it. We lived so intimately together that there would have been one evening when he was sort of drunk and so on. It would have been in his character to do that. But we didn't really talk about that.

I remember sitting in his car one night talking about a girl that he'd once sort of loved at RADA and this was his lost love. His family hadn't liked her. She'd not been up to par or something. Brian had a bit of sorrow about this. I don't know what the strength of it was but we talked a long time about that and he seemed quite sad that it had not worked out. But that was the extent of that. From then on he was just kind of openly gay and none of us minded, really.

We were quite naïve. Sometimes on the road we would go to a late-night drinking club which was great because we'd worked long and wanted to relax. There were often all men there. I don't think any of us went, 'Oh, there's all men here.' It just sort of happened. I don't think it was till years later we said, 'Oh, that was probably a gay hangout.'

I don't think we inquired too much of Brian. We knew he had certain friends and we knew who they were and what the relationship was but we didn't really talk too much about it. I think it was probably better that way. He had his own life and we had ours. I didn't tell him about every girl I went with.

I think in many ways it was a plus because there's a gay network in show business. There are a lot of people who are gay so that a lot of the TV producers we would find ourselves working with we'd later find out were gay. So now I can see that Brian was networking. I think it was only ever a plus. It was never negative.

Peter Brown: My sense of the trip to Barcelona is that it was an intriguing situation because John left his wife to go on this holiday, who was still in hospital having given birth to her first child. So it was an extraordinary thing, but John wanted to go on holiday with Brian and there was a great bond between them. John knew that Brian was going and he also knew that Brian was very attracted to him and I think this intrigued John. My understanding only comes from Brian. I never discussed this with John but I heard that there were lots of discussions about the business of homosexuality and Brian's homosexuality. But I think it's wrong to discuss something which is really rather significant when I only know one side of the picture.

Aunt Stella: I think everyone was very proud when the Beatles became famous and I know that Queenie and Harry were very thrilled with what Brian was doing.

Derek Taylor: Queenie was a very respectable Jewish mother, daughter of a rich Sheffield businessman. I had a Sunday lunch at their house once when I first met Brian. He took me there to show me the house and meet his parents. They were very well-to-do, well-behaved, rather anxious parents. They must have been immensely proud. His parents had to put up with him being dumped from the army. I read somewhere that he'd left the army because of homosexual behaviour, but I'm not at all sure that's true. He never told me that. There was some trouble at RADA too, but if you had to leave RADA for being gay, I'll eat my hat. He hadn't settled down, although what he did for his father and in the shops and NEMS with his cataloguing was very good.

I think the thing about Brian that is often missed is that he was a success in formal mainstream terms, as a businessman, as a shopkeeper. They can complain about the business deals, but it's easy to be wise after the event about business deals. He couldn't have known that this was going to happen because, right through to the end, the Beatles were still breaking new ground.

Rex Makin: Bob Wooler, who was the original disc jockey and well known in Liverpool, went to the twenty-first birthday party of Paul McCartney, and at the birthday party everybody had a lot to drink and John Lennon thought or perceived that Wooler had made a pass at him, whereupon he socked him and broke his nose and gave him a black eye. Bob Wooler came to see me and, of course, having regard to the identity of the assailant I got in touch with Brian.

Brian said, 'Well, can you represent all of us?' So I said, 'Well, it's a bit difficult. 'If you're going to pay there's no difficulty because I'll advise Bob what's a reasonable amount.' 'Fine,' said Brian. And we proceeded to negotiate a settlement of the claim made by Wooler against Lennon and the cheque came from NEMS Enterprises Limited on behalf of John and that was the end of the story.

This wasn't the only bit of advice I had to give to Brian. Once he'd descended upon me in the office and asked me could I give him the name of a good venereologist because one of the boys, or some of them, or all of them, had got involved in a social situation, and I gave him the name of a venereologist because in those days we used to use venereologists in connection with divorce proceedings.

George Martin: Brian wanted to be a star himself. That was the essential part of Brian. He couldn't do it as an actor and now he was able to do it as a man who was a manipulator, a puppeteer if you like. He loved this role of being the power behind the scenes. It's a pretty heady wine when everything you do becomes successful, and inevitably he was having a good time. He loved it.

Derek Taylor: I met him at the NEMS office the day after Paul's twenty-first birthday. I went and did a *Daily Express* interview with the man behind the Beatles. Svengali stuff. We got on awfully well, considering what a front he had. He was awfully remote. He did like the interview but also had this kind of sniffy front. But that didn't fool me because I was from Liverpool and I did know he was Jewish. He wouldn't tell me where he was from in Liverpool. I told him I was from Aigburth. Eventually he said Queens Drive. I should have known but he was most resistant to saying where he was from.

He was a bit rum about being Jewish. We got such an easy relationship so quickly that he could say such awful things. 'I hate Jewish golf clubs,' he said, 'they're so noisy.' He'd tell me almost anything but he wouldn't say where he was from. I didn't ask him anything very cheeky. I just wanted to be nice about him and the Beatles because I was truly stunned by how marvellous they'd been at that concert I'd seen in Manchester.

Brian was slightly plump. A very soft appearance, he didn't look as if he did any exercise, but then a lot of people didn't then. I was smoking cigarettes and so was he. Very nervy. Very well dressed, very good suit, lovely shirt. These were the differences, what made people different, the buckled shoes, the monogrammed shirt. The detail. Good short haircut.

He had plenty of friends in Liverpool, all that gay community, although I didn't know anything about him being gay then. He went to a very good bar called the Basnett Bar, a really important place in the story. It was close to cotton Liverpool, traders' Liverpool. I think there was a gay aspect without being a gay bar. It was full of fun, and in the context Brian Epstein would meet all kinds of wonderful people, rough people, knockabout people, gay people, people in the trade he was in, which was the retail trade. Don't forget, although he was fancy and gay and theatrical and artistic, he was a shopkeeper. So he wasn't isolated.

The lads were making money and the lads were looking after the parents. He was the type that all the parents knew. The stratification of Liverpool society was plain to see and everybody knew it. He was this Jewish chap from Queens Drive who had that nice shop in Whitechapel, treated you well; you went in there and ordered a record and he got it in. And he'd got good manners and his father was well behaved, a nice mother. Perfect.

I probably saw him two or three times in 1963 for dinner after the first interview. We'd talk about the boys. One day he said he was worried about what they should do in the mid-term. I'd recently met Ken Dodd, who was very hot, and he'd said, 'I like those lads, they're very cheeky. They should learn to dance.' I said to Brian that's what Ken Dodd said. Brian said, 'I've never heard such nonsense. How dare Ken Dodd offer such advice!'

Lionel Bart: He was beginning to be interested in the music scene and I think he wanted to get to know some people in London. He knew of my association with rock and roll, and he knew what Larry Parnes was doing with his stable of rock and rollers, and I think that he was trying to find out what the network was in London. It's good that he did come to London. I was able to introduce him to a number of people.

I think it was important for him. My girlfriend then was Alma Cogan. Her little flat in High Street Ken was a kind of centrifugal place that people used to go to. There would be all manner of people: major stars from America – Hollywood and New York – and London.

You'd sort of pitch up at two in the morning. After some delay, a face would appear at the window. The keys would come down and you'd let yourself into this small apartment. Alma lived there with her sister, Sandra, and her mother, Faye, who was always chain-smoking. We'd often see Laurence Olivier there, also Noel Coward, Danny Kaye – all the Americans that used to play the Palladium. God knows when Alma ever slept. Brian was very taken with her, as we all were. John Lennon used to love coming up there when the boys came to London.

I'd been up to Liverpool before and Brian had taken me to the Cavern. I remember his colleague Peter Brown had this little apartment that was freezing cold. He'd have to put shillings in the meter and try to get it warm. I wrote a show called *Maggie May* and I wanted to get some Liverpool colour. Brian said, 'Come to Liverpool,' and I lived there for a year.

Paul McCartney: Brian was very honest and we would always honour the not very good deals.

Early on we had some engagements around Cheshire. We thought that was really touring. We were half an hour out of Liverpool and, man, that was nearly Broadway. So we did deals with these people and said, 'Where are we going to get fifty pounds a night?' and later on we would honour them. That was quite a nice thing. After we started making records, we wouldn't say, 'Hey, you've got to pay £500.' We'd say, 'No, no, no, the deal was for fifty. We'll do it for fifty.' Brian was keen that we do that and be quite honourable about all that. He was an honourable businessman.

George Martin: The publishing of 'Love Me Do' was handled by EMI through the fellow who introduced me to Brian, Sid Coleman. After that record was out, Brian had obviously spent a great deal of time and effort trying to get it into the charts, but it only got to number 17. I don't know how many records he bought to do even that.

Brian came to me and said, 'We didn't get any help from your publishers on this at all. We got no promotion. I'm going to take it to somebody else.' I said, 'Who are you going to take it to?' He said he thought he'd go to Hill & Range. They were American publishers with a base in London who handled most of Elvis Presley's material and that was the reason he was going to give it to them. And I said, 'Don't do that, that's silly. If you give it to them you'll be just another little fish in a big pond. What you want is someone who's going to work their guts out for you, and I'd like you to have a British publisher. Don't fall into the hands of an American company.'

I gave him three names. The first one he went to was Dick James. Dick immediately saw the potential. Dick used to be a singer with me. I handled him on records and he was terribly enthusiastic. He thought that 'Please Please Me', which was the first record he had the opportunity of working on, was a hit. Dick worked very hard with promotion and I think he was the main person who got the boys their first big television show. I think it was *Ready, Steady, Go*.

That did the trick. Seeing them on television performing this work, the build-up started happening, and Dick was a tremendous help. Now Dick was also quite clever in suggesting to Brian that, instead of a publishing deal like Brian had had with the previous publisher, just a song-by-song job, why not sign the Beatles' future writings to a company that the Beatles would partly own?

This was a radical idea, and Brian thought it was wonderful. He said, 'I tell you what. If I handle it, my company will take half of it and your company will take the other half.' So Northern Songs began as 20 per cent to John, 20 per cent to Paul, 10 per cent to Brian and the other half to the Dick James camp.

At the time it seemed a good deal, but it was unusual for artists to write their own material. It was also unusual because the record business and publishing business in those days was a very rigid establishment feature and publishers were very strong. If you wrote a song and you had it published by somebody you expected to get 50 per cent of the performing rights, 50 per cent of mechanicals and 10 per cent of sheet music, and that was the kind of standard contract. So you were giving away a lot. In today's terms if you accepted that you'd be considered to be an idiot. But that was the deal and it was against that background that the Beatles were signed to Dick James's companies.

Paul McCartney: It was put to us that we would have our own company, so naturally John and I thought it was half his, half mine.

In actual fact, it was a company within a company that was run by our song publisher, Dick James. This meant that, for practical purposes, Dick owned 51 per cent and we owned 49 per cent, and therein lies the catch. He can outvote and they can do anything they want. I have a dim memory of going into a mews flat in Liverpool with cobbles outside, the kind of place I didn't really know existed in Liverpool. There was a lawyer there who I now know was our lawyer but it was never pointed out to us that he was our man. I assumed he was Brian's lawyer or something. Very quickly they sort of said, 'Da, da, da, song-writing, da, da, da. This is what we should do, da, da, da. That's the deal, da da. Do you want it?'

Like any young writers wanting to be published, we said yes. They asked if we wanted to read the contract and we said, 'Well, no.' The lawyer came all da, da, da, and so that is virtually the deal that I'm under today with the songs, and that's not quite fair.

Dick James, born Richard Leon Vapnick, had been a singer. His biggest success was the theme song to the popular English TV series *Robin Hood*. He soon realized that the chances of making money were much better in publishing than singing. When Brian and he met, he was working from a small office on Charing Cross Road.

The Northern Songs deal made him rich beyond his wildest expectations and established his career as British pop's most famous music publisher. He was sued successfully by Elton John in the eighties after years of benefiting from a publishing deal so one-sided that a court demanded John receive a retrospective payment in the millions.

Derek Taylor: Generally speaking, Brian got lucky, never mind the deals. At the time, Dick James was a good workmanlike publisher who wasn't rich like Chappell, so he worked those copyrights like buggery. George Martin was a perfect bit of casting, a cloudless sky.

George Martin: The record contract that I gave him in the first instance wasn't a very fair one either. It was a very poor deal. I had nothing to lose and Brian needed this record deal. The contract required them only to sing eight songs per year if I wanted it. They would only get one penny per doubled-sided single, which they shared between them, and that was an old penny too.

At the end of the first year – June '63, so it was quite early on – I was conscious of the success we'd had and I went to my boss at EMI and said, 'Look, I want to change this deal.' Although the contract said I'd give them increases of 25 per cent each year if we signed again, it was patently unfair. I told EMI I'd like to double their royalty right away. And my boss said, 'Yeah, OK, get another five-year option out of them and double the royalty.' I said, 'No, you don't understand. I don't want to ask for anything; I want to give it to them.'

From that moment on I was considered a traitor within EMI. The new negotiation was taken out of my hands and EMI negotiated directly with Brian. Now EMI are pretty powerful people and Brian had a solid contract which bound the boys for four years. They did renegotiate and they did get a much better deal but he was negotiating with one arm tied behind his back.

I don't think Brian could have tried to negotiate the new contract earlier, not without jeopardizing the success that was going on. He did try to renegotiate the contract without much success, and then as the contract got nearer and nearer its expiry he was able to negotiate another deal.

Peter Brown: In the original record deals he had very little room for negotiation because all he wanted to do was to get the deal. Of course, there were standard deals in those days. Stars were not strong enough ever to make their own demands and I think he made the best deal he could, and in everything else he was very straightforward. Whenever you talk to any of the people who did business with Brian, they will tell you that he was a very, very straightforward man as far as his deals and his word were concerned.

It's a standard procedure now in the music business that you have a contract and the moment you have a big hit you go back and renegotiate. But we were doing things for the first time, so what he did was he waited till the end of the contract and then renegotiated for infinitely better terms and made them retrospective.

George Martin: He was pitchforked into the rough end of the business without a great deal of training or experience, and he did remarkably well. Suddenly, from being a kind of failed dramatic student, he found something that he felt he could cope with. Being unsure for most of his life up to that time, suddenly he realized that there was something that he could do really rather well.

Brian never seemed to lack confidence. He just took it in his stride. He realized that he'd done extraordinarily well and the Beatles had done extraordinarily well. It was just irritating that he couldn't get a better deal for them.

Robert Stigwood: I think it's tosh and nonsense to say that he didn't make good business deals. I think anyone can look today and see the deals that were made then and the deals today. To his best ability he did the best deals for them and anyone can look back and be critical. I know it well. So, you can get 15 per cent today. In those days you got 2 per cent. He did what was correct for the market. I'd like to know anyone today who could say Brian should have renegotiated a contract before he did. I'd tell them it's hindsight and not good. I think he has to be remembered for what he did because no one wanted to know the Beatles and Brian had the faith and belief to make them a success.

Lionel Bart: Brian certainly could get the bit between his teeth. When the Beatles had taken off, they were making a new album with some Tamla Motown titles, Brian phoned Berry Gordy and said the boys were interested in doing a couple of the titles. The only thing is they wanted a big chunk of the music publishing. It was early days to insist on that sort of thing. Berry Gordy said he'd think about it. And a day later he said he'd do it because it could give the Tamla Motown sound a new angle and new kind of credibility. But the album was out three days later. They'd already made it regardless of what Berry Gordy said. It was a real stroke that Brian pulled off, a top hustler's order. He could do that.

Gerry Marsden: Brian was not a financial genius, but he could see things other people couldn't.

When Brian took the Beatles and made 'Love Me Do', people looked up. 'What's that? What's happening?' Then they made 'Please Please Me' and we made 'How Do You Do It?', which got to number one. Then people thought 'Hello', and Brian realized, 'Cor, what have we got here?' Massive. Then everybody in Liverpool said, 'Oh, Brian, will you manage us, please?' Brian said, 'No, hang on.' So he only managed ourselves, Billy J. Kramer and a couple of other groups. Then London started invading Liverpool for all this untapped talent. Brian got a bit peeved because he had discovered it all and he was a bit annoyed that he was losing people that he thought he could make famous. But Brian enjoyed it. Brian had more fans than we did. He'd sign more photographs than I ever did, God bless him, and send them all over the world.

Billy J. Kramer: NEMS arranged all our travel for us. They arranged our hotels, just about everything. It was amazing because, no matter where we were in the world, Brian always made sure that we were taken care of financially. There would be this registered envelope that would arrive every Saturday morning with a cash float and we would all have a check of the balance, of what we'd earned, to be sent to our accountants. It was very well organized.

Brian was the first agent I ever had, and I still think he was the most organized.

Johnny Gustafson: We were just hard rockers, trying to play rock and roll as rough and ready as we could. We didn't wear the suits he provided. If we went away on tour the suits would stay in the van and we'd wear whatever we liked, the jeans and the scruffy shoes. Sometimes we'd forget our gear and literally leave it on the pavement and borrow stuff when we got to a club. We never had a PA. He used to give us money to go in hotels but we used to sleep in the van and spend the money in the pub. He didn't take too kindly to things like that. So he just fired us.

6. Big-time Operator

Always America seemed too big, too vast, too remote and too American. I remember the night we heard about the number-one position on Cashbox. *I said to John Lennon, 'There can be nothing more important than this,' adding a tentative 'Can there?'*

BRIAN EPSTEIN, *A CELLARFUL OF NOISE*

Geoffrey Ellis: In the beginning of November 1963, Brian wrote to me and said he was coming to New York and he hoped to see something of me. In fact he asked me to recommend a hotel where he should stay in New York and I recommended one quite near where I lived at the time in New York, where I was working as a lawyer.

I had mentioned to him a number of times before that one of the pleasures of living in New York was that you could get a drink at any time of day. The licensing laws were not the same as they were in England in those days. It happened, though, that Brian arrived in New York on Election Day in November 1963. Election Day is the one day in America where all the bars are closed and you can't get a drop of alcohol until the polls have closed at nine at night. So he was a bit disappointed at that, though he probably made up for it later.

He came the day after the Beatles' Royal Command Variety Performance that year at the Prince of Wales Theatre, and he was on a big high because it was their splashiest performance to date. He brought with him Billy J. Kramer, I think largely for company, because at that time I don't think he had any plans to launch Billy in the States, but he did have plans, very substantial plans, to launch the Beatles in the States.

So he told me a lot about what they'd been doing and what he wanted to do. I, of course, was working in my office in New York at the time and I didn't know what he did during the days. But one day he told me that he'd been to meet Ed Sullivan and that he was arranging for the Beatles to appear on *Ed Sullivan* in early 1964. So he wanted to have a small tour at the same time to see what the flavour of the Beatles would be like in the States. I was very interested to hear about all this, though I knew nothing about the business side of it at all. During that first visit to the States, we did spend time together in the evenings. We went out to restaurants, and night-clubs and so on.

Billy J. Kramer: In about '63 Brian had this thing that he thought I had the kind of appeal that was right for the American market. I didn't have this mop-top hairdo and I was smart and I had the boy-next-door image, and he thought maybe I was the one that was going to do it. At that time I didn't think I was going to do it but I wasn't going to turn down a trip to New York. So I came to New York and I did TV and radio and met a lot of different people in the industry.

When I got off the plane at JFK I wanted to fly back to England because it was just too much. I had had a whole year of travelling all over the place and doing all these tours and hysteria and girls screaming. I looked at the skyline of New York and all the cars and everything and I just thought I was going to have a breakdown.

We met up with Geoffrey Ellis and people like Lionel Bart. Then Brian gave me a big lecture one night in a restaurant about how if I just lost some weight we could make some fantastic movies and I could have a different career. I said, 'Hey, Brian, I have a hard time miming to records on TV, never mind making movies.'

I always thought, 'Why would people in American want to know about English bands when they've had Eddie Cochran and Little Richard and Jerry Lee Lewis and Chuck Berry? What do they want to listen to us for?'

And there I am walking down Broadway with a list of albums and Brian Epstein's doing the same thing. We're going through these stores buying all these albums to take back. We both went back with loads of albums.

Geoffrey Ellis: I was walking with Brian and Billy J. Kramer through Times Square, I think fairly late one night after a theatre, and Billy caught sight in one of the shop windows of a Western-style fringed shirt. 'Oh,' he said to Brian, 'I'd like that.' Brian said, 'No, Billy, not your style at all.' So Billy didn't get the shirt. Brian was always very conscious of how his artists ought to look and Billy's style was rather clean-cut and that's the image that Brian wanted him to retain, certainly no sort of country and western look.

Derek Taylor: Paul has a recollection that the Beatles said they wouldn't go to America without a number one. But the counter-theory is that they were booked into the *Ed Sullivan Show* with billing and fee arranged long before 'I Want to Hold Your Hand'. There might have been a bit of a to-and-fro over the fee, but if it was a case of doing it or not doing it, I don't think that Brian would have done *Ed Sullivan* without top billing. He had it worked out. I can give you a quote which is a bit too neat and tidy to be entirely accurate, but he said, 'One day they will be bigger than Elvis.' He really did say that.

Thinking big. This is what bound Brian and the boys together. They all did think big. Very high notions of themselves and very high expectations. They always felt they were going to be OK.

Towards the end of 1963, Ed Sullivan was one of the few Americans who was aware of Beatlemania. He witnessed it first hand on a stop-over at Heathrow Airport in September, returning to America from a talent-finding European tour on a day when the Beatles were arriving home.

Sullivan's Sunday night variety show had an insatiable appetite for talent and he relied on European and British acts to fill up his weekly TV hour. The biggest American stars from Elvis Presley to Leonard Bernstein would perform between appearances from Topo Gigio (a popular Italian mouse puppet), the Moscow State Circus or even the British ventriloquist Arthur Worsley.

Sullivan agreed to meet Epstein on his visit to New York. To his astonishment, Epstein offered him the Beatles but only on condition that they have top billing on the show. The demand seemed preposterous at first but Brian was not prepared to accept any other terms.

Money, however, was not the point. Since Sullivan was only prepared to pay the Beatles their air fare in addition to a low fee for performing, Brian effectively agreed to subsidize the Beatles' appearance.

Sid Bernstein: I first heard about the Beatles as a night student at the New School in the Village. The professor was the distinguished journalist Max Lerner. He told us at the very first session to pick up an English newspaper once a week to see how the government in England works.

And I got lucky – there it was in the first week, a little story about a new group out of Liverpool creating a sensation in the north of England.

Then the next week I picked up another newspaper. The story was three times as large. On the third week, I was looking forward to reading some news about these boys called the Beatles. I said to myself, 'What an odd name!' There was also a picture of the boys with the long hair. The article talked about them turning away about a thousand people at a showcase in the south of England, somewhere away from Liverpool. I couldn't wait for the next week.

I was an agent at General Artists Corporation and we had an agency in London. I had been sending memos to the heads of the agency telling them to sign the Beatles, but all they did was wire back to me and to the head of our agency, Buddy Hall, saying I was bugging them too much and that the group didn't mean a thing in America.

I decided to take matters into my own hands. I called a friend of mine who just coincidentally had been hired by Brian Epstein to do some record promotion. He gave me Brian's home number. Brian was still working out of his home at the time so I called him in Liverpool at Childwall 6518 – I'll never forget that number. Queenie Epstein answered. We talked about the book review section of the Sunday *New York Times* and finally she said, 'I must be costing you an awful lot of money, Mr Bernstein. Let me get my son to the phone.' I heard footsteps, which was Brian coming down from his workshop in the lovely Tudor house they lived in. 'Mr Bernstein, could I help you?' And I said, 'Yes, I'm interested in your group.' He said, 'Why would you want to commit suicide? We can't get any air play in New York.' And I just ad-libbed, 'Oh, you will. I'm just sure you will.'

I'd never heard a note of their music but I had become obsessed with the idea of presenting them for the first time. Brian said, 'Where would you present them?' I said, 'I'd like to present them at Carnegie Hall.' Luckily he had just seen an old film whose title was *Carnegie Hall*. He asked when and I said, 'How about three months from now?' Now this call was made in February 1963 and he said three months would be much too soon, and he asked if I knew how much money the Beatles got. He said, 'We get the equivalent of $2,000 a night for one show in all the music halls in Great Britain and we can't fill the dates. We're superstars here in England.' I said, 'Mr Epstein, I will give you $6,500 for one day for two shows.' He said, 'Wait till I tell the boys. But not three months from now.' I said, 'How about five months?' We settled on twelve months from then, February 1964. But there was one proviso. If there was no air play or chart action nine months from then, meaning November 1963, he could cancel. I said, 'That's fine.'

I had never been to Carnegie Hall in my life so I rang them and found out that I needed a $500 deposit. I didn't have it and had to borrow the money from my old friend Abe Margolis, a very successful jeweller. He said, 'Who do you want to present?' I said, 'I've got a group from England. You wouldn't know them. They're called the Beatles.' And Abe said, 'Sid, in my last stages of syphilis will I ever be crazy enough to back you with a group with a name like that.' But I got the money and ran to Carnegie Hall to deposit the money with the bookers. I told the lady who booked the shows, Mrs Satasky, that I was going to present four young men who are a phenomenon in Great Britain, so she accepted the money.

George Martin: The success of both Billy J. and Gerry was meteoric, actually. They were riding on the coat-tails of the Beatles, obviously, but they also had the talent to do it and they had the songs to do it and they had the records to do it.

It was a kind of whirlwind of success, really, and I was working non-stop in the studios. That year of 1963 I had thirty-seven weeks in the number-one spot. I had a situation where I would have the record I'd made with one artist drop down from number one, then another record I'd made would come up to replace the last one. And the Beatles were just a small part of that.

All of these acts were Epstein acts. He then realized that he had the makings of a kind of latter-day Diaghilev. He saw himself as an impresario with a stable of great stars, and certainly it was a great kick-off to a career like that.

I think it was a whirlwind of a year and nobody had time to stop and start thinking about things. Strategy wasn't a long-term job. It was tactics. It was, 'How do we deal with next week?' 'Where will Gerry be?' 'Can we book him in the Hippodrome?' 'I've got to think about the Beatles breaking in America.' There were so many things to think about. Brian coped with it remarkably well considering he'd had no experience. Inevitably he made mistakes, but at the same time I think he did a frightfully good job with what he had to do.

Brian was developing in the same way that the Beatles were so he didn't know where he was going to end up. When you're young, you don't have a grand strategy like, 'By the time I'm fifty-five I'll be president of ICI.' You don't think like that; you just take it as it comes. He did and hoped that it would become bigger and bigger and he would become more and more important.

Alan Livingston: When EMI bought Capitol we made an agreement between us. We had right of first refusal, and they the same in reverse, on any of EMI's English artists, or any artists around the world that they had. EMI could use, had first right or first refusal on any Capitol records and of course it worked very well for EMI because we had Nat Cole and we had many of the big bands who did very well. However, we were not successful with English records. Occasionally some hit would come out of France or even India but we just never got off the ground with English artists.

The funny thing is I didn't even hear the first Beatles record. In order to satisfy EMI, who were really our parent company, I named a producer at Capitol to have the responsibility to screen every EMI artist that was sent to us for consideration for release in the United States. Out of courtesy we would occasionally put out an English artist but we never had any success with them. At this time, the producer was Dave Dexter.

One day I held the weekly A&R meeting, which I went to even though I was president, but I had come up through A&R so I had an interest in these meetings. I would decide, with the producers' help, which records to release, which artists to sign, what elements to put together and so forth. I had been reading the English music press, and I read about the success of a group called the Beatles. So I said to Dexter, 'What about the Beatles? Shouldn't we put them out?' He said, 'Alan, they're a bunch of long-haired kids. They're nothing. Forget it.' I thought that was OK. We hadn't had any success with English artists so why should I question him?

Two weeks later I asked again because there was so much going on in England and he said, 'Alan, please, they're nothing. Forget it.' So we passed on them. We passed on the right of first refusal so EMI then went trying to find another place to get them to put their records out. They took the Beatles to CBS, then Columbia Records, to RCA, then RCA Victor records, to Decca Records, which in those days was a very big company, and every one of them turned them down.

They finally found a small company in Philadelphia called Swan Records, who put out two sides. Two records and nothing happened so Swan gave them up. They didn't want them any more. EMI then got VeeJay Records, a very small company in serious financial trouble, black-owned. It was a free album to them, so they said, 'OK, we'll put it out.' And they couldn't pay the royalty dues to EMI, so lost their rights. They didn't seem to care because the album didn't sell; nothing happened. And that was the end of it. The Beatles could have been dead in the United States.

I was sitting in my office one day when my secretary told me I had a call from a man named Brian Epstein. I didn't know who he was. I picked up the phone and he said, 'Mr Livingston, we don't understand why you don't put out the Beatles records. Have you heard them?' I told him I hadn't. So he said, 'Would you please listen and call me back?' I said, 'Sure.' And I went downstairs and I heard 'I Want to Hold Your Hand'. I can't honestly say I knew how big they would be but I heard something and I saw the look of them. Also, I liked Brian just then on the telephone. He was a gentleman and he was persuasive. I called him back and said, 'OK, we'll put them out.' Brian said, 'Wait a minute. I'm not going to give them to you unless you spend $40,000 to promote their first single.'

Well, that was pretty much unheard-of in the early sixties. You just didn't spend that kind of money because it wasn't necessary. For whatever reason, I said OK. I took it down to our A&R meeting and I said that we would put the Beatles out on our label.

Everyone at the meeting thought that was OK and selected 'I Want to Hold Your Hand' as the first record. I then took the record home to my wife Nancy Olson, who was very musical, an actress, talented and interested in popular music. I told her I thought this group would change the whole music business if it happens. She said, 'Really? Let me hear it.' And I played it for her. She said, '"I Want to Hold Your Hand". Are you kidding?' So I thought maybe I had made a mistake. Anyway we put the record out and I never got through the $40,000. I didn't need to. The record exploded and of course the rest is history.

Capitol released 'I Want to Hold Your Hand' on 26 December 1963. Although the record may have been heard as an import on a few local stations, this was the first time most people in the United States heard the Beatles' music. *Life* magazine ran an article on the band at the end of the year and a short piece of BBC footage was shown on Jack Parr's late-night programme on 4 January 1964.

Once Capitol committed themselves to promoting national radio air play, it took three weeks for 'I Want to Hold Your Hand' to become the number-one record in the States. The Beatles were in Paris playing at the Olympia Theatre when they got the news.

Alan Livingston: It was obviously something different. The other British groups were either into their own style of music, which didn't appeal to me for play here for the United States, or they were imitative of the US music and not too good. Here was a different sound and of course the boys had a different look and had great promotional possibilities in the teenage market. I just believed in the group for whatever reason. In this business you fly by the seat of your pants.

In those days in the record business, if I put out a record, it automatically got air play. The different thing about the record business is that it's the only form of entertainment that people buy for repetition. They don't buy it to hear it once. When you go to a motion picture, you pay your money. If you don't like it it's too bad. The same with the theatre. But when you buy a record you want to play it again and again. Therefore, the best promotion is to have it played on the air, so somebody can hear it. If nobody can hear it, to hell with it.

It was very easy at that time to get air play. Particularly for Capitol, who had a good following. So that was the promotion. As far as the press was concerned it was almost automatic. You had to fend them off because the Beatles became so big.

The time frame was as short as you want to make it. A week, two weeks. I mean it happened so fast. It happened overnight. We put out the album on top of the single, and of course that sold more than the single. It broke out overnight. It was the easiest promotion I've ever seen.

Paul McCartney: We were very surprised when we arrived in America because we hadn't anticipated the reaction, although one of the early things we'd said to Brian was that we wouldn't go to America unless we were number one. I have a clear memory of saying this. A couple of the other guys don't remember, so maybe it was me and Brian talking.

I'd noticed that a lot of British acts came over to America. Cliff Richard, Adam Faith, who were quite big in England, had come over and gone on bills with people like Fabian and Frankie Avalon, only to be third or fourth on the bill. We didn't really reckon Fabian and Frankie Avalon. They weren't anywhere as good as Elvis, and we thought there was almost a little lack of pride about Cliff coming back and saying, 'Wow, I went to America.' It was like, yeah, but you were fourth on the bill and what's all that about?

So I remember saying to Brian, probably John and I said it to him, 'Look, don't send us to America till we're number one. We're not going to America till then.' We knew then that we'd be able to walk in and not have to bang the door down. The door would open for us and whatever anybody said to us we would then be able to say, 'Yeah, but we're number one. Check it out.' There's not a lot you can say about that. People can't say, 'Well, you're not very good.' We could say, 'Well, you mean American people's judgement is wrong on this one?' So we waited till we were number one. But we didn't expect that airport reaction, although some of the journalists and the pilots had radioed ahead and they said, 'Hey, there's a big crowd there.' So we were starting to think it might be big but not quite as big as that. And we thought Brian was doing a great job for us.

The Maysles brothers, Albert and David, had established a reputation as two of America's most adventurous *cinéma vérité* documentary film-makers. Two hours before the Beatles landed at the newly named Kennedy International Airport on 7 February 1964, the Maysles brothers received a call from Granada Television asking them to be at the airport to film the Beatles as they arrived.

Virtually the whole of the Beatles' first visit to America was recorded by the Maysles brothers' cameras. The film they shot became the inspiration for much of *A Hard Day's Night*, the Beatles' first film, released in the summer of 1964.

Albert Maysles: I didn't know who they were, so I put my hand over the phone and said to my brother, 'Who are the Beatles? Are they any good?' He said he thought they were.

We had to rush to the airport. We arrived there just in time to see this little speck in the sky coming down. When it landed, we were already filming.

They were just kids. They didn't really know just exactly what was going to happen; it could have been that nobody showed up at the airport. As it turned out, it was something like four or five thousand people. Most Americans had never heard of them.

The Beatles film that we made in '64, full of promise, energy and the innocence of youth, was like the start of something. Then the film we made with the Rolling Stones at the end of 1969 was *Gimme Shelter*. That marked the end, when everything fell apart.

Geoffrey Ellis: Brian brought the Beatles for their first visit to New York in February 1964, and there was tremendous excitement in New York at the time. It was amazing to me because I knew nothing of the pop music business at all and it seemed to me that all the lamp standards were plastered with fliers about THE BEATLES ARE COMING, THE BEATLES ARE COMING. On the day they arrived, I happened to be in a cab and the cab driver said to me, 'Those Beatles are coming to New York.' I said, 'Yes, I know they are,' and it was the first item on the news that day. I saw Brian and the Beatles stepping out of the plane.

A free Beatles T-shirt had been promised to anyone who turned up at Kennedy Airport to welcome the band. This and other promotions were the brain-children of Nicky Byrne, a London entrepreneur, who three weeks before had concluded a deal with Epstein giving him the right to license and distribute Beatles merchandise. This deal was to have a profound impact on Epstein's life.

The American branch of Byrne's organization was called Seltaeb – Beatles spelled backwards.

Sid Bernstein: When the Beatles arrived in New York, I went down to the Plaza Hotel and stood outside with all those kids. There were 1,500 to 2,000 kids there and I was one of them. Nobody knew who I was. When they pulled up in their limos, it was an unbelievable sight.

I met the Beatles for the first time at a reception given by Capitol Records that afternoon. Brian couldn't believe it. He said, 'This is bigger even than Great Britain.' But he was collected, very self-contained, very in charge of himself.

Geoffrey Ellis: When they'd settled in at the Plaza Hotel, Brian telephoned me and asked if I would like to come over and meet them and have dinner. I said, 'Yes, I certainly would.' So I walked over to the Plaza, which wasn't far from where I was living. The hotel was surrounded by screaming fans and some of New York's finest cops on horseback, keeping the fans back. No one was allowed into the Plaza unless they were guests or could prove they had business there.

I managed to get in without too much difficulty. Perhaps I didn't look very much like a screaming fan at the time. I went up to Brian's suite, which he had arranged very sensibly to be on a different floor from the Beatles. He wanted to have a little bit of privacy. We chatted for a time and I had a drink. Then he said, 'Come down and meet the boys.' I went down a couple of floors with him into the Beatles' suite where three of them were, John, Paul and Ringo. George had an indisposition at the time.

It was a very curious sight because they were lolling about on the beds in one of the bedrooms with the TV set on showing them arriving and shots of the Plaza Hotel which we were in at the same time. But the sound was off and they were playing transistor radios because all the radio stations were playing Beatle music at the same time. Cynthia Lennon was there as well. She was kept very much in the background because at that time, again under Brian's influence, it was not generally known that John Lennon was married. Brian thought it would be bad for the image of any of the Beatles to be married and he wanted to keep the fans' enthusiasm for the Beatles at fever pitch.

We stayed there for a time. Brian introduced me to them: 'This is Geoffrey Ellis from Liverpool.' I don't think they were very interested, but it was interesting for me. Then Brian suggested that we go out to dinner. As we were leaving the boys' suite, one of his henchmen said, 'You better take this,' and handed Brian an envelope which he put into his pocket.

Before going out we went up to Brian's suite for him to get his coat. In the room was one of his NEMS employees who had to stay in for the evening and just ordered an enormous dinner from the Plaza Hotel room service. Brian was a little bit incensed at this and said, 'That is going to cost a fortune.' This was one of the first times I saw him being somewhat imperious with a member of his staff, and the member of staff in point of fact left Brian's employ a few weeks later, though whether that was connected with the large meal at the Plaza I don't know.

Anyhow, we went out to dinner. We went to the Four Seasons, which is a very up-market New York restaurant, very grand. When we settled down at the table, Brian pulled the envelope that he'd been given on leaving out of his pocket. It had 'The Four Seasons' written on it. He handed it to the *maître d'hôtel* and said, 'What's this all about?' The *maître d'hôtel* opened the envelope and inside was an invitation to the Beatles to have dinner at the Four Seasons for free up to a value of $100, which was quite a lot in 1964. Brian said to the *maître d'hôtel*, 'The Beatles can't come but I am their manager and we will have the dinner.' So we did. He said to me, 'How much is $100 in pounds?' I told him. In those days it was about £42, which was an incredible amount in those days for two people to eat, but we managed it.

Albert Maysles: It's hard to tell exactly who Brian was because I think in a situation like that he's so busy, so distracted with the details of the management of the tour. But I came to think that even out of those activities he was somebody that – I wouldn't say he had problems, I don't know about that, but his mind seemed to be somewhere else. And that to me suggests somebody who isn't content with himself, isn't at ease. But there would be lot of that unease for anybody in that situation not knowing what was coming up next, having to make plans on the run.

I don't think we offered any problems and he never seemed to have any irritation from us being there. From their experiences in England, I think the boys and he were, as young as they were, used to the press and all that kind of stuff. In fact, we had a kind of a problem that we never would otherwise have met. The Beatles had got used to being asked by the press to do this, to do that, so it was almost impossible for us to get them out of that sort of mode.

They were doing things for us only because that's the way they thought they were supposed to behave. They were asked to do all these things for the camera all the time. There were some very informal moments where they got out of that performing mode, thank goodness. There was a moment I remember with Paul reflecting on things and he said that he felt somewhat depressed.

And also I can't say that I really got to know Brian that well. In the course of filming the Beatles, I assumed the best. After all, he had a good name, Brian Epstein. My mother's name was Epstein before she got married and then I had a cousin whom we called Eppie. So I took him as a member of the family and I think that helped. We hit it off well.

The Beatles' first appearance on the *Ed Sullivan Show* was on 9 February 1964. It had the most viewers of any programme in American television history up till that time. Epstein's gamble had paid off. The Beatles were suddenly the most famous group in America.

Sid Bernstein: There was mayhem after the *Ed Sullivan Show*. Everyone was calling me and begging for tickets. Even Abe Margolis called me and said, 'Sid, you've got to get me 300 tickets. They're tearing my phone apart. I can't do business.' How could I not help him? Finally, I had to put 300 seats on the stage just to accommodate people.

During the intermission, Mrs Sataski, the lady who had okayed the date [at the Carnegie Hall], came over to me. She was livid. She said, 'Mr Bernstein, I've never seen anything like this. A lot of people are standing on chairs and screaming. Why did you do this to me? When you told me they were a phenomenon, I assumed you were talking about a string ensemble.' I said, 'But I never said that.' She said, 'Don't ever come back here again.'

I paid Brian the guarantee of $6,500 and I wound up making $10,000 on the two shows. So it turned out that my gamble paid off quite well for myself. Brian Epstein was most pleased and said, 'Sid, whenever the Beatles play in New York, because you did everything I asked you to, you'll be the man we talk to when we come here again.'

Alan Livingston: With all due respect to Brian, I think his one major contribution was to pick up the phone and call me and convince me to put the album out and to insist that I spend $40,000 to promote the first single. That was a major contribution and I think from that point on the only one. And I can't say I made any major contribution there either. It was a momentum that you couldn't stop if you tried.

After the *Ed Sullivan Show*, we would press a million copies of every record in advance and of course they'd sell more than that. We wanted to cover the immediate demand. From then on every album we put out was at least a million in front before we even got it out to the market. Ordinarily with a new artist, or with any artist, you might press 5,000 records in advance. For a big artist that had a following, you might press 25,000, 50,000. To press a million copies in advance was unheard-of, but for the Beatles it was their audience. A lot of our artists complained that our factories were so inundated with Beatles pressings that they felt they were being forgotten.

And to an extent that was true. They suffered somewhat. We became known as the Beatles company.

Geoffrey Ellis: The effect of the adulation of the Beatles and his apparent control of them was to give Brian a great deal more self-confidence, certainly on the exterior. He knew what he wanted to do. He knew he had a world-beating act. He knew he could get virtually anything he wanted for the Beatles and he did certainly project far more a self-confident appearance than he had done when I knew him in Liverpool, before all this started to happen.

7. The Talk of the Town

BILL GRUNDY: *Mr Epstein, what sort of size of empire have you got now?*

EPSTEIN: We have seven acts; I call them acts because five of those are groups and two of them are soloists. That's Billy J. Kramer and the Dakotas, which are a separate entity – his backing group, Gerry and the Pacemakers, Tommy Quickly, the Fourmost, Cilla Black and Sounds Incorporated.

GRUNDY: *What about the administrative staff to support all this?*

EPSTEIN: Well, it varies slightly, because we've just moved to London and we're gathering new staff, but it's approximately twenty-five.

GRUNDY: *What sort of size of empire is it in terms of money? One's read some staggering figures that the Beatles have earned for their recording company in the last year. What sort of turnover does this empire produce?*

EPSTEIN: I couldn't give you an answer to that, I really don't know. Because, don't forget, the companies which manage these artists have only been in operation since June 1962.

GRUNDY: *The papers have been accusing you of being Mr 25 per cent. If the turnover's as big as you were implying then this means a very large income for you. Is it, in fact, a lot in the entertainment business, is it a high percentage?*

EPSTEIN: It isn't. And one's profits from that 25 per cent in this business are not really fantastic because my own personal expenses in connection with the management of artists are quite fantastic. Really.

INTERVIEW, BBC HOME SERVICE, 7 MARCH 1964

Derek Taylor: At the height of it all, in 1963/4/5, the waves did part as he came into a big throng. They would all peel back to let this man through. Brian Epstein was very, very famous. As close as I was to him, I would have spotted any self-aggrandizement, but there was none. All the offers came in and an enormous amount of it was rejected, particularly if it was naff. He would do a *Panorama* and an interview with Kenneth Harris, but there were a lot of crude things he would never dream of doing. But he would never ever try to compete with the Beatles. You'd call it sad today, his humility.

But still, as a man of enormous personal vanity, he liked to go and get his

1 A promising family unit: Brian (right) with his mother
Queenie and his brother Clive at their home in Queens Drive.
2 Harry Epstein had high hopes that his eldest son would
follow him and his father into the family business.

3 Brian in the army: 'a compulsive civilian'.

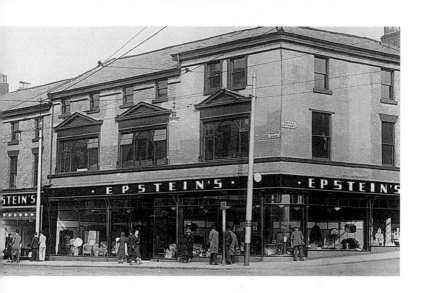

4 NEMS: North End Music Stores, the family firm.
5 The Beatles: the Leather Years.

6 The Beatles in Epstein's London flat: Whaddon House, Knightsbridge.
7 The new Svengali of pop with producer George Martin – together they would
have thirty-seven weeks at the No. 1 position in 1963.

8 The Epstein stable.
9 High roller.

10 High life:
Lonnie Trimble serves
Epstein his breakfast.
11 Relaxing with
Lennon.

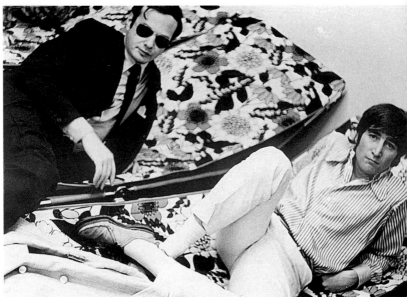

12 Taking time out in Japan during the fraught tour of 1966.
13 Letting his hair down in the last few months.

14 El Cordobes, one of Epstein's favourite matadors.
His youth and style earned him the nickname 'El Beatle'.
15 Epstein's county retreat in Sussex, Kingsley Hill.

hair cut by a very special barber. He liked eating well, he liked the high life, the car with electric windows.

Paul McCartney: He was a great gentleman. He was a great dresser. He was very proud of the way he dressed and his look. But he was a very genuine person. Whenever we talked together, I think we got it honestly.

Brian's greatest expression was 'Ohh!' throwing his hands in the air. 'What do you think of it? Ohh!' Everything was 'Ohh!' And you knew exactly what he meant.

Geoffrey Ellis: Brian told me about the fact that he was having to move his business to London, because London was the centre of the entertainment business in the UK, and that he had to expand a great deal. There was a great deal of work for him to do. He didn't like office work at all, and he did like to have round him people that he knew.

He said that there were lots of people in London who would love to come and work for the management of the Beatles but he was very leery of a lot of people's motives in this respect.

Alistair Taylor: We had to go to London. Brian decided that, whether we liked it or not. It wasn't falling out with Liverpool or not liking Liverpool but everything happened in London. I don't think Liverpool's really forgiven him yet.

It had to be and we tightened the ship up. It just suddenly became a big business machine. You know, the staff increased. There we were in West End offices. There's a marvellous memo that Brian sent to all the artists and to all the other staff saying, 'Please come and see our new offices because we want to be the best management company.' And we were damned good. You know, the whole team was great.

Our offices were on Argyll Street, next to the London Palladium. Brian said he wanted our neighbours to be the biggest stars in the world.

LETTER TO STAFF ON MOVING TO ARGYLL STREET, LONDON W1,

Welcome to the new offices! 9 March 1964

Attached is a copy of a letter which is being sent out to all artistes. I hope you will note its most important message: 'That NEMS Enterprises provides the finest and most efficient management/direction of artistes in the world'. This must be without question our principal aim and should be borne in mind by all staff.

Alistair Taylor will be advising you of the details of operating the new offices, but I would like personally to point out one or two things.

First of all as our organization is very much in the public eye, it is most important that we present the best possible 'front'. By this I mean that all visitors must be treated with utmost courtesy. That work must be carried out smoothly and efficiently without fuss. And most important, that the offices themselves must be kept tidy and clean at all times.

Another matter which I must ask you to treat with considerable care is the question of divulging to unauthorized or persons outside the organization information concerning the company. It is strictly out of order for anyone to discuss with the press any business (however slight or remotely connected) whatsoever. Your adherence to this ruling is of great importance.

I really hope that you will be happy and as comfortable as possible in our new surroundings.

With best wishes for the future,

Aunt Stella: I didn't see Brian too often once he went to London. He was very occupied and we were in Southport. He would probably come to Liverpool to see his parents or they would go to see him.

We were in touch occasionally. I remember him sending me a beautiful arrangement of flowers for Rosh Hashanah, for the New Year, and he was very helpful when we wanted tickets for the theatre, but I didn't see him much.

Gerry Marsden: I didn't go to London. I stayed in Liverpool. It didn't matter to me. Brian was doing the business. I never used to go into the office of NEMS every day when he was in Liverpool. Brian would ring and we'd work. I'd see Brian in London and he'd come up to see me at home. I just didn't want to live in London.

Billy J. Kramer: I think there is a big change from Liverpool to London. My father would say to me, 'They won't like you down there, you know.' But I think that plays on your head. You've been tearing the world apart and you go to London and you're shaking in your boots until you get a bit of experience in music. But when NEMS moved to London, I always sort of went off on my own. I hung out with the Dakotas and that was about it. Brian moved to London but then we were always off doing tours.

I've moved to London with great reluctance because I like Liverpool and I like its people. I owe the city quite a lot, but the trouble was it was becoming almost impossible to organize my own life and to do the best that I could for the artists. The artists perform often in London and they make their records in London. So I suppose I was forced into it. I'm not terribly unhappy about it, though it's sad in a way.

But it doesn't mean we think any less of Liverpool or we want to be in Liverpool any less. My home is in Liverpool and I intend to return there as much as I can.

EPSTEIN, BBC HOME SERVICE, 7 MARCH 1964

Peter Brown: I think Brian lived in Grosvenor House when he first started to visit London and then he found a new apartment off Lowndes Square in a place called Williams Mews. It was a new building called Whaddon House and he took the top apartment. At the time George and Ringo were bachelors and had nowhere to live, so he found accommodations for them in the same building on the lower floor.

I think that he wanted to live in one of the more exclusive residential areas. He was newly rich and at the time Brian was very into modern architecture and modern furniture. So Whaddon House suited him perfectly 'cause it was a brand-new building and considered rather splendid in those days of the early sixties. When I looked at it recently it didn't look quite so splendid, though.

He has enormous respect for the Beatles. They're always called the boys and the other people he looks after are called 'my other artists'. And the boys call him Eppie.

He seems to have a genuine respect for them and their music. Unlike a lot of other managers in this business who make a lot of money out of the people they look after and I think at rock bottom despise them.

He really admires them and has always thought they would be greater than Elvis Presley. He has great faith in what they can do and I think this shows in the way he's exposed them to merciless publicity the whole time. In fact, I said to him round about last October, 'Don't you think they're doing too much?' And he said, 'They can stand it.' I think he's been proved right.

I think it's very difficult for him to affect the Beatles as far as taste goes. I think they admire him because clearly he's got some. They rather like the fact that he has a Bentley and a Jaguar and a coloured manservant. They like the richness and the glamour that his life seems to have. They also like the fact that he talks differently from the way they do and the fact that he's well off anyway. They like this. They like the fact that he's used to wearing a dinner jacket. They think he's sort of different – a cut above.

POP JOURNALIST MAUREEN CLEAVE, *PANORAMA*, BBC, 30 MARCH 1964

Derek Taylor: If you hear his accent now, it's quite weird. An upper working-class, lower middle-class Liverpool accent. Anyone from up there will know that it isn't a public-school accent. They'd know it's what is called Liverpool posh.

Brian was impressive. He was undoubtedly very impressive. He's not the sad figure you might have read about. It's not for me to say that he didn't have a lot of sadness, but he was much more optimistic and cheerful and happy than sad, lonely and isolated. A lot of trouble came from being mucked about and blackmailed – if indeed he was really blackmailed. He was certainly mucked about and thrown about a few rooms. This was a repeat pattern which he brought on by living too dangerously and drinking too much and there were quite a few pills knocking about.

The separate life of his being gay and living dangerously was not furtive. No questions were asked. There was no nudgy, 'Oh, what a night I had last night with him.' He was entirely discreet in his own way. The Queens Drive thing. You would have found no homosexual relationships among his professional contacts. He was a terribly professional businessman, terribly stiff with all the Mr Brian and Mr Clive stuff.

There was a bit of the 1930s and 40s in him. His father was a Victorian, as mine was, and we carried a lot of rather stuffy old formalities. Brian had been in the army, as I had, and we were not as free as the lot that came later. It got easier and easier and looser and looser for them.

Lonnie Trimble: He wanted me to look after his flat, as a cook/houseman sort of thing, but in the end he didn't want me to cook, once we'd discussed the terms. So I said, 'Fine.' Then he asked me how much money I wanted. I asked how much was he offering, which he told me would be ten pounds a week. I said I was expecting twelve, he agreed and with that we said goodbye. And I started to work in February '64.

He said I was his personal man. But he'd never had anybody as a servant for himself, so he was just learning how to get on with life, with all this money that he was making.

I wore my own clothes when I started and then he decided that, with a bit of help from Wendy Hanson, that I should be in a uniform, to open the door for guests. So I put my uniform on. Black trousers, black tie, white jacket, white shirt.

Wendy Hanson was Brian's personal assistant and could be very snooty. She was the cousin of Lord Hanson and she was always able to tell everybody what to do. And they'd do it.

Well, when I went to work for him he wasn't well dressed. He was wearing something like Burton suits and I think it was the time when winkle pickers were in and he had some cheap, winkle picker shoes.

I'm sure in Liverpool he had style; he wore suits and he did have a nice overcoat. But then I don't know that much about Liverpool. When he came to London he didn't have the style for London. I mean, London was swinging then and I considered myself a better-dressed person than he was.

He was learning. We hear that Epstein came from this well-to-do family, but if you looked at his apartment in the day it was all G-plan, stainless steel and stuff.

My daily routine was always the same. I arrived about quarter to eight. I knocked on his bedroom door at half past eight to say good morning and that I was there. He would thank me and then I would go about getting his breakfast, which was grapefruit and tea. Nothing else. I usually had it on the table when he came out for breakfast. The grapefruit was in place, but I brought the tea out afterwards. After breakfast was cleared away, I cleaned up the flat, the lounge, dining room, kitchen, everything, and then I left. I did the shopping at Harrods if we needed anything.

He didn't entertain a lot, but he entertained his parents when they came down. He also entertained a few celebrities like Alma Cogan and Lionel Bart and David Jacobs, all the people that were in the music business, like the disc jockey Alan Freeman. When he would entertain, I cooked a meal.

We were basically standard as far as the dinner menu went. We would probably start off with the grapefruit, as a first course. With his parents it would usually be a grilled Dover sole and vegetables for the main course, then ice cream or something simple like that for dessert. When other people were there, we had caviar and smoked-salmon canapés and champagne. We also had beef on occasions, but it was never really extravagant because the man wasn't used to entertaining.

Alistair Taylor: It didn't make any difference when we moved to London, I can assure you. Brian could be the loveliest guy and he could be the biggest you-know-what in the world because you never quite knew exactly where you were with him.

I resigned twice over the years and he sacked me four times. At one particular point he sacked the entire management company over the phone from Heathrow because he was upset with them. I can remember standing there saying, 'Brian, am I included in that?' 'Yes, of course you are.' So that's it. That was one time when I resigned.

These things of his were over ten minutes later. It's fascinating talking to the few who are left that worked closely with him. We've all got stories to tell about what a 'b' he was and how he'd upset us and we'd say, 'Never again. That's it,' and yet at the end of the day everyone ends up saying, 'Yes, but we loved him.'

Another reason he sacked me . . . Sometimes the only thing managers and agents cared about was getting gigs, regardless of where they were. So bands could play Monday night in Exeter, Tuesday night in Leeds, Wednesday night in Plymouth. I made a mistake once when I was doing a bit of booking because our booker was off. I did that usual kind of schedule. Brian found out and I promptly was sacked because he believed you should go round in a circle not up and down around the country. I was reinstated about half an hour later, but at the time he said, 'I think that warrants resignation, Alistair.' So I said, 'Well, I'm not resigning. You know I'm not really a booker anyway.' So he said, 'Right, then you're sacked.' So I said, 'Fine, Brian. I'll go and clear my desk.' And of course I went back to my desk. This happened every time, and I'd just carry on working and the phone would go. 'Alistair, can you come in a minute.' I'd say, 'No, Brian, I'm sorry. I'm busy. I'm clearing my desk. You just sacked me. Remember?' 'Alistair, come in here.' And more than once he'd put his arm round my shoulder and say, 'Look out of the window. Isn't this a beautiful day? You know I didn't mean it.'

Nat Weiss: I think he saw NEMS Enterprises in sort of imperial or royal terms. Derek Taylor named him the Emperor of NEMS, contracted to Nemperor, which became their cable address and the name of various companies afterwards. He dealt in almost a Gaullist manner. He spoke from the top and there was no collegiality in dealing with Brian. This was what fascinated me most. His answers or solutions to problems were the last ones I would expect. If I thought the answer was that or this is it, I would have to say that on almost every occasion he was right. He had his own way of thinking and his insights were amazing.

Derek Taylor: He got me to do *A Cellarful of Noise* through the publisher Ernest Hecht. Hecht had asked Brian to do his autobiography and I was to write it with him.

We drove down to Torquay in a car with electric windows. I'd never seen such a thing. So down to Torquay where I set about the taping in a very big suite in a five-star hotel. In the first lunch Brian said, 'I'm going to have to tell you now, did you know I was queer?' 'No,' I said, 'I didn't.' 'Well,' he said, 'I am, and if we're going to do this book I'm going to have to stop buggering about saying I was with this girl when I would not be with a girl, when I was with a boy. Does that make any difference.' 'No,' I said, 'it does not make any difference. It'll make it a lot easier. So you mustn't worry any more, difficult as it may be to convince you perhaps, but I won't ever let you down.' It all came out long years afterwards.

There was only one thing I had to censor. When he was talking about Rita, whoever it was, this girl was a boy. He couldn't have anything in there that implied or hinted at homosexuality because of the dangers of jail. This was only ten years after the Lord Montague thing, which was a frightening, horrible witch-hunt.

To a considerable degree he was very easy about the gay thing. He was prepared to tell me about it when we were writing *Cellarful of Noise* and he didn't really know me all that well. It was a risk. I'm not sure whether he minded at all if he wasn't in the middle of a blackmail thing. He had a great fondness for slim gold watches and he must have lost half a dozen that I know of. But when there was nothing like that going on, I found him to be completely relaxed and happy and I didn't find him troubled by homosexuality at all.

Lonnie Trimble: He started to dress in a different way when Wendy Hanson introduced him to the tailor Huntsman. I remember the first day that he got his first suit from Huntsman. He came home and he peacocked around the apartment like mad in this new suit. Wendy tried to tell him that he looked absolutely wonderful. But all he said was, 'But I never knew you could pay so much for one suit.' He had spent £125 for that first one.

Marianne Faithfull: I know we looked at them as being very provincial, very straight, sort of a little bit behind London people, which is very patronizing and not really true.

What Brian Epstein realized is that we were almost a new form. There wasn't much that had gone before that was like me, John Lennon or Mick Jagger. The only person that was like Mick, and I remember talking about this with Brian, would have been somebody like Nijinsky or Nureyev or Valentino maybe.

At that time it was a form that was not much understood and it still isn't. But Brian understood it.

He had such immense charm. If you were measuring him up against someone like Robert Stigwood or Andrew Oldham, Brian Epstein's strongest card was that he actually cared for the community he served – which was us, this group of young, artistic free spirits ranging from Mick Jagger to John

Lennon to Joe Orton to Edward Bond, Andy Warhol – all of them. It was all connected. Brian was going to be the synthesizing force, with the help of the Beatles. He needed them.

BILL GRUNDY: *Do you think modern pop is good music?*
EPSTEIN: I don't know about it being good music, but it's an art form.

GRUNDY: *An art form. You pitch it as high as that?*
EPSTEIN: Yes, yes.

BBC HOME SERVICE, 7 MARCH 1964

Geoffrey Ellis: Brian was very careful in his treatment of the Beatles. He not only informed them of everything that he was doing and got their consent and agreement to all the deals that he did, he respected their views and he respected them as artists. He put them on a pedestal for the public as well as for himself, really. He respected them. They respected him.

Peter Brown: Brian and I would always go on holiday together. The first big holiday we took since he'd become this big rich impresario was in that spring of '64, when we went to Spain for the bullfights.

Brian wasn't an ordinary man and he got fascinated by things and ran with them 100 per cent. I suppose it's not surprising that he loved bullfighting. It's a spectacle. It's grandiose and it's attracted a lot of other highly intellectual and interesting people.

That year Brian got a feeler from the manager of El Cordobes. He was this handsome, working-class kid with a poverty background who had been picked up by a manager called El Pipo.

The thing in the Spanish bullfighting structure was that a lot of these matadors actually came from poverty-stricken families and were found and developed by powerful managers, who would look after the matadors. They would be provided for and they would be trained and they were brave because they had nothing to lose. They were kids and this was their way to fame and fortune.

Cordobes was the epitome of this syndrome. He was this handsome kid who wore his hair long and he became the Beatle bullfighter that everyone knew and there was talk about him being part of the next Beatle movie. Brian and I went to visit him at his farm in Cordoba where we were treated like very important people. They were all very courteous. But Pipo was a monster and Cordobes was very tied up with him. We did examine the whole business about whether it was possible to do the movie. It just didn't work out, but it was wonderful for us to go to this farm.

Nat Weiss: I think his fascination with bullfighting and bullfighters has something to do with his strange preoccupation with the concept of death and dying.

Bullfighting is dangerous and Brian was always fascinated by dangerous situations. It was almost as if danger was a turn-on for him and bullfighting provided the opportunity for him to witness danger. It was a psychological confrontation with danger and death right before his eyes.

Bullfighters were to Brian what the Beatles were to music fans. They were his idols.

Peter Brown: Going to Spain in the early sixties was like going back in a time warp, because Franco was still running the country and nothing had changed since the Civil War.

They were wonderful trips. We had a great time and we were on our own. Every day there was a bullfight and we stayed up all night because the Spanish are late people. This was holiday time and we met wonderful people there. We met Ken Tynan there who we knew from London, who introduced us to Orson Welles. They were all part of these aficionados who went from bullring to bullring. We became sort of part of them and there was a great feeling of enjoyment. It was like going to a soccer game.

It was great fun for Brian to be hanging out with these people who respected him. He was a known quantity then. He'd become famous and they respected what he had done. He'd turned the world around as far as British entertainment was concerned, and so they were fascinated to meet him.

BILL GRUNDY: *Do you get on very well with a lot of people?*
EPSTEIN: On the whole yes. Obviously one gets on well with people unless one doesn't like them.

GRUNDY: *But do you go out of your way to get on well with people?*
EPSTEIN: Yes.

GRUNDY: *In this peculiar business, the world of the impresario, you still seem to me to be a strange fish in a very weird sort of sea. Do you get on well with the impresarios you have to mix with?*
EPSTEIN: On the whole I think so. There may be quite a lot of envy about. I'm aware of that and for that reason I think it's up to me to try personally to make up for that envy. It isn't a particularly nice thing for other people to feel.

BBC HOME SERVICE, 7 MARCH 1964

Ken Partridge: Brian wanted a typical Belgravia party. He said, 'I don't want any gimmicks.' I said, 'You mean you want white tablecloths, silver candelabra, white flowers?' 'Perfect,' he said. I said, 'Pink and white striped?' 'Yes. Want all that,' he said.

I went away and did a drawing for him which was just what he wanted. He then started to worry about catering because at that time there were not many people you could go to for catering. We got Mr Capella, who ran the bar at Covent Garden.

He was a very portly man who came up to Chapel Street and said he could do the party. Brian said, 'Well, I want two kinds of food. I want gentile food and I want kosher food.' 'No problem at all,' he said. 'We shall arrange all that, Mr Epstein.' Then he went down and said, 'I've never done anything like this quite before in my life. I'll do my best.'

I thought Brian was quite wonderful to work for. He would suddenly become a little petulant over some slight thing, but it could always be ironed out. But the worst thing of all was when the party was completed and I'd said nobody was allowed up on the roof until the party began.

It was in the afternoon that Brian said, 'My mother's downstairs and she's just back from the hairdresser and she'd love to come and see it.' I said, 'No.' He said, 'Please.' So I said, 'Well, all right. Just this once, then.'

The marquee and everything were finished, completely finished. Everybody was disappearing off. Suddenly up came Queenie and said, 'Oh, it's magnificent but it's unlucky. It's red and white.' It was red carnations and white carnations. Brian said, 'What are we going to do?' I said 'What are we going to do? Nothing.' I said to Pam Foster who did the flowers, 'What are we going to do?' and she said, 'It's a bit late in the day isn't it, but we could dye some white carnations.' She went to Harrods to get some ink and dyed the carnations in buckets. The flowers were dripping on the floor when they came up the stairs but luckily Brian had a dark red floor.

I don't think anybody got wet from the dripping carnations and nobody noticed at all and Queenie was happy.

Peter Brown: Judy Garland wasn't on the original invitation list because Brian had met her a couple of nights before at Lionel Bart's and invited her but then forgot to put her on the list, so when she turned up nobody would let her in, so she was standing at the door and you rescued her.

KP: And I was told there was a woman trying to get in . So I said, 'Who is the woman?' I went down and there was this little woman in a pink coat who said, 'Brian met me last night in the restaurant.' I said, 'Judy Garland, please come in. You're my guest.'

PB: You were the only one that cared.

KP: Nobody else cared. She came and saw the room downstairs where everybody had drinks and it looked as if a bomb had hit it. Everybody had gone and there was hundreds of dirty glasses, cigarette butts, everything around. She said, 'Oh my God, I'm late.' I said, 'No, they're on the roof.' So she said, 'Gosh, what are they doing on the roof?' 'Well, they're not jumping off. They're having dinner.' Then she asked me for some orange juice.

PB: Orange juice?

KP: That's all she was drinking then. She had an orange juice and she was with Mark Heron. I don't know if she was married to him or not. So after a few minutes we came upstairs. There was no table for her at all until I saw David Jacobs. He saw Judy and how he cleared a table I will never know. But he immediately got Lionel Bart to sit there. Brian came over and everybody gathered around Judy who said, 'Hold my hand, I'm so frightened,' and as I put my hand out for her she stubbed a cigarette out on the back of it. She said, 'I've never burned anybody before.' I said, 'I shall treasure it for the rest of my life.'

David Jacobs was a powerful London show-business lawyer. He had eccentric habits, invariably appearing in public wearing full make-up.

PB: But none of the other people cared about Judy Garland 'cause they were all rock and rollers.

KP: They were all, yes.

PB: The Stones, the Searchers.

KP: Dusty Springfield.

PB: Dusty Springfield, right.

KP: They really didn't know who Judy Garland was, did they?

PB: He had the NEMS Company to run, but at night he would have dinner and then go to the clubs. They were very small, incredibly small and they were extraordinarily exclusive. I mean they were exclusive to pop stars.

The Ad-Lib was the first of that kind of calibre. Then there was the Scotch. Later there was the Cromwellian. It was very difficult to get into them. You had to be a rock star. You had to be a Rolling Stone or a Beatle or some such person. Later on, it could be people like the Who and models like Jean Shrimpton.

Not a lot of conversation went on because these clubs were very noisy, very small. We'd go at least three times a week because there was nowhere else for us to go. The nature of rock and roll is that you stay out late and go to dinner. The pubs shut early, so you had to go somewhere. But pop stars couldn't go just anywhere because they'd be mobbed, so this whole exclusive environment for this new breed of pop stars was created where they could hang out together. It was their club.

But it was inevitable that it would change. It wasn't that wonderful being stuck in that little environment. Everyone would have got tired of it sooner or later, just hanging out every night in the same place with the same people. Eventually you'd want more interesting and wider choices.

Lonnie Trimble: His apartment was his sanctuary, where he could do his own thing. He wasn't a very camp person. It was only when he was with camp people such as Peter Brown that he seemed camp.

8. Private Lives

BILL GRUNDY: *What's the pleasure of management then? What kick do you get out of it?*

BRIAN EPSTEIN: Lots. First, the development of an artist. I suppose there must be something in the actual dependence of an artist and their tremendous loyalty which is very gratifying in a way. I like my artists as people very much. I think they're all great people. It was recently written about me that I probably enjoy the company of my artists most of all. I think it's quite true. It was written in the context of my not having much of a social life so that most of my time is spent with my artists.

BBC HOME SERVICE, 7 MARCH 1964

Derek Taylor: He would drop in and out of a tour. Sometimes he would go off for two or three days. If you were in an industrial town – Cincinnati, Cleveland – they weren't of much interest to him, so he'd show up again when we got to New Orleans so he could have dinner at Antoine's.

I once met him at the airport in Cleveland and he had a very dark mien. I thought, 'Christ. What's happened?' In the car he said, 'Derek, I have a bone to pick with you and it can't wait. You've been making off-colour jokes with John in someone else's hearing and it's got back to me.' I said, 'It's impossible because I would never talk to any of them about each other, nor would I talk about you to them, nor would I talk about them to you. It's trouble-making and it's familiar to me. Those of us who are really on your side, like Mal, Neil* and one or two others, we can walk around without fear or favour. It hasn't happened.' But Brian was extremely angry, or rather disappointed, I think. I wasn't homophobic but he supposed I was. The Beatles, on the other hand, did say terrible things about homosexuality, but to him. In front of him.

He found it impossible to delegate all the time I knew him. He was a frightfully bossy man. He wasn't malicious. He didn't bear grudges. He was very tight with money, very punctilious, but if he thought he'd done anything that he shouldn't have done, he made up for it. I had a good deal with *A*

---

* Before there was Brian Epstein, there was Mal Evans and Neil Aspinall. They were a crucial part of the Beatles family: roadies, minders, gofers and best friends. They were part of the group's daily life. Mal Evans was killed in an incident with the Los Angeles police in 1976. Neil Apsinall is now the CEO of Apple PLC.

Cellarful of Noise, but I think he gave me a poor percentage. He took me out to lunch in Beverly Hills later and said, 'That wasn't good enough, that deal. I want to give you £1,000 or $2,000,' so he'd feel better. But in business and as an employer he was very stingy. He was the shopkeeper.

Paul McCartney: We were in New York and Bob Dylan came round to visit with a couple of other people, including a guy called Al Aronowitz who was a friend of his. I think they were the people who had the pot, actually. Bob kind of gets blamed for it, and I'm not sure he's too happy with that rap.

That night, anyway, was the first time all of us smoked pot. I have a great memory of Brian sitting on one of the twin beds in the hotel room. Ringo sort of went out first and the rest of us dived in when he looked all goofy and stuff. We said, 'We've got to try this.' George and I were sitting on this bed and Brian was sort of lying there rather grandly as he would, very beautifully dressed and everything. I have this image of him with a tiny little bit of a butt in his mouth like an old tramp, trying to be graceful with this terrible little fag end.

We actually all got stoned and we were giggling. It was giggling time and we were uncontrollable. And Brian was looking at himself. He was going hysterical pointing to himself, saying, 'Jew! Jew!' He saw the funny side of it. It was as if he was finally sort of talking about the fact. 'Oh, I'm Jewish. I forgot.' I don't think he smoked it a lot. I think the band smoked much more.

Nat Weiss: When I first met him there was really a mental block to him. He still saw homosexuality as something you do in back alleys and out of the side of the pub and something you just didn't talk about. When he started going to bars in New York and meeting people he became notoriously open about the whole thing.

There was a bar, called Kelly's Bar, on 45th Street between 6th Avenue and Broadway, which originally was very famous as a servicemen's bar, but then began to collect all kinds of people. We used to go there a lot because a lot of male hustlers used to hang out there with the servicemen and the girls that were around.

What these hustlers used to do was pick up someone gay, make their money and then take out a girl. Like the food chain, so to speak. There was another country and western place called the Wagon Wheel right across the street. We used to go there. It was a rough and wild place and Brian really liked that. It was a great street because that famous club the Peppermint Lounge, where the twist started, was there. What really ruined 45th Street was the twist becoming popular. Then all these limos with all the people you wanted to avoid started arriving on the street.

Derek Taylor: I left him at the end of the 1964 tour of America. One night we were all tired and he took my limo because I must have been in his. It was a terrible experience because of his noise. He was shouting, 'I'm not having it. I'm absolutely not having it.' He could go on for twenty minutes like that. And the regrets would follow pretty quickly. He hated having trouble with people he really liked. I got a letter under my door. 'This really is too bad, Derek. We must be friends.' I thought he must be pissed, not pissed off, pissed since it was the end of the final night of the first big American tour. I wanted to go down to the bar with Neil [Aspinall] and Al Aronowitz, Bob Freeman, and just relax, not have all the stress and pressure and 'Mr Brian'.

After the business with the limo, there was this three months' notice to be worked out. But on the following day on the plane coming back, he came through to economy to get Mal [Evans] and Neil [Aspinall] and me out into first class. He was sent through by the Beatles actually. 'What are they doing back there? We made a fucking fortune on the tour. Get them up here. You go and get them.'

When we got to first class, he called me over. I was the Beatles' press officer, but he still saw me as a PA and he said, 'About last night, I want it to be over. I want you to be my friend.' But I felt such freedom having resigned. That's what the note that went through the door was, my resignation – and I got a bit weepy. I put my hand on his and said, 'I am very fond of you. It's been a hell of a year, but I can't take any more of this business.' So I didn't go back and we got to be friends very quickly, but I never did work for him again. We stayed friends. He used to come over to our house in LA and use it for events and parties. It was a good friendship.

Nat Weiss: With the advantage of looking back thirty years now and knowing what we know about certain things, I would say he certainly had all the symptoms of someone who was manic depressive. His mood swings were not frequent but immediate. He was either very elated or he was withdrawn and these mood swings were triggered by very small things. Like if someone came in and said they'd read a bad review of the Beatles, he would shut down completely and stare at you. Or if you said something he just couldn't relate to he'd suddenly become silent and you'd get the starey look. Then it would stop.

When he was more manic, he was creative, bright, full of enthusiasm. When he talked about music or people he always used his hands. He had these tremendous expressions as if he was talking about some imperial court. Brian felt that he had a miniature empire that he was running and he had the same rules that a royal scene would have.

Geoffrey Ellis: During 1964, Brian came back to New York a number of times. I think he came once more with the Beatles when they did a slightly longer tour and several times on business, seeing the record companies, talking to promoters and so on. On each occasion I saw him, we would spend evenings together and time together. There was a great deal of work for him to do. He didn't like office work at all, and he did like to have round him people that he knew. Eventually he suggested to me that I should come and work for him in London.

To me this was a remarkable suggestion. I knew nothing about pop music, the music business, the entertainment business. I didn't like pop music and I told him I didn't know that I was qualified to do so. But he said he would like me to do so very much because much of the work would be administration and working with contracts. I'd been trained as a lawyer and insurance policies are contracts, also.

I thought about it quite a lot because I'd be giving up what seemed to be a reasonable career. Although Brian's offer at the time appeared to be very attractive, one could never know quite how it would turn out in the long run. However, I thought it was worth taking a risk and I was fascinated, as everybody was, by the Beatles; and not only the Beatles, all the other acts he had by then, most of which were successful. So I agreed that I would go and work for him.

Lonnie Trimble: I thought he was all right with his homosexuality because I had a relationship and he said to me, 'How is it that you and Patrick are so happy?' I said, 'Because we love each other.' I don't think Brian found love. He found people that would use him but he used them as well, for sexual reasons.

Brian had rough trade. He brought them in and I discovered them all on a sofa in the lounge. I questioned him about it and said, 'Don't you feel nervous about bringing these people in here?' He said, 'Oh no. They wouldn't hurt me. I'm Brian Epstein.'

So he listened to my advice from time to time. Then he had this lover boy that he picked up in California and brought back from the second tour of America.

Nat Weiss: Diz Gillespie was a young man that Brian had met in New York, I believe, before I'd met Brian. He was a rather good-looking, sophisticated male hustler and Brian got to like him. He was from the mid-west and obviously he seduced Brian into thinking that he really cared about him.

Brian had never really been seduced that way before and he really fell for it.

Lonnie Trimble: Diz looked a bit like Gene Pitney, a clean-cut sort of young man. I arrived one morning and found the second bedroom occupied. Then at breakfast time, Epstein came out and introduced me to Diz. As far as I was concerned it was a nice time because Epstein was playing house. He would go to the office after his breakfast and then he would come home at six o'clock and there was smiles all around because he was having a bit of happiness.

They were fine together. I saw them at breakfast, and then occasionally I was asked to come in and cook dinner for them. It was like happy families, which pleased me, because while Diz was there my life was very easy. While he was being good Diz, things were great, and then he could suddenly turn.

They fought about drugs and his trollops that Diz brought in. Diz was bisexual and he didn't really want to play the homosexual bit. I went in one day and the place was all messed up with girls all over the place. I caught Diz and I told him, 'You're making my life a misery. There's too much work because of this and Epstein doesn't like it.' And I also said, 'By the way, Diz, you're not playing your role. You don't have to love him but at least you ought to sleep with him once a week and give him a kiss when he comes home in the evening and then we'll all be happy.' But Diz did not do it. He went the other way. He started to steal things and do anything he could to upset Epstein.

One evening Brian wanted me to cook dinner for his mother and father while Diz was there. I went out and did the usual thing, grapefruit, large Dover soles, veg and a simple pudding. We were halfway through the meal when Diz stood up and said something nasty to Epstein and walked out of the flat, whereupon Queenie and Harry were sitting there dumbfounded, not knowing what to do. Then Epstein left the flat, leaving me and Harry and Queenie there.

They decided to get their coats because there wasn't going to be a complete meal that evening. As they got ready to leave the flat, Queenie said to me, 'Lonnie, look after my son.' Now, I was a bit annoyed with this because that was the second mother to ask me to look after her son. First was Peter O'Toole's mother and then here's Epstein's mother asking me to look after her son. They realized that I could look after myself.

Billy J. Kramer: I think it must have been very difficult being gay back then because you couldn't go out and tell the world. I used to feel like saying to him, 'You know, Brian, I know you're gay. I'm cool about it. If you want to talk about it it's fine.' But I think he was very nervous about that and very nervous about the world finding out about it and it must have been very hard on him.

Geoffrey Ellis: At the time I joined NEMS, as well as familiarizing myself with the day-to-day aspects of running the business, there were a number of outstanding problems to deal with. There was a new recording contract to be dealt with and there were very important publishing matters to be considered. But one of the most difficult items to understand was that concerning the merchandising of Beatles-related objects – wigs, pens, guitars, heaven knows what, all sorts of stuff that people wanted to make money out of.

This all started before I joined NEMS. It transpired, I found out, that manufacturers had approached Brian and asked him for the rights to manufacture and sell Beatles-related objects. Brian, not knowing anything about that business, and frankly at that time not realizing how important it could be financially and being concerned with the Beatles' image, had in effect brushed it off and said, 'Well, you'll have to deal with my lawyer about that.' He realized that it was a technical matter of copyright and likenesses. His lawyers at the time had not dealt with it entirely properly or with the degree of efficiency which they ought to have done. They had issued certain licences to manufacturers – I think almost entirely in England or the UK – to manufacture various things like Beatles watches, for example.

Brian was then approached by a group of young men who had the bright idea of licensing the manufacture and overseeing this business for Brian and the Beatles. Brian had agreed that these people should take on the work of doing this licensing. This was an English company called Stramsact, which is an anagram of Smartacts, not inappropriate. There was also an American company formed in association with Stramsact called Seltaeb.

Both companies were headed by an Englishman called Nicky Byrne, who had his headquarters in America, and he went around and secured many lucrative licensing deals in America. The deal which they had done with Brian was for them to do a licensing, collect the income and pay NEMS for the account of the Beatles 10 per cent of the proceeds. Looking at it now, and indeed looking at it then, this was an extraordinary deal. It should have been the other way round. The Beatles should have got 90 per cent and Nicky Byrne, who was in fact no more than an agent, should have got a small agency commission. But the deal was done and they proceeded to license many, many items, mostly in America.

David Jacobs had been highly recommended to Brian because of his reputation as a sophisticated expert in entertainment law.

Epstein gave Jacobs complete control of the Stramsact negotiations in the winter of 1963–4.

Nat Weiss: If you take the attitude that the buck stops here, it's Brian's fault. He never denied that he didn't know about merchandising, no one did. But since he took the credit for so much he had to acknowledge his mistakes. Secondly, I think it was David Jacobs's fault. The attorney is really supposed to look into deals and check things out.

There were certainly many merchandising companies in New York at the time. There were companies that merchandised fictional characters, things like that. Disney had a merchandising company and Jacobs should have looked into that.

Geoffrey Ellis: Almost immediately trouble had ensued because some of the licences Seltaeb issued were in conflict with some of the earlier licences which had been issued by our solicitors in London. There had been a lack of communication between them. It had not been handled very efficiently or very effectively either, and at the time I joined there were mutterings on both sides. Brian was beginning to realize that it was a bad deal, that he was only getting 10 per cent of the account of the Beatles from all these enormous payments being made principally in America. Also, the Seltaeb people were becoming irritated by the conflicting licences, some of which had been already issued in the UK before they took on the business.

Meetings were held which I was not myself involved with. In fact, they may have been before I joined, I'm not sure. The deal was somewhat improved so that Seltaeb paid NEMS something under 50 per cent, around 45 to 47 per cent, instead of the 10 per cent. Still a bad deal, I must say, because they retained more than 50 per cent of the income that was coming in.

But having renegotiated that, it had little effect because it seemed to us that Seltaeb was still not accounting properly. There were stories of the Seltaeb people living very high off the hog in America, spending all the money and enjoying life to the full, and at the same time not accounting and not paying NEMS.

So eventually Brian and I, with our solicitors in London, decided that we ought to sue Seltaeb for unaccounting and payment. The writs were issued in New York with the inevitable result that Seltaeb counter-sued. They sued NEMS on account of the conflicting licensing, saying that they had been prevented from carrying on their business properly and effectively.

Nat Weiss: The Beatles never made any money on merchandising in the United States. It had all been dissipated by the time the level of Beatlemania that would have generated the merchandising was over. After 1965, there was no possibility of any income. No one who dealt in these things would touch

Beatles merchandising at that time, in view of all the experiences they had had with the confused licensing of the original lunch-box companies, T-shirt companies, wig companies and things like that. It had been a total loss for the Beatles and they lost millions.

Paul McCartney: The problems arose because, in as much as he was from Liverpool, he hadn't done this kind of business before. He had a great theatricality but I think some of the deals he got us were great for the time but not so great, as it turned out. I can look back on it now and say he could have done that, he could have asked for that. But I just don't think any of us knew about it then. It was very early days. So I think for what he knew and what he could bring us he was really excellent, and I don't think the Beatles would have been the same without him.

You can't go back and change things. I'm not upset, but now that I'm more aware of the way business works I can see one or two things we really should have done better. Brian would not know about those kind of things. British people didn't know that stuff at that time. I think the rest of the time Brian did good deals. I think he looked to his dad for business advice and his dad really knew how to run a furniture store in Liverpool. This was a little bigger than that.

Geoffrey Ellis: The lawsuits proceeded with a great deal of acrimony and rather slowly initially. There were hearings in New York where statements of evidence were given. Eventually there was a hearing in New York which our then attorney, the late Walter Hofer, handled for us. He told Brian that he was summoned to appear in court in New York.

Brian hid his head in the sand and refused to appear. Although our New York attorney said they could get over this problem, this was not the case. A finding was recorded against NEMS in the amount of $5 million.

Nat Weiss: I was in court that day and found that a full judgement of $5 million had been taken against the Beatles. Brian was not familiar with these things. When I called him and said, 'Are you aware of the fact there's a $5 million judgement against the Beatles?' he said 'Is that good or bad?' I said, 'That's very bad.'

Geoffrey Ellis: So Brian and I set off to New York together with our London solicitor, David Jacobs. We met with Nat Weiss on arrival and the next day we went to see Louis Nizer in his office, which was in the old Paramount Building in Times Square. This was not the place where you would usually expect to find a prominent New York attorney's firm. But I assume the office was at this location because they handled a lot of film business and Times Square was the centre of the entertainment part of New York.

And when we went to see Louis Nizer, his office appeared rather cathedral-like with stained-glass windows. He himself sat on his desk on a small dais. He was a small man and I think that's why he had his desk on a dais. But this making an impression wasn't necessary at all because he had a very strong personality and one could see how he could impress a jury by his performance.

Nat Weiss: It was very funny when I brought Brian in to meet Louis Nizer because Nizer was a rather short person and he sat on a stage in his office. When Brian came in Mr Nizer said, 'Oh, Mr Epstein, have you ever read my book?' He'd written a best seller about jury trials. And Brian said, 'No. Have you ever read my book?' Nizer said no and it started the whole conversation. Nizer told me how difficult the case would be and that the initial retainer would be $50,000, which was a substantial retainer at that time. Brian said, 'It's my responsibility. I'm going to pay all of this,' which he did. Nizer was able to take care of the judgement and the case proceeded from there.

At the end of 1964, Brian was given the accolade of an appearance on BBC Radio's *Desert Island Discs*. The programme had been running since 1942 and Epstein joined the glittering roster of stars who had indulged themselves in the programme's premise: if you were cast away alone on a desert island, which eight records, one book and one luxury would you choose to take with you? Previous castaways had included Noel Coward, Princess Margaret, Alec Guinness and Cary Grant.

ROY PLOMLEY: *How do you do, ladies and gentlemen. Our castaway this week is the young man who's been called the Czar of Pop and the Emperor of Beat. He's the man behind the Beatles, Gerry and the Pacemakers, Cilla Black and other recording stars – Brian Epstein.*

PLOMLEY: *Brian, do you call yourself a musical person? Is music important to you?*
EPSTEIN: Most important to me. I don't think I'm a musical person, though.

PLOMLEY: *Have you ever studied it?*
EPSTEIN: Yes, I studied the violin when I was in school, when I was very young. But I don't think I could play it now.

PLOMLEY: *Do you think you'd be able to face solitude?*
EPSTEIN: Yes, to a degree. But I would miss people. Though I wouldn't mind a bit of solitude right now.

PLOMLEY: *Do you have any religious philosophy that would help?*
EPSTEIN: No.

BRIAN EPSTEIN'S DESERT ISLAND DISCS

1 *All My Loving* – 'It's a splendid song by John Lennon and Paul McCartney and here rerecorded by George Martin and his Orchestra. George Martin, the man who actually makes the Beatles' records in the studio, has brought a great deal of love to this number and I think it's a very fine song and easy to listen to and very, very pleasant.'

2 *Bach's Brandenburg* – 'The fifth actually. It happens my mother gave them all to me for my birthday when I was nineteen . . . It's a very basic, truthful music.'

3 *Kilimanjaro by the Quartette Trés Bien.*

4 *The Beatles, She's A Woman* – 'I think it's tremendously good. It has a lot of feeling and soul about it and marks a tremendous change in their recorded sound.'

5 *Sibelius 2nd Symphony* – 'It expresses a great deal of passion, fire and sort of keeps one's thoughts a long way off.'

6 *Odun de! Odun de! by Michael Olatunji.*

7 *Violin Concerto No. 1 in G Minor by Max Bruch* – 'I have a very deep feeling for this. Max Bruch is a Jewish man and this probably brings out some early instincts within me.'

8 *Ritmo de Carmen Amaya* – 'I must have some flamenco.'

PLOMLEY: *If you could have just one disc of the eight, which would it be?*
EPSTEIN: Unquestionably, the Kilimanjaro.

PLOMLEY: *And one luxury to take with you?*
EPSTEIN: A set of oils, canvas and brushes.

PLOMLEY: *And one book apart from the Bible and Shakespeare?*
EPSTEIN: *Elected Silence,* by Thomas Merton.

PLOMLEY: *What is that, a novel?*
EPSTEIN: Yes.

PLOMLEY: *What's it about?*
EPSTEIN: It's about Roman Catholicism.

DESERT ISLAND DISCS, BBC, 18 NOVEMBER 1964

9. Uncharted Waters

BILL GRUNDY: *Aren't you a bit timid about going into new areas, highly technical areas, for example, without a great deal of knowledge and experience.*
BRIAN EPSTEIN: Not really, because one studies quite a lot from an outsider's point of view. After all, I started to manage the Beatles without any experience at all.

BBC HOME SERVICE, 7 MARCH 1964

Sid Bernstein: Brian never asked how I got the money for Shea Stadium and I never told him.

The guy at Carnegie Hall told me that I could have sold out thirty days of tickets, two shows a day, and he asked me if I could get the Beatles again. That meant to me as a promoter I could have sold close to 200,000 seats – I knew the man's experience and wisdom. So when I called Brian, it was not about Madison Square Garden. I said, 'Brian, would you be interested in doing a show at Shea Stadium?' He said, 'Wait a minute, how many seats does that have?' I said, 'Brian, it has 55,000 and we'll sell it out.' He said, 'I don't want my boys playing to empty seats.' I said, 'Brian, I will give you ten dollars for every seat that's empty.' He said, 'You're on.' That showed his elegance, his class, his word – no contract.

He said, 'Sid, what I'd like for the boys is a $100,000 guarantee against 60 per cent of the gross.' I said, 'Fine.' He said, 'Sidney, I will need half deposit,' meaning $50,000, 'before we agree on the exact date and the deal.' I didn't have $50,000 and I said to him that my money was all tied up and could I have some time to get the money. This was on January 10 1965. He said, 'I'll be in New York on April 10th. I'll be at the Waldorf Towers. Why don't you call me there and present the cheque to me? But you cannot advertise this. You cannot do any publicity, no interviews, until you pay me the $50,000.' I said, 'Agreed. But may I talk to my friends about this?' He said, 'I can't stop you from talking.'

By this time I had presented the Beatles, the Rolling Stones, the Dave Clark Five, the Animals and eight other British groups in New York so I became an identifiable picture, particularly in the Village. When I'd take my little boy Adam to Washington Square Park on weekends, all the kids would come up to me and say, 'Mr Bernstein, what's the next concert?' So after that conversation with Brian, I told them, 'The Beatles at Shea Stadium.' There was pandemonium. I got the idea I should get a post office box and on my next walk with Adam, I let the kids know they could order the tickets by mail with a cheque or money order at PO Box 21 in Chelsea, New York. I did this for three weeks in a row.

After three weeks, I went to the post office and said, 'I'm here to pick up my mail at PO Box 21.' The clerk in the front of the office looked at me and said, 'Hey, buddy, what's your racket? What do you do?' He called to the man in the back, 'Hey Bill, Bernstein Box 21 is here.' This big man said to me, 'Hey, you really got something hot going for you.' So he and the other guy came back with the three biggest duffel bags I'd ever seen.

I used to pay my phone bill at this post office, so I figured these guys had confused my box with the telephone company's mail. I said, 'Wait a minute. That's not my mail.' So they pulled out some sample letters, 'Yeah, Box 21. Yeah, Mr Bernstein.' Well I couldn't believe this and by the time April 10 rolled around, and I was supposed to see Brian Epstein at the Waldorf Astoria Towers, I had already banked $185,000 and I hadn't even scratched the surface yet.

I came to Brian's suite and instead of giving him the $50,000, which was half the deposit, I gave him a cheque that read $100,000. He said, 'Sid, you made a mistake.' I said, 'No, I didn't.' He said, 'Oh, you must be liquid now. Your funds must have loosened up.' He figured I was in Wall Street and had an investment that paid off. I said, 'I'm in good shape, Brian. Thank you very much.'

No one had ever done this kind of concert before. I had no experience about what the stage would cost. I had no idea what the unions would want, the electricians, the stagehands, the security people, the ushers. Finally, the budget just skyrocketed to where I wound up making a net of $6,500 on a show that grossed $304,000. Instead of a $100,000 guarantee against 60 per cent of the gross, the boys walked out with $180,000 for what I realized was twenty-eight minutes of concert.

Geoffrey Ellis: The time came all too soon when Brian and I had to go to New York for pre-trial examinations in connection with the Seltaeb lawsuit. These would normally be held in the offices of the attorneys for one or other of the parties, but by then our attorneys had become so incensed at the attitude of the Seltaeb attorneys, and vice versa, that they decided that they would hold the examinations in a room in the courthouse in downtown Manhattan. A retired judge had to be called in as a referee.

Brian went first and he spent, I think, about two days being examined by the Seltaeb's attorneys. Most unhappily, he didn't know the answers to perhaps the majority of the questions that were asked.

They were highly technical questions to do with the licences which had been issued, the terms of the licences, the proceeds, the items manufactured and so on. Brian, of course, had always tried to keep himself rather apart from this type of technical business. He was highly embarrassed at not being able to answer most of his questions and embarrassed and annoyed at the attitude of the other side's attorneys. They would say, 'Why, Mr Epstein, didn't you know about this deal which could net the Beatles, your managed artists, millions of dollars?' Brian had to say that he didn't, and felt a feeling almost of shame.

This went on for about two days. In the intervals and in the evenings, I would say to him, 'Tell them that, if you don't know the answers, Geoffrey Ellis will provide the answers when his turn comes.' So he did. He would say, 'Well, Mr Ellis can tell you about this. I was not concerned with the detail.'

I don't think this did anything to mitigate his own feelings of embarrassment. But at the same time Seltaeb's lawyers knew that they weren't going to get answers out of him at that stage. After his pre-trial examination was over, he went back to London and I think I accompanied him. Then I had to go back to New York in a couple of weeks' time for my own pre-trial examination.

In the interim, in London, I had immersed myself in the details, the complexities of the Seltaeb licensing, what it was all about and how they had been working. So when my turn came – I was examined for only one day, mercifully – I did have a lot of the answers. But, of course, this was not as exciting to the other side's attorneys as having the Beatles' actual manager, Brian Epstein, at their mercy.

Following these pre-trial examinations we redoubled our efforts to settle. Seltaeb at the same time wanted to settle. However, they didn't let up. They were still producing more and more accountings for ridiculous sums. It approached something like $100 million, which in today's terms would be, heaven knows, getting on for a billion dollars. They were idiotic, ludicrous, headline figures which made no sense at all. But they made headlines, in point of fact. It's exactly what they did do: 'Beatles sued for blah-blah-blah.'

The whole legal battle went on for about a year and a half, and the settlement was finalized in early 1967.

Simon Napier-Bell: About two or three years into the life of the Beatles, one heard people say at the time, 'Oh, Brian's hopeless,' or 'Brian's useless.' But that's because they were way beyond the stage of being broken. Brian had been a sensational manager. He had taken on an unknown group of people who everyone else had ignored and in one way or another, through his own enthusiasm, had broken them and made them into this enormous group.

But it's a completely different situation once a group has happened from the work that has to be done to break them initially. As he began more and more to be the business manager, looking after things on a high level with high finance, people saw weakness in him.

George Martin: I was increasingly worried that everything that Brian brought to me was gradually getting not quite so good. I had the Beatles to begin with, Gerry and the Pacemakers, Billy J. Kramer, Cilla Black, the Fourmost. After that we started going downhill with other acts which weren't as good as those. It was part of Brian's attempt to build up his empire. Brian thought that all you had to do was to get a good song and a reasonable artist. Then I would come along, get them into the studio, sprinkle a little bit of fairy dust and we'd have number-one records. He wasn't involved in the hard grind of making a record a success. He was the one who put the things into place and expected them to lock in and become gems. And when they didn't, he didn't quite understand why.

Nat Weiss: As time went by there were so many acts that they could never get the attention that was warranted from Brian, and of course every act that went to NEMS expected to be treated like the Beatles, and consequently there was a string of acts that didn't happen. But Brian felt he had the magic touch when he signed somebody. He had this grandiose description of how he was going to work it. He was a very controlling person. In this day and age we talk about people who like to control and Brian was obsessed with controlling a situation. Anything done outside his area of control he was contemptuous of, or certainly it brought about a tirade of abuse.

Gerry Marsden: We were competitive with the Beatles. I would get annoyed with Brian because he spent so much time with the Beatles, more than he did with us. That was what some of my arguments were with him. I said, 'Brian, how come you've got a week with the Beatles, when we haven't seen you come one day with me?' And he would say, 'Gerry, please realize these four guys are the biggest in the world. They're stars. You're a little light bulb.' And then I would hit him very hard. Boom boom! Brian would say he had to devote more time to them because they were always more popular than we were. I used to get jealous, but then I realized in the end that Brian was correct. He had to spend more time with the Beatles. I would get annoyed and we were deadly rivals onstage. Offstage, great mates. John was my best pal. But onstage we'd want to bury them. Too bad we didn't have two Brian Epsteins. If we did, we might have carried on a bit longer as a band.

If Brian would have given us more time we would have more records. We stopped recording in 1966 or we stopped making hits in 1966. Maybe if Brian would have devoted more time to us we could have been bigger.

Billy J. Kramer: I was always a bit annoyed because I used to see different members of his stable on *Juke Box Jury*. The Beatles would be on and Cilla Black would be on and Gerry Marsden would be on. I would ask Brian, 'Why can't I do *Juke Box Jury*?' And he said, 'Because you don't speak well enough. Your diction and the way you speak are terrible and you need to have elocution lessons.' And I said, and that was one thing I did say to Brian, 'You know, if people can't accept me the way I am then it's too bad.' But I never took elocution lessons and I never did *Juke Box Jury*.

Lonnie Trimble: People couldn't get really close to Brian, because he didn't let them. He was a lonely man who wanted friendship but he could never find it. He had two affairs that I knew of, one was an actor called Michael and it was absolutely wonderful, and then he had Diz. Nobody but them seemed to care for him. Still, each time after they had a nice week, I'd come in and find the house empty: lover boy has gone. But he had friendships with DJs and things like that, all the people that knew what was going to be number one in the hit parade before it actually was published.

Johnny Gustafson: I knew about Brian's way but he never approached me in that way apart from one time at his flat. There was a party there with John Lennon and some of the Beatles and their girlfriends. I was staying in a flat in Bayswater and I was pretty broke. They all went and I lingered on. I probably hoped for another drink or something.

He kind of put his arm round my shoulder in a friendly way and said something along the lines of, 'You know, John, I can really help you if . . .' The implied 'if' was there. So I said something like, 'I know you can help me, Brian, but I can't really help you and I really have to go now.' And so off I went. So that was the last time I really saw him.

I could have gone away and thought about it and decided on some way to get round what I felt was a problem, but I didn't. At that time his homosexuality meant a lot more to me than it would now. It was more of a powerful influence on me. So I decided not to go back or phone him again about it, and that was probably my mistake. But we make these mistakes.

Lonnie Trimble: One day Epstein telephoned me at home to tell me not to come to work. I thought it was strange that this man's gonna pay me for a day's work and I'm not working. So I telephoned his chauffeur, Alf Blackburn, and said, 'What's happened?' And Alf said he'd been told not to come to work as well.

Of course, curiosity was killing us. So when I went in the next day, half past eight, I couldn't wait to get to find out what was going on. I knocked on his bedroom door and said, 'Good morning, Mr Epstein. It's half past eight,' and then I went to look in the spare bedroom. It was empty.

So I figured out what had happened. Diz was gone. Mr Epstein came out to have his breakfast. He sat there and he said, 'You can have everything and still be unhappy,' and then he started to cry. I'd never seen him cry before, so what am I supposed to do? I put my arm around his shoulder, which I'd never done the whole time, and said, 'Snap out of it.' He said, 'I've got this important meeting.' I said, 'Well, either you got to cancel the meeting or you snap out of it and get to it.' He snapped out of it. He left the flat, and I carried on cleaning up.

Next morning, there's a picture of Brian Epstein in full feature when he took over the Saville Theatre from Lew Grade and Bernard Delfont. He was an upstart as far as they were concerned and this really upset a lot of people at the time, but Epstein was very happy that he had a theatre.

Marianne Faithfull: He bought the Saville Theatre, which was a very beautiful theatre. It was a moment where people were a bit insecure about the West End and what was going to happen. I think he had a vision that this is what we must do with the West End. We must open it up. He was absolutely right; this is exactly what was going on at the time.

Without being pretentious, all these different *métiers* – film, painting, sculpture, rock'n'roll, classical music, everything, photography – were opening up and you could switch, you could go from one to another. You didn't have to say, 'I'm a painter. I'm an actor. I'm a musician,' like you didn't have to say, 'I'm straight,' or 'I'm gay.' You could be both. You could be everything.

I think that what Brian Epstein realized was that we were almost a new form. We had to relate our new form to people like Robin Fox and Roz Chatto. It's important for critical and historical context to put new work in a framework, to relate it to the past. But in some ways the actual artists, and I consider myself one of them, were completely different. I never think anybody is exclusively anything, specially Englishmen. I just don't believe in this all-consuming, 'I'm this and that cuts everything else out.' I think everybody has got all possibilities if they want them. The tension was the secret. Though I think he would have been very much happier in a more open sort of bisexual world. Like now maybe.

But this was a perfect situation for Brian Epstein and a perfect situation for me and a perfect situation for all of us. He was the one with the vision and class, much more than somebody like Andrew Oldham, who was too self-centred, really. It's almost embarrassing to talk about it, but the mass consciousness had to be raised and Brian Epstein was in the perfect position to do that. Just as the Beatles were, in a way, through their record sales.

Aunt Stella: We were invited to the opening of a show that he put on at the Saville Theatre and we went to that. I remember seeing him there. He seemed absolutely fine. He was full of beans, very pleased with himself. After all he'd just bought this theatre and he was quite thrilled with what was going on.

Lonnie Trimble: He sat me down once after he'd gotten rid of Diz. It was the first time I ever went into his bedroom when he was actually in bed, and he said, 'Sit down. I want to talk to you. I want to tell you about this and that.' I said, 'Wait a minute, now. Do you really want my opinion of what you're gonna tell me?' He said he did and I made sure to ask him three times if he really wanted my opinion. So eventually I laid it on the line.

I said, 'Diz is in California now. Leave him there out of harm's way.' Then Epstein said, 'Oh, I'm gonna make him a star. He wouldn't harm me.' It was during the same discussion that he told me that he and John Lennon had been lovers. Now that's too much for me to take on. We'd never talked about his personal life before, so I left the room.

A week or two later, who's back in London? Diz, worse than he was the first time. I thought, 'Oh my God, Epstein's going crazy.'

Nat Weiss: The Diz Gillespie scene was something that approached a successful relationship before he realized who he was dealing with.

Simon Napier-Bell: In the music industry everybody knew Brian was gay without any doubt. Probably everyone in the country knew, because newspapers carried some strongly hinting stories. Most people realized that it was something in his sexuality which had energized him to really fall in love with the Beatles, not individually, necessarily, but as a group and as an image and to see them dress up as he'd like to see boys like that dressed up.

Now I think everyone recognized that and even people who weren't gay would have respected that that was a large part of what had made it happen for him.

Straight people often think that gays should be slightly sorry for themselves, but I've never met a single gay person in my entire life who would
want to be straight for one fraction of a second. I've never met a black man
who wanted to be white. I've never met a Jewish person who wished he
wasn't Jewish. I doubt that Brian was the exception to this rule.

Peter Brown: Brian was an extremely private person, particularly with the gay
side of his life, which was something that he wasn't happy with. He didn't
discuss it with the Beatles. He didn't discuss it with Cilla. He considered it a
very private matter and he didn't want it generally discussed.

There was an element certainly on the gay side that he didn't wish to admit
to his prodigies, but it's not that illogical because he regarded them as part of
his business life and the gambling or the gay part as part of his private life.
Why would a successful businessman tell his clients all about his other
interests in his private life?

Of course the Beatles knew Brian was gay, but Brian lived in denial about
their knowing. We're talking about the dark ages but he probably didn't
rationalize it too well. After all, they had lived in the seedy parts of Hamburg
and seen all there was to see there, so nothing really bothered them.

Certainly their respect for him would not have been lessened by a
discussion or open knowledge of this. But he couldn't see this because of his
own insecurity about being gay.

What was important to him – and that was the same thing that was
important to the Beatles – was the next number one. That's how you judged
the success of what you were doing. You were struggling for the next hit song
and the next hit single and that's what it was all about. Brian could do a good
deal with the records and with the film deals and whatever other deals he was
doing, the touring deals and everything, but essentially it always came down
to positioning, choosing the next record.

There's no question that Brian was a totally honest person. He was aware of
the fact that the business was sharp but I don't think that he had particularly
sharp practices, and of course, as we were dealing with new situations, he was
in the vanguard of what was developing.

Nat Weiss: Brian really sailed into uncharted waters. When Brian came to
America, there were no groups that could fill stadiums. There were no groups
that could fill Madison Square Garden. There were no groups of that nature. We
had Elvis, but Brian said they would be bigger than Elvis back in '61, which I'm
sure in some cases was misconstrued. The idea of putting together stadiums
and large arenas, all these things were new. He created a lot of these things.

Nobody has come near to fashioning a phenomenon like he did, and it's not a learned process. His very essence is what made it work. He wasn't like someone who can get a Harvard MA and become a business manager. The very nature of the Beatles' career required a personality like his, and he was the one. Until Brian's entrance to the scene, the Beatles were a good act but may never have gotten out of Liverpool, may never have gotten out of England. Brian was the fuse that created the explosion or set it off – not only set it off but controlled it and made it work.

You discover it all when it goes in all different directions and you still have to contain it and make it work. And that's what Brian did, and he made it work out of pure instinct and with no precedent.

Sid Bernstein: I wanted to create the Beatles of America. They were a new young group called the Young Rascals. I learned a lot from Brian and it helped me a lot in the development of the Rascals.

The managing director of Shea Stadium, William Tooley, came over to me and said, 'Sid, is there any message you'd like to put on the scoreboard?' 'Yes, Mr Tooley. I would like real quick, like in fifteen, twenty seconds, a few times, "The Rascals Are Coming".'

Brian came out on the field upset. 'Sid, you've got to take that message off or the boys won't go on.' However, that message in front of 55,000 people prior to show time got me phone calls from record companies all over the world. Even the great Phil Spector called from California. He had heard about the Rascals on the scoreboard.'

Again, the magic of Brian turned my life around.

He referred to the Beatles, and I loved it, as 'my boys'. It was always 'the boys'. He always worried, 'Is security right? Have you taken care of this?' He was always planning in advance for their safety.

Before Brian the music business was limited to local clubs or, if you made it big, to theatres and music halls. This is what the Beatles were playing in England, 1,200 or 1,500 seats at maximum. But these weren't big enough. Brian broadened the landscape of show business.

What Brian Epstein did was turn the music business totally around. It came out of the Copacabanas of the world into the arenas of the world, the Shea Stadiums of the world. Brian, just by saying yes, took a chance that turned the music business around. The total picture of entertainment changed.

Nat Weiss: There was a promoter in Kansas City who wanted to do a Beatles concert in Kansas City and offered Brian $50,000 without knowing anything about gross potentials, seats and things like that. Brian just said, 'A hundred and fifty thousand,' and he got it. That's not the way you would do it today but that's how it was done then. But every tour was a success. The Beatles continued to grow.

Simon Napier-Bell: He told me that just once he allowed himself to go and stand at the back with all the girls in a concert in America. It think it was one of the stadiums where there were probably 25,000, 30,000 people, and he went into the crowd of girls and he just screamed like one of the girls, which he said is what he'd always wanted to do from the first minute he'd ever seen them. He had spent his whole life being restrained and wearing suits and suddenly he just screamed and became the mad fan he wanted to be.

What he liked was being one of the Beatles. That's what he wanted from the beginning. A lot of stress has been laid on being gay or fancying John Lennon or somebody else, but I think it was far more his being a loner and suddenly finding he was part of a group. I think that was much more of what he was interested in, and in some way that brought him into another group: show business. But what he wanted was to feel he was one of them and that's what he could never have.

Paul McCartney: He was a very private person and like good managers he didn't put himself up front. He was only up there if he had to be there. You were more likely to see him standing enigmatically. It's a great memory of mine: Brian in his polka-dot scarf at the back of the crowd, holding himself very proud, very proud of his boys.

Nat Weiss: I think the image of Brian was that of a very soft, sensitive person, which was not the case. He was a very strong-willed person. I remember when John Lennon refused to do an interview during a tour because the people out there were fascists or something like that. Brian went nose to nose with him. He took his tie and said, 'John, you're soft,' and stared him down. And you could see it, John backed away. Brian had full control and they respected his thinking. Brian, in a way, saw them like his children. He understood them. When one of them complained, he would say, 'I know he loves me and I love him.'

He used to go on about their relative talents and things like that. He had great insights into their personalities. He once gave me a précis of the Beatles in Cleveland. George was always concerned about publishing and things like that. Paul was concerned about the Beatles' image, the fan clubs, the opposite of a counterculture approach. John and Brian related perfectly because they saw eye to eye. Ringo was the least talented but was not uptight about it.

Brian was the total manager of the Beatles. He kept a circle around the Beatles. Nobody got to the Beatles without having to go through Brian and he controlled every facet of their professional career. No press conference was run without Brian having it under his control. No statements were made, no deals were made without Brian being in complete control. It was a one-man operation.

Paul McCartney: Brian was the first theatrical person we'd met. It was an image he wanted to project. But it was never in public. In public we were at the front, but when we'd go back for a party afterwards Brian would come to life, because then he could now show himself. He was not on show in the public arena. He wanted to remain very dignified. As the manager you have to deal with all these business people who he didn't want to look goofy in front of so there was always that very straightforward image. But you would get back to the party and his 'Ohh!' would emerge again. He was witty and intelligent and a great partier. All his friends liked him a lot, you could tell.

Nat Weiss: When Brian was on he had an amazing sense of humour, and when Brian would come into the room with the four Beatles it was Brian who was the star. He would light up the room. He was very good-looking, very well dressed and had this infectious smile. He was filled with witticisms and he could be very funny and when he started to get funny he became outrageously funny. He was such an iconoclast and nothing was sacred to him. Then again, when it went the other way it really went the other way. He was a full roller-coaster ride on any visit.

10. High Stakes

I think that the Beatles believe that MBE stands for Mr Brian Epstein.
PRINCESS MARGARET, OCTOBER 1965

Joanne Petersen: I remember going in to see him. The first impression was that he was very young, very handsome and he seemed very shy. I was pretty shy being in there too, so I don't think either of us really looked at each other much. He kind of looked down and I looked down and occasionally we connected. It wasn't a very long interview. He asked me a bit about what I'd done and he asked me about my musical influences and if there'd been any music in my life. I told him something I had no intention telling him: that Joe Loss was my uncle. I was a bit apprehensive about that 'cause I thought it was a bit uncool in the sixties to say Joe Loss was your uncle. But Queenie told me after Brian died that he was enormously impressed that I was Joe Loss's niece. It was one of the contributing factors to me getting the job. So I was rather glad I said it.

This was in '65 and NEMS was a thriving operation in Argyll Street. He decided to take a private suite of offices in Hille House in Albemarle Street off Green Park. When I went to NEMS for the interview, the first thing that struck me was that this was everything that was happening in the sixties. It was so exciting. When you walked into NEMS you felt that this was the centre of it. This was the eye of the storm. This was where it was happening. Sitting in the reception it felt like the walls were pulsating. There was this awesome energy, this force. I looked around the walls at Gerry and the Pacemakers and Billy J. Kramer and Cilla and the Beatles and I was just in awe. I just couldn't believe I was there. The building wasn't anything flash but the energy – that was there. But I also think that he felt like he'd created this monster. It was incredibly active in there. He wanted to get back to the basics of running the Beatles. So he took this private suite of offices in Hille House and that was where I started work with Wendy Hanson and Brian. We also had a receptionist, Jill.

Geoffrey Ellis: When I came in I was given a very small office to start with, but Brian wanted to move away from the main office where he felt he was very vulnerable to all these visitors, casual or otherwise. So he took a small suite half a mile away in Mayfair. I inherited his large, fairly impressive office. The offices were busy from morning till night. There were piles of mail, there were contracts to be read – for me, that is. There were problems to be resolved and there were staff matters to be dealt with. It was a normal busy office atmosphere.

Joanne Petersen: I think there was some disappointment when he moved out of Argyll Street. It was always exciting when he came in. He created a different atmosphere. Nothing changed in the day-to-day workings of that office, but I think everyone there missed his presence a little when he first took Hille House.

Geoffrey Ellis: At that time he was very fond of gambling. He used to gamble quite heavily and I accompanied him several times to Crockford's, to the Clermont, where we would have an excellent dinner for which no bill was presented because he was a high roller at the time in those clubs. We'd really gorge ourselves rather on good food and wine. Then I would accompany him to the gaming rooms and quietly slip away because he wanted to gamble and I wanted to go home to bed.

Peter Brown: We were this tight little community, which didn't have much contact with the outside world, and there was no idea at the time how we were affecting the rest of the world. Going out to the rock clubs every night was not very satisfactory in the end. Brian and I started to go off looking for other places, and it usually turned out that because Brian was interested in gambling we would go to the more exclusive gambling clubs.

The most interesting one at that time was the one that John Aspinall ran in Berkeley Square called the Clermont Club, and it was very very chic. They treated Brian very well there. It was very exclusive and at times they would play for quite high stakes. Those figures don't necessarily sound that high these days because of inflation, but we're talking about tens of thousands of pounds and we're talking about games that can escalate into big figures.

It was very very grand in those days. You used to see people like Lord Lucan and Charles Churchill at the Clermont. We used to stay there quite late. I'd leave Brian there often because I had to get up in the morning and he didn't. He had his choice, his option not to leave if he didn't want to, but we would stay there very late. I don't think we met lots of people that we subsequently became friendly with, but there was a camaraderie amongst that group of people in gambling. There were high stakes; it was big drama.

I think he was a good gambler. He did lose heavily a few times but he didn't lose lots and lots of money. He wasn't one of those gamblers where he had to turn up every day and really kind of hit the boards. I don't know what he'd be prepared to lose, but I do remember one night when he lost £17,000, which in those days was an immense amount of money. He was more embarrassed than anything else. I think that he felt embarrassed that he'd thrown that kind of money away. I was not allowed to tell anyone because he was embarrassed. I mean, it was not a thing that he was proud of.

There was an element of danger-seeker but I think there was the element of the gambling instinct. He had a gambling trait.

Geoffrey Ellis: I think perhaps Brian's love of gambling was symptomatic of the fact that he did like to take risks in his personal life as well as he did initially in his business life. His whole management of the Beatles was in a sense a gamble from the beginning. He put a fair amount of money into them before he started getting anything like a decent return. So I suppose he was a gambler.

When the Beatles received their MBEs, Brian was still living at Whaddon House despite his purchase of 24 Chapel Street in the summer of 1965. It took six months for the new home to be ready.

Lonnie Trimble: People think that the Beatles spent a lot of time at his apartment at Whaddon House, but I only saw them there on a couple of occasions. Once was for their MBE morning, where they sort of preened themselves in the mirror and had a look at a breakfast. They came to two other parties. One was Cilla Black's twenty-first birthday party, which I catered, and another was a roof-garden party which I didn't cater for. But I didn't see the Beatles around hardly ever.

Marianne Faithfull: I think I could read character and social class very well. I could see exactly where he was from. His background helped him because it helped him to talk to intellectuals and to a very wide range of people, but I think his charm and his intelligence would have been the same whatever background he came from.

Peter Brown: Brian liked modern things and everything but I don't think he ever thought of Whaddon House as a permanent place. I think that the idea of having a proper house in Belgravia gave some kind of long-term view. It was a nice solid house. It was Grosvenor Estates.

He moved to Belgravia mainly because it was near to the centre of London and it's not as congested as Mayfair. I think that Belgravia is just more pleasant and not so busy and that Brian aspired to having his own style. I was never conscious of the fact that he was copying anything or wanted to be the standard old-fashioned English gentleman.

He went to Huntsman, the classic old tailor, and to Turnbull & Asser, the best shirt-makers, but I don't think that he was ever aping the idea of being a member of the upper class. From what we thought of the upper class they weren't very attractive. We had our own thing going for us, and I don't know how consciously we were doing this but we had our own gig. It was a great gig and we got on with it and sort of created our own environment.

We were rather unique in that we didn't want to aspire to being part of the grand upper class. What we were doing was interesting and we weren't going to blend anyway. And there is, of course, the Liverpool attitude, you know: fuck them, we don't need them, we'll get on with it. I think that, if any of us had tried to do anything like that, John Lennon for one would have rapped us over the knuckles.

Lonnie Trimble: He had money everywhere, so much money he couldn't use it. He did mention once that he could lay his hands on £1 million in cash. Now in 1965 that was a lot of money to put your hands on without cashing in stocks and bonds.

Ken Partridge: When I was doing John Lennon's house sometimes I'd spend all day down there and occasionally John would say, 'How's Ep doing? I heard there was a party there last night and he didn't invite me.' Then I'd come back to London in the evening and Brian would ring me to say, 'What happened down there today? Did John talk about me?' I would say, 'Well, matter of fact, no, he didn't mention you.' 'Oh, that's very odd.' He seemed to be rather jealous of the fact that I was down there. Brian got his house halfway through before John's was finished actually, and said, 'You can't work on both houses, you know,' and I said, 'Well, I can,' which I did.

Chapel Street was pretty good structurally except we had to put a new staircase in. There was the most hideous filled-in staircase there. I had to get a magnificent one made up by Crowthers. It was a curved staircase, which was beautiful, but I must say it didn't last for long after Brian had moved in.

There was some trouble one evening with two guests he took back. I think they had a fight on the stairs like they do in a Western. Somebody fell through it and Joanne, the secretary, called me the next morning at eight o'clock and said, 'Can you come to look at the staircase? It's fallen down.' I said, 'Well, it can't possibly fall down. It's magnificently made,' but when I went in it was like a pile of sticks on the floor. I mean, it really had been wrecked. I went upstairs and banged on Brian's door and said, 'What happened?' He said, 'Go away. Get the builders in. This is a badly made staircase.' It wasn't badly made and finally I think it took me to the end of the day to find out what really happened on that staircase.

Peter Brown: Brian's way was not to settle down and not to see anyone more than a few times. It was just to move on and continue one unsatisfactory relationship after another.

It's part of his generosity that I did have relationships and he was never unkind about them. He was always happy that I had them and never resented them. When best friends have a relationship often it means that you don't see as much of the other person as you had before. But there was never any of that side in Brian. He was always very generous and very supportive of me having relationships with people. I think maybe inwardly he recognized that that wasn't what he wanted.

Joanne Petersen: Right downstairs was the staff quarters. This was where his housekeeper and her husband lived. Then as you came in you walked straight into the kitchen, straight ahead, and to your right was the dining room. You went up the stairs to the sitting room, and behind the sitting room was Brian's study. It was a panelled study, where he had his music and his stereo and where most of his work was. The stereo was set behind wood panelling, had large speakers and it was mostly played at very loud volume. One of my jobs was to get them repaired after a very hectic night of frivolity and music in Chapel Street.

He played anything from the Four Tops to the Beatles, the latest singles that he got from America – just lots of great music of the time. We were all into Motown: Smokey Robinson and the Miracles.

The second floor was his bedroom suite. You went in through double doors to his dressing room, and then into his bedroom and then through there to his bathroom. The bathroom was pretty unique. It was totally white with a picture of El Cordobes on one wall. It was very imposing.

From there you went up again. On the next floor was the guest bedroom, which was blue. The rest of the top floor was two rooms knocked into one, and that was where I worked in one corner. It was the office by day and the playroom by night. It was where he had all his memorabilia and his present from Elvis. It was just full of treasures of Brian's. It was also where everybody went up at night and at the weekends to play. I used to put my typewriter under my desk because then it wasn't the office any more. From there, there were some very rickety pull-down stairs. They went up to the roof garden where the Beatles would come and hang out and we would all spend sunny afternoons.

It was amazing how really and truly there was just the two of us running this thing and we ran it with two phones and a typewriter and a very small filing cabinet.

Bryan Barrett: I just took the bull by the horns, went in, got the interview. He was a bit surprised. He thought I was from an agency and I wasn't, but I got the job.

I started chauffeuring him and there were the Rolls, the Silver Cloud, the Bentley and I think one of the 1100s that had all been tarted up, really a nice little car. He got rid of that and then he got himself a Mini Cooper Radford conversion. He wasn't happy at all with that car and he crashed it in the finish. He decided to get rid of it; it was too dangerous. It was like a rocket, a wonderful machine. Then he bought a second-hand Phantom Five. It had belonged to John Bloom and I said, 'It's no good. Don't buy this one, sir.' But he put the deposit on it. He said, 'Yes, yes, I'm gonna have it. It's a Rolls-Royce.' I said, 'I don't care. It's not a good Rolls-Royce,' slammed the door and a quarter of the door fell off. It had been filled up with China plate and we got rid of that one in the finish.

Image, that's what he wanted, image. The Silver Cloud was the same colour as Buckingham Palace cars: burgundy. It had dark windows, and just by coincidence it had EXR, not ER but EXR 100c plates, and that worked wonders sometimes with the police.

He had a tiny little record-player in the car. I think it must have been about ten inches across and about three or four inches deep, and you just slid the record into it and you popped it out. It was the forerunner of the tape. Plus he had one of the very, very first videos, which were two gigantic cabinets. I remember carting them buggers at the top of house, nearly breaking my back getting them up there. Two men had to lift them.

Lonnie Trimble: He started to disrespect me and I felt right it was time to go. We'd been in Chapel Street two weeks before Christmas, and he hadn't mentioned a rise. He had said that he was going to give me a rise once we moved in. The Christmas box he gave me was the same that he'd given me when I had only worked for him for ten months, a week's wages and a twenty-pound Christmas bonus. We spoke on Boxing Day, which was my day off, and I told him I didn't think it was worth working for him any more.

He said, 'Are you coming in tomorrow?' I said, 'Maybe.' But then he asked me again so I said I would. When I got there, it was like walking through hell. The Grassinis, who were the housekeeper and cook, were furious with me because they had worked all over the Christmas period.

Queenie walked into the kitchen before it was time for his breakfast. We greeted each other and I got on the intercom and rang Brian up to say breakfast was ready. I took it up to his suite and put it on the carpet because he didn't open his door. Then I went back to the kitchen and waited till he'd finished breakfast.

After breakfast, he summoned me up to the study and said, 'Lonnie, I will never have a Christmas like this again. As far as your rise is concerned, it will be in your pay packet next week.' With that I was dismissed from the room. A week or two after that, we got to the stage where he would leave a note for me rather than speak to me. We'd pass each other on the stairs and he would just walk past me and I'd find a note telling me what to do. And I thought, 'Right, it's time for me to go. I'm gonna try and be clever.'

I left him a note to ask if I could have my holiday in February. The last time he spoke to me was coming down the stairs. He said, 'No, you can't take your holiday in February. You take it like the office staff, between May and September.' He made me work on that Saturday, which I wasn't supposed to be working. The Grassinis were absolutely pleased as they could be because I was in the shit.

So I worked and knew I was leaving there. His new chauffeur, Bryan Barrett, told me not to quit. I said, 'Look, I have a life of my own, not Brian Epstein and the Beatles.' He said, 'But you're making good money.' I said, 'So?' Bryan Barrett drove me home after I'd written my resignation. I'd typed out a little note saying to please accept my resignation because I've had enough.

When I got home the telephone rang three times. I refused to answer because I knew it was Brian Epstein, upset. If I had answered the phone, he would have offered me more money to come back, and me being human I might have accepted it. So I refused to speak to him.

Bryan Barrett: He never called me anything other than Mr Barrett. I called him Mr Epstein or sir. All the lower echelons said, 'Brian, Brian, Brian.' He didn't like it but he went along with it because of 'free' pop people and all that. But he used to tell me things about these people calling him Brian.

The first time we had a planned trip, first time ever, we got to Liverpool, his parents' house, and started unloading the baggage. It was a long trip in those days. The old gardener appeared that used to drive Harry. Now he'd drive Harry in an old brown engineer's overall and wellington boots, because Harry wouldn't buy him a uniform.

He was a typical Liverpudlian. He said to me, 'Did you come up from London, pal?' I said, 'Yeah.' He said, 'You're on for a feast.' 'Oh great,' I said, 'I'm starving.' 'Yeah,' he said. 'You're gonna get a boiled egg and two slices.'

Well, I thought it was funny. Then Brian came out and said, 'Go and have something to eat. You can go back to the house for it.' So I said, 'OK, sir. Will you need me?' He said, 'I'll call you.' So that was it. I went in and there was the one boiled egg, cup of tea, two slices of bread and that was it.

Geoffrey Ellis: He enjoyed the fame and the recognition that he was accorded in public and private. He liked being recognized in the streets and in restaurants as the famous Mr Epstein, the manager of the Beatles. But he wanted to be a star himself. He knew he couldn't act, but he wanted to have some connection whereby he would become an individual star of the theatre and of show business.

To that end he directed the play *Smashing Day* by Alan Plater at the Arts Theatre Club in the West End of London and he made his occasional appearances on television. He certainly wanted to present himself as a personality in show business as well as being a businessman.

Marianne Faithfull: He would find a way of saying something to everybody that made them feel included, and maybe the best thing was that he wasn't on acid. That was also very important. It was very smart of him not to do that. I think he did take a bit of acid but not much and not in public.

He took it all very seriously, his social responsibilities. Actually it was a very social thing, what he was doing. It was a way of helping the whole thing to mature, really. There's a limit to what you can plan when you're exhausted and drunk and stoned up in the Ad Lib. That's not the most creative moment for talking about what we're going to do next. But in the afternoon, you could go round to lunch with Brian Epstein and you could actually think quite straight and things could get done.

I would have asked him to be part of what I knew I was going to do. I wanted to play the London stage, play it in the full sense of the word. I wasn't prepared to be a Vivien Leigh type, although I tried, but I wasn't really going to be happy like that.

I flirted with Brian but I like to flirt with people. He was a very good flirt. I'm not sure if he was really comfortable, but he would have learned. Things don't all have to end up in bed, especially in creative relationships. In fact, if they end up in bed it can even be a disadvantage. It's like sort of not having sex before a fight or something. So the sort of slightly sexual tone in a relationship didn't mean that you then actually had sex. That's one of the big mistakes people make about the sixties, that everybody was just endlessly jumping into bed. They weren't. Firstly, a lot of the time we were too stoned. Also some relationships were too good and you didn't want to destroy anything with too much indiscriminate bed-hopping.

Joanne Petersen: Most of the time he was fine. I often have thought back and wondered why he had me in his house. I think what it was was that he felt comfortable having me there. He felt he could trust having me there. There was an in-built loyalty and I think he sensed that. He could also feel my desire to protect him. I think those really close to him, like Bryan Barrett and myself, were very, very protective of Brian and wanted nothing bad to happen to him. He had to be able to trust us. There were a lot of goings-on in his house and he had to be sure that nothing left his house in terms of leaks. Things were very confidential.

You never really knew what mood Brian was going to be in. There were two fairly distinct moods – he could be warm and charming and effusive and really sweet, or he could be cold and aloof and imperial and distant. You picked up on that pretty quickly and I would relate to that and think, 'OK, this is the mood for today.' It could change halfway through the day. It was a bit of a seesaw ride, but we got to know it and we got to read the signs and we acted accordingly.

I was fairly intuitive about things like that. I could walk into a room and sense the atmosphere in the room and what the vibe was, and that stood me in good stead for how it was to be around Brian. You just learned pretty quickly.

One time he wanted a phone number in the South of France. He was down in the lounge room when he buzzed me up and asked me to get the phone number. I found the letterhead with the phone number on it and I went down and I gave him the phone number. He wrote it down and tried several times to get through. Then he buzzed me up and said I had not given him the right phone number.

I looked again at the piece of paper and I realized what I'd done was give him how many feet up the mountainside the place was. I went down and told him and he just went wild. He was holding a teapot and he threw it at me. I was standing there covered in tea leaves. I think I burst into tears and fled out the room. He was mortified and I was mortified, but it was just a snap moment.

There were times when it was very stressful, when it would upset me. I was sensitive to these things, but then he would leave me really sweet notes. They'd say things like, 'Be a bit patient of me when I'm at my worst. I don't want to hurt you. I don't want to hurt anyone. I'm really sorry.' He would be really, really upset next day or after an incident like that. It didn't happen all the time. They happened sometimes but other times he was so warm and nice and I liked being around him a lot. That kind of made up for it.

Bryan Barrett: One night there was a session going on around at Paul's house with George. I took Brian up there in the old Phantom Five. Then suddenly, after a while, they asked me to go and collect a package from Archer Street. I thought, 'Archer Street musicians, music, yeah,' and off I went. They gave me an address that was an old Peabody Trust type building, so I asked a policeman if he could help me out since the Phantom Five was such a bloody great thing. I said, 'I'll only be a couple of minutes. I've just got to go collect a package down there. It's all set up.' So up I went to collect this package. I came down with it, threw it in the car, off I went. When I got to Piccadilly, I was sniffing and I could smell it was grass. I thought, 'Christ, and I asked a policeman to look after the car.'

I took it back to the house and then I had a big row with Brian coming back in the car. I told him, 'Don't ever do that to me again. I've got three children and I don't want to go to prison. I don't want to get pulled for that.'

He said, 'Oh no, you'd have been all right,' and I said, 'No. I'd have gone down and you'd have probably denied it.' So he said, 'Oh, you'd have had a lawyer.' I said, 'I don't care, the best lawyers. I've got three children. Don't ever do that to me again, ever,' and he said, 'Oh, yes, all right.'

Geoffrey Ellis: It was well known that Brian was taking drugs, certainly during the last two years of his life. He secured drugs from a number of sources, both in America and this country. I was, of course, aware that he was taking drugs. Personally I have no knowledge of drugs and he did not educate me. I never saw him taking drugs. He never referred to his drug-taking to me personally. Thinking back on it, I'm very glad that he didn't, because it does show that our relationship at least was one which did not involve this type of behaviour.

Nat Weiss: Prior to the '66 tour he had this boy he'd known long before I knew him who was sort of an American hustler. He began to create problems just before the tour about creating scenes on the tour, blackmail and things. It was really a bit scary. I asked Brian if I could take care of it, which I did. I told Brian to give him a certain amount of money, not as a pay-off, but because he'd been with him. I said, 'Get him the car and get rid of him.' I said to the boy, 'You can have your car but never come back,' and he didn't come back. After that, I began to deal with Brian's personal problems.

The problem was that Brian was not a predatory type of person. When it came to meeting people that he might have a liaison with, they had to be the moving party. Brian would never attempt to seduce any man under any circumstances. He was almost shy. He was like the girl that drops the handkerchief: 'I'm available but you come after me,' which they did.

Still, Brian was always attracted to the sort of very masculine construction worker type of person. He was not attracted to people who were effeminate or very young people. He liked the macho look, like the image the guys projected at the Cavern: leather jackets, cigarettes dangling out of the mouth, rough talk. That attracted Brian. It was the exact opposite of what he was, in many respects. As a result, even when he met people who were very masculine, he was never able to sustain a long-term relationship.

I think it was like the syndrome of the rich girl who says that she's always suspicious that all anyone wants is her money. Brian was always concerned that someone only liked him for being Brian Epstein, who, incidentally, was a very handsome, sharp, good-looking person. I saw it happen many times. Brian would think the relationship was developing and then the person would say, 'Now, tell me what they're like, Brian, and when can I meet them?' That would terminate the relationship right then and there.

That was sad, because he would be very optimistic, then he'd become depressed and disillusioned by the fact that he'd believe that it was not him they wanted but who he was. It's unfortunate because we're all a combination of everything we are. But he had that sense of paranoia, and in this country he never had a successful long-term relationship.

Bryan Barrett: He was relaxed with his mother completely but he never seemed fully relaxed with his father. The disapproval of old was still there, even though he'd made it and there was a bit of reflected glory in that 'My son is Brian Epstein,' but basically I don't think it was the happiest of relationships.

There always seemed to be a lot of strain between him and his brother. He'd been caught out once by Clive. I had answered the door and said to Clive, 'You can't go upstairs, sir. Do you mind waiting in the reception, in the dining room?' He said, 'Why can't I go up?' and I said, 'Well, Mr Epstein is bathing or something or talking to somebody and he'd rather you didn't go up.' I don't know what I said, something I made up on the spot. Brian came down about half an hour later. He wouldn't let his brother stay in his house, though he had a guest room where he'd let certain people stay. His father and Clive never stayed there. They got a flat in Hill Street, and the same with Queenie.

Joanne Petersen: I really, really liked Queenie. We got along well and I thought she was a really interesting, very elegant, very sweet lady. Lots of people have said different things about Queenie, but the Queenie I knew was the one who came to stay in the house.

Brian always regulated his life when Queenie was around. He would get up and have breakfast with her. He loved Queenie a lot and she adored Brian. He was a lot like Queenie. She was quite vague and quite fey at times and Brian was too. They were quite similar and I can see a lot of Brian's characteristics came from Queenie. Queenie would go out shopping during the day and Brian would go to work. Then she would come home and we'd have afternoon tea together and chat about things.

She'd talk about Brian and she'd always ask about my family and about how my mother was. My father had died the previous year and that concerned her. She was a very caring person, and we came from similar backgrounds, Brian and I. I came from a fairly traditional middle-class Jewish family in North London and he came from a similar family in Liverpool. Queenie related to me through that, I guess.

If Brian knew his parents were coming to town he would make sure that he led a more regulated life. But he was always calm and relaxed around them.

I think he was in conflict all the time. There was a lot of internal turmoil. He had to lead a double life, at least hiding a side of himself from Clive and Queenie. He especially had to hide it from Harry while he was alive. He had to be secretive and cover things up. This all weighed heavily on him.

Queenie never discussed Brian's homosexuality. I think she knew but she just didn't want to see. She was a mum that went into denial. I don't think she wanted to deal with it, and she used to talk about ladies that she'd met that would be nice for Brian. She talked about Brian one day getting married. There was an artist she liked and thought would be rather nice for Brian, and she kind of used to plot that perhaps he should take her to the theatre.

I think Brian was amused by his mother's endeavours. This was not a constant thing. It just would come up every so often, and Brian always had this very sort of bemused look around his mother, a sort of a warmth around her. He'd just look benignly at her and played along with it to a certain degree. I think they both knew it was play-acting.

Marianne Faithfull: I connect Brian with this very golden, happy, civilized, exciting time in London, when I was very, very sure that everything was going to be wonderful. He was very important in that. I think in many ways he may not have been the greatest businessman in the world. He may well have made a lot of mistakes. I know he did. But I couldn't care less about things like licensing T-shirts. It just isn't interesting. I don't think it's so bad to not be good at that sort of thing. But he obviously wasn't very good at that and so you could pick endless holes in Brian Epstein if you wanted to. But I could see that he had this golden future, which wasn't necessarily going to be just managing the Beatles.

He was in a tradition, a sort of English impresario tradition. I can't remember all the names but the name Binkie Beaumont comes to mind here, and all those kind of guys. That's where Brian fits into the Noel Coward genre. He really was in that sort of great actor-manager tradition and his greatest moment, for me, was his supper theatre. It didn't last very long. Everybody's forgotten about it.

But he wasn't rigid about things, you know. He could see that things were going to change, especially with his relationship with the Beatles. He would have been able to handle it, I know. He's been castigated so much for not knowing about T-shirt sales, but his job in our group at that time was really more a sort of spiritual psychic force.

He was really great with them. He was, and this is before this word got its negative connotations, a grown-up and we needed a few people like that. He was quite a lot in the grown-up world but also able to play with us more.

The Beatles treated Brian with awe and respect. I'm sure they teased him and I know he teased them but there really was, I think, a lot of mutual affection.

He didn't court personal publicity at all, so he wouldn't have gone and talked to Maureen Cleave openly about his plans for the Saville. He wouldn't have even talked to the *Observer* like Peter Hall was doing at the time. He was going on a hunch, an idea, and he was very afraid always of being shot down in flames and being unmasked. If you think about the period of England at this time and being gay and being powerful and being rich and having a vision, it was all quite a combustible and dangerous mix.

BILL GRUNDY: *Were you ever good at acting?*
BRIAN EPSTEIN: Not at the time. I like to think I may have been.

GRUNDY: *Has it left you with a distaste for or a real taste for theatre?*
EPSTEIN: A real taste for theatre.

GRUNDY: *Real theatre?*
EPSTEIN: Yes, very much so. I would like so much to produce and, dare I say it, act in a straight play.

GRUNDY: *What sort of plays?*

EPSTEIN: Possibly something by Chekhov or a modern straight drama.

GRUNDY: *What sort of dramatist?*

EPSTEIN: I don't know. Osborne. Something that one knows about.

BBC HOME SERVICE, 7 MARCH 1964

11. The Fire This Time

'Nat, how much would it cost to cancel this tour?'
BRIAN EPSTEIN TO NAT WEISS, AUGUST 1966

In the summer of 1966, Brian Epstein and the Beatles undertook their biggest ever tour.

Peter Brown: Everything became very difficult. There was Germany, which we'd done on the train. That wasn't easy but it wasn't terrible. It was all that business of hiding away in rooms with sealed doors with wet towels so nobody could smell the marijuana being smoked.

Paul McCartney: We once got on a train in Germany which was the Queen's train, which we were all amused by. It was very nice, the royal train. It was an overnight trip and of course Brian loved it. It was just about right for him. As we set off from the station we started a card game and a few drinks before going to bed.

Brian would pull out his Dunhill lighter, a gold one, very posh at the time. He'd put that on the table because it was poker or something and said, 'Dunhill lighter raise you,' and he played with his things – pill case, lighters. It wouldn't be money. It would be some gesture. He'd say, 'I can't raise you a Dunhill. You know I'm folding.'

Peter Brown: Then we went to Japan where there was an attempt on the Beatles' lives by a right-wing group who promised to assassinate them.

The Japanese security measures were so stringent that the Beatles could never leave their hotel rooms except to go to the concert. The whole of the route from the hotel was sealed by the army so that we could get from one place to the other. It was horrendous.

This was immediately followed by the Philippines where the awful Mrs Marcos had invited us to lunch. It was Brian's policy not to go to events after they had the unfortunate experience at the British Embassy in Washington where some deb had tried to cut Ringo's hair and treated him like some zombie. So Brian had made this policy that we don't go to official functions or anything.

We politely declined to go to the Presidential Palace with the Beatles for lunch. She turned the situation around as if it was a slap in the face to the Philippine people. All our security was removed.

There was a very serious riot at the airport where we were pushed around very nastily and I think our lives were in danger. Mal Evans was knocked down. It was very frightening, and after all of this nasty business we got on a plane which was stopped from taking off. By the time we got away from this thirty-six hours of horror in the Philippines we flew to India. It was the first time any of us had been to India. Brian was so ill with nerves and felt that it was all his fault because it was his responsibility to look after everyone and these horrible things had happened.

When we got to Delhi, Brian never went anywhere. The rest of us went to all these various places but Brian stayed in his room. Then on the plane from Delhi to London he came out in hives all over his skin. His condition was so bad that the pilot radioed ahead to have an ambulance meet us at the airport. From Heathrow, Brian was taken straight to hospital.

Nat Weiss: When John Lennon gave his interview to Maureen Cleave saying that the Beatles were more popular than Christ, an American magazine picked it up. I was in the office. This was about two weeks before the Beatles tour and I got a call from Birmingham, Alabama, saying they were burning Beatles records. Then came a call from Memphis that they were burning Beatles records also. I couldn't imagine why until someone told me those Bible states were up in arms and DJs were suggesting people destroy their Beatles records because of John Lennon's statement.

At the time, Brian was in Portmeirion, Wales, and he was ill. As the evening went on and I was getting all these calls, I called Portmeirion in the middle of the night and said, 'Something has to be done about this.' And he said, 'Is it serious?' And I said, 'I think it's so serious that you have to come over here.'

The next day he flew over and I met him at the airport. The first thing he said to me was, 'How much would it take to cancel the tour?' And I said, 'I don't know. Maybe a million dollars.' He was so concerned about anything happening to any of the Beatles. For two days John and Brian were on the phone working out a statement to the effect that John certainly intended to hurt no one. When it was worked out, Brian set up a press conference, read the statement, and that ended the situation. Of course, when we got to Memphis, Brian was very sure that no one got near the Beatles, in their dressing room or anywhere. This man was very protective of them.

Paul McCartney: We'd had our big success in America. Now we were sort of going again and again and the novelty had begun to wear off a bit. And we were starting to get a bit of flak because they only put you up to knock you down. Then John made this inadvertent remark about Jesus, saying that the Beatles were bigger than Jesus. What he meant was that it was a pity that we get millions of kids to our shows and the churches don't. And in the spirit of that he said, 'I think at the moment we're bigger than Jesus.' It was just a flippant remark, but of course when it was pulled out and used as a headline, particularly in the southern states in America, it was a biggy and John got in a lot of trouble over that.

Brian advised him to own up and try to explain it, but it was the most nervous I'd ever seen John because normally he didn't really care.

Nat Weiss: We were not allowed to bring up anything that might be considered to create a nervous effect on any of the Beatles. In almost every city you have many cases of people being brought backstage on stretchers and in wheelchairs, some saying this is the last day and things like that. Certainly Brian was sympathetic. He would look at this and it would break anyone's heart but he also had this idea that if he brought the Beatles into this scene before they went onstage, it would have created a very depressing attitude. He would just arrange for autographed photographs to be given to the sick people but he had to stand firm on that. He would protect the Beatles from all sights that would affect their ability to perform.

It was only in the last tour in one place, Atlanta, that the Beatles used a sound system. That was a beginning but the Beatles didn't even know about it. In those days the main concern for Brian was not the sound checks, the money and things like that, but the safety of the Beatles. Security was the main concern at any given date – getting into the stadium and getting out of the stadium. The hazards were immense, enormous. Those were his main concerns.

Still, during that tour I observed that after each performance Brian would wait for the Beatles to come offstage. Then he would sit and critique the whole performance as to whether they bowed correctly, whether the pacing was correct and things like that.

During that tour, people started bringing drugs around because people are always trying to be hip by bringing around the latest drug. Access to any artist of the time consisted of, 'Here's some acid. Here's some of this. Here's some of that,' and all of a sudden you were members of the same fraternity.

Brian began to get involved with Nembutals and Seconals and things like that. Brian had always taken certain amphetamines which kept him up, and suddenly the seesaw thing began. Down with the Nembutals, up with the amphetamines, until he had to go to the hospital at one point and be given some induced sleep so he could balance himself out. Depression began to set in and he found his haven in some of these downers.

Peter Brown: During the tour, Paul had this phobia that they were going to get shot while they were onstage.

Nat Weiss: We were in California in August of 1966. The Beatles were playing their last show at Candlelight Park in San Francisco, and we were at the house where the Beatles were staying in Los Angeles. On that day, Diz showed up miraculously and Brian was thrilled to see him. And I warned Brian that nothing changes, but Brian assured me that Diz had changed. He was there in LA because he loved Brian. I just threw cold water on that. I said, 'You're dealing with one of the most professional hustlers that I've ever come across and there's no emotion involved, only money.'

That afternoon, Brian had said, 'This will be the last time.' I'll never forget that. He said, 'This will be the last time the Beatles will ever perform together. They will never tour again.' Which was strange because I just thought it was something not to be taken lightly.

That evening when I went to get my briefcase it was gone. So was Brian's briefcase and so was Diz. Apparently, when we were out to dinner, he got into the rooms and took both briefcases, which were later recovered, and appropriate action was taken against him.

But that depressed Brian and it accounts for his first major depression. But he didn't want us to pursue Diz. He felt it would be embarrassing. The briefcase contained things he didn't want people to know about. There were Beatle contracts in there; there were pills in there, and things like that, that were potentially damaging at the time, and Brian was very much afraid of what could happen. So he asked me not to pursue the matter. I said, 'Look, he took *my* briefcase,' and I was outraged. While I had no right to go against Brian for his briefcase, I had every right to go against Diz for my briefcase. Which I did, and Diz was arrested and things taken were returned. But that was the beginning Brian's loss of self-confidence.

Geoffrey Ellis: Brian was subject to mood cycles. He would be high from time to time. People would take problems to him and he'd say, 'But no, this is easily resolved. We'll resolve this. Don't worry, everything will be fine.' Other times he would retreat to his home and not come out, just refuse to take calls and refuse to attend meetings. To what extent this was endemic in his character and to what extent it was exacerbated by his dependence on pills in his later years, I can't tell.

The main task he had to face in 1966 was to renegotiate the Beatles' contract with EMI. Despite his psychological condition, this was a matter he took most seriously indeed, as he did all matters concerning the Beatles.

The first contract Brian signed with EMI in 1962 gave EMI three one-year options on the Beatles. Initially, the Beatles received a standard low royalty, commonly given to newly signed acts.

At the end of the first year, Epstein was able to renegotiate for a higher rate because EMI wanted to extend their option further. Epstein said he could only give EMI one more year because his own contract with the Beatles would expire in the autumn of 1967. He made no further attempts to renegotiate the contract after that, even though the Beatles became increasingly successful.

So here was Brian's opportunity to make up for three years of the Beatles not getting their proper percentage of the enormous profits they had generated.

Nat Weiss: When the EMI contract was ending and Brian spoke to other record companies, they never discussed money. Brian went to the head of Columbia Records, who told him the Beatles had peaked. So he just walked out of the meeting.

We went to RCA, who told us they were the type of company that could be the home for the Beatles, so they gave him an album called *Chet Atkins Picks the Beatles*. Brian looked and just said, 'These are cabbage heads,' and walked out. He loved Ahmet Ertegun and Jerry Wexler at Atlantic Records. He knew they were record people but he was more concerned about the record company being a home for the Beatles. He felt he could deal with the money thereafter.

Alan Livingston: After the peak of the Beatlemania, when the Beatles' contract with EMI expired, Brian Epstein very brightly said to EMI, 'I'll negotiate with you for England but I will negotiate directly with Capitol for the United States.' That's what I had to face. I gave them a $2 million bonus, and a royalty of 9 per cent, which was unheard-of at that time; 5 per cent was the maximum. So the Beatles got their contract for nine years and I gave them a $2 million bonus. That was quite a commitment but I didn't worry about it a bit. I did get a call from Sir Joseph Lockwood, chairman of EMI, who said, 'Alan, I think you're crazy. They've peaked.' I said, 'I'll get it back on the first album, Joe,' and of course history took care of it.

Nat Weiss: Brian definitely wanted to negotiate a longer contract. At that point I think he was really interested in seeing if another record company would make a fabulous offer to get the Beatles, and it never got to that. And I think Brian was sort of content to be with EMI. The extended contract was too long and was not that great an increase to make anyone feel happy. Later on, that contract changed again. But Brian wasn't the kind to play games about holding back product.

I just don't think it was in him to play that card. I just don't think he had that degree of sophistication. Brian was always concerned about the very fair contract but never overreaching, never hitting it too hard. I think in that case he didn't hit hard enough. I don't think he realized his leverage.

Brian was vulnerable to criticism for not having done that. He was more concerned about artistic freedoms and things like that. Today we would negotiate a record contract and you don't talk about anything but money and commitment. There's nothing to do with quality of life for the artist. It's all money, and unless you've really pushed the record company to the wall you're not considered a successful manager or lawyer. But that was not his mentality at the time.

That's the stuff that Allen Klein later provoked, saying he would have withheld product and things like that. The answer to that is if you do that you harm an artist's career. The Beatles couldn't hold back product. Today, that's how it's done. If you have a hit record, a company will come to you and renegotiate, but it was different then.

Alan Livingston: Once, a certain album called *Yesterday and Today* was about to come out in the US only. Brian sent us an album cover, which was a picture of the four boys in white coats with pieces of meat and bones and baby dolls dismembered. I had no idea of what it was supposed to be. I called Brian and he said, 'Well, that's what the boys want. It's their comment on war.' I said, 'It may be, but I don't know that I can put this out.' A few days later Brian came back to me saying that the Beatles absolutely insisted on this cover.

I wanted to maintain a good relationship, so I told Brian I'd test the cover and see what happened. I printed a few hundred, maybe 500, covers and albums and sent them out as advance copies to the sales force to take to the retailers and get orders. The word came back very fast that the dealers would not touch it. They would not put the album in their stores. That wouldn't happen today, but at that time that was the reaction. I had to call Brian and tell him I couldn't put the album out. It was out of my hands. They finally sent us another album cover that we could put out.

Brian was there to represent their interests and wanted the Beatles to have the cover they wanted. But he also was concerned about money, so when it got to the point where Capitol just absolutely refused to put out the album with that cover, he eventually gave in.

Paul McCartney: When we actually did finish touring, I suppose Brian felt that his role was decreasing and I think that was a sadness to him. I think that was what was happening. We'd had enough of the trouble we were running into. I finally agreed with the other guys because it took me a little while to come round. I thought we'd tour for ever but I started to realize it was going to be a problem.

There was no question in our minds that we would stay with Brian. We didn't want another manager. We didn't think it was necessary. If anything, I think the problem was we were starting to feel we didn't really need much management. We were now in the studio making *Sgt Pepper* and Brian kept out. To give him his credit, he kept out of our face in the studio. In fact, we actually wanted him to visit a little more, because we liked him and it was always nice when he showed up. But he was very 'No, no, I won't interrupt. I'm just going to take two seconds, da da da da. Gotta go.' So he kept out of the way.

Alistair Taylor: I think he was getting the feeling that the boys didn't need him quite so much now. It was not a matter of falling out with them, and I don't believe they would ever have parted company, but I think he got a bit depressed. He suddenly felt he wasn't needed and he adored them so much and they were the light of his life. What he should have done, and I think at one time I actually tried to talk to him about it, was to look after some of our other acts. We had all the other great artists on our books and some of them were beginning to feel a bit neglected. He was almost tunnel vision about the Beatles. People like myself were left to look after the others. I don't mean he neglected them or ignored them, far from it, but they weren't quite getting the attention. And when the boys suddenly didn't need it quite so much, I think that's when the depression started to come and get heavier. That was the real dreadful phase, the beginning of the end, I think.

But he loved what he was doing and he had a good company of people round him. Not just himself but a good press office, a good accounts departments, good lawyers, good accountants. The whole team of us were doing our damnedest and very often trying to protect him from any undue pressure.

Gerry Marsden: Brian was losing it. Brian didn't like to delegate. That was Brian's problem. He wanted to be there doing it and he didn't want to feel as though he was letting you down. I think the whole thing was getting a little too much for Brian in those days, but he was still working very hard.

George Martin: I think Brian was enthusiastic about what the Beatles were doing. He always thought they were the bee's knees. They'd never disappointed him and they've never disappointed me. What had happened, of course, was that they insisted that they were fed up with touring by the end of '66, and this embarrassed Brian. He'd actually booked them into tours, which they refused to do. They were fed up being in a goldfish bowl and said they were not going to appear in public again, and this was a terrible blow to him, really.

He realized they wanted to concentrate more on working in the studio with me. The result of that was *Sgt Pepper*. We started work on *Sgt Pepper* in November, December 1966, and went through to about March or April, about five months. During that time obviously Brian concentrated on other things, but the boys were locked away. They weren't a problem, but it did mean that his overt sense of empire was folding up because he wasn't going to have the Beatles performing any more. I think it was a bit of a shock to him and he felt he might have been losing touch because he didn't have the control in the studio.

Nat Weiss: About the time of the end of the Beatles tour in August and their return to England, Brian began to see that the next major project of his would be the next Beatle movie. He was busy thinking of directors and concepts. That's was what interested him most at the time and he spoke to Antonioni about it. Paul McCartney agreed that was a very good choice. Brian's next big thing was to do another Beatle movie as soon as *Sgt Pepper* was finished. Brian saw his future in films. He also saw that, with no touring and just records and a movie, there could be a future for himself touring the United States lecturing or hosting a programme.

He was the Pied Piper of any new drug or any new attitude at the time. Unfortunately, he was not the best master of his own use of these things, and I think what was happening, between the down and the ups, was the pressure began to get worse.

By this time (August 1966), Epstein had begun to work almost exclusively from his home in Chapel Street, with only the help of Joanne Petersen as his assistant. He hardly ever went to Argyll Street, which continued to be NEMS headquarters, or to Hille House, which he left to Peter Brown.

Bryan Barrett: If Brian was in silly situations I had to shield him. There were one or two people who used to eff and blind at him. I just had to get between them and him. I threw some guys out the house once. Two of them were trying to smash the bedroom door down. Brian got on the phone to me and I was there in ten minutes. I only lived ten minutes down the road and I crept in behind them and got them out.

I don't know what he did at night because he didn't like his personal staff, such as myself and butlers, to get too fully involved in what he was doing in clubs and things like that. I never went into any of the clubs with him. I just dropped him off and left the keys of the car with the doorman, which I always resented because I thought it was a dangerous to leave the key with anyone.

One night we had a row. He was very very depressed, terribly depressed and he was all on his own. I took him out to a restaurant. He was looking around the restaurants and every place we went, he would say, 'No. So and so will probably be in there. I don't want to meet them.' So I finally took him to the Beefeater in Knightsbridge. He told me to leave the car there. Well, the state he was in, I said, 'No. I'm not leaving the car keys.' He said, 'Leave the car keys.' I said, 'I'm not leaving them, sir.' So we had a bit of an argument. He went in and I said to the manager, 'Call me. This is my number. I'll be here in five minutes.' Then I went back to the house which was only round the corner.

He came out. I took him home to the foot of the stairs and he went in. Then he said, 'Leave the car keys. I'm going out again.' I said, 'You're not driving the car.' It was the Cooper, bloody dangerous car. He said, 'Well, I'll get the Bentley out.' So I said, 'I doubt if you'll get it out the garage, sir. Why do you want to drive? Go to bed. Go to sleep.'

It was the first time I had a real argument with him. When he said to leave the keys again, I threw the keys on the side table. Then I went out and I waited five minutes, crept in again and picked up the keys. He put his head round the stairs and said, 'All right, I'm not going out. Take 'em anyway.'

Joanne Petersen: A typical day for me was to get to work at ten, go up to the office, make some calls, check in with the office on Argyll Street and sort out any correspondence left over from the day before or any notes Brian had left.

. As I passed his bedroom on the way up, there were often notes left for me under the door. They could be anything: 'Wake me up at three o'clock with breakfast.' That meant three o'clock in the afternoon. Or it might be some money in an envelope saying something like, 'Please bank my happiness.' That would be last night's happiness because he may have gone to the Clermont or the White Elephant and won some money gambling.

There were various instructions about what to do if he wasn't around. Then often he would bound up the stairs at three o'clock and say, 'Right, let's get into the day.' The day would often start at three but it could start at ten or one. It really could start at any time. It started at whatever time Brian showed up.

12. Uppers and Downers

BILL GRUNDY: *Do they need you as a manager or have they got to the stage now when anybody can manage them, who knew the technical side of the thing?*
BRIAN EPSTEIN: I don't think that anybody could manage them because I don't think that the Beatles would be managed by anybody else.

GRUNDY: *Is this a personal relationship?*
EPSTEIN: I don't know that I should be saying this actually, but I think that it's true.

GRUNDY: *Do you get much satisfaction from a sense of power from running this organization?*
EPSTEIN: No and I don't feel it particularly. I suppose it could be said that controlling human beings is a powerful thing, but I don't think of it as such. I don't even try not to. I just don't.

GRUNDY: *Are you, in your own opinion, a good businessman?*
EPSTEIN: Fair as a businessman, fair. I've got a businessman background and probably a good business brain. But I'm no sort of genius.

GRUNDY: *What are your defects then? Why aren't you better than you apparently think you are?*
EPSTEIN: I'm probably sort of too conscious of ideas rather than finance behind the ideas.

BBC HOME SERVICE, 7 MARCH 1964

Geoffrey Ellis: Brian was very ambitious for his business and he wanted to diversify a great deal, hence his acquisition of the Saville Theatre and his interest in assisting in production of films and, of course, his encouragement of the Beatles' film career. I think perhaps in 1966 he was – and this is with benefit of hindsight – diversifying too fast and what with his depressions and the problems caused by matters such as Seltaeb – Seltaeb being perhaps the most important and most difficult problem that arose at that time – he felt that he needed help and that he wanted to lessen his responsibilities. It was around that time his agreement with Robert Stigwood went into effect.

This was not entirely a popular move among NEMS staff. In fact, we who worked at NEMS were quite distressed about it, partly because it meant that we would lose Brian as the constant presence and mentor and he was very well liked, I have to say, by all the people who worked for him, and partly because we really didn't want someone else coming in from outside and bringing in his people to us. The deal that he did with Robert Stigwood was a little complex to start, but it did mean that Robert Stigwood came into our offices with his own staff and brought in his own acts. Some of them were very successful indeed: the Bee Gees, Cream and so forth.

Robert Stigwood: I knew Brian socially, and he wanted to retire from the music business and actually manage bullfighters in Spain. And that was for real because he used to go to Spain a lot. So he approached me to see if I would become joint manager and director of NEMS, and look after everything there except the Beatles.

Peter Brown: Brian had met Robert Stigwood at a party through Chris Stamp, who was managing the Who. Brian immediately got on very well with Stigwood. He saw what Robert was all about, which was that he was savvy to the music business and he was very good with artists. One of the things Brian wanted to do was get out of the day-to-day activity, which he knew he wasn't any good at any longer. He didn't have the fire, and the depression thing was getting deeper and deeper. So the thing was to eliminate the day-to-day business of having to look after all of the other groups, managing them, agenting for them and so forth. It was a big business by then.

So the idea was to bring Stigwood in, to make him co-managing director and have him run the operation excluding the Beatles and Cilla, who Brian would still control and maintain the management of.

Robert Stigwood: It was quite simple. We'd be joint managing directors together and he would give me an option, I think it was for six months. If I paid him half a million pounds then the controlling shares would be transferred to me and my company. In other words, I would control the company – including the Beatles. My percentage would be 51 per cent of the company because Brian's brother and a few other people were involved. In the interim I agreed to go and work with him on the company. There were a lot of Beatles matters involved but not their day-to-day dealings.

I was doing business with Polygram over Cream. I think I was also doing a Who record at the time when they were in some record dispute. So Polygram offered me a loan of half a million but they wanted to acquire a minority shareholding in NEMS. But that was fine. It took a lot of faith in those days for someone to give you a cheque for that much money.

Brian received a letter saying that I was taking up the option and that the funds would be there at the end of the option period. When he got the letter we had a wonderful dinner and laughed and joked about the future and talked. He was thrilled. He wasn't sad.

Apple was being set up at the time. Brian stood aside and said, 'It's their money. They can do whatever they want to do, but, Robert, would you give them any advice they need?' I set up their own publishing company for them because in those days they were tied to Dick James.

I don't think the Beatles really knew the whole arrangement. I think Brian had said to them that I was taking over everything except their personal arrangements between Brian and the Beatles. They found out that I was going to take over NEMS the day after he died.

George Martin: Brian thought the arrangement with Robert Stigwood was strengthening his arm and it seemed it was going to be a strengthening alliance if it could be controlled. I wasn't terribly happy about it and the Beatles weren't at all happy about it because they saw it as a weakening of their strength within the group. But Brian saw it as a build-up, really.

That would have been a sell-out as far as the Beatles were concerned, in the same way that the Dick James thing was. They didn't want to be controlled by anybody except Brian; they didn't want to work with anybody except Brian in the general field and myself in the recording studio. It was an uncomfortable business.

Joanne Petersen: It didn't have any effect on my life because I worked for Brian, and as far as I was concerned Brian was still running the whole show. It was a very curious time, a lot of people were very surprised when Robert was brought in. They were shocked and amazed. Why would Brian have brought someone else in to run something that he had built up? Clearly Brian felt that NEMS had become too big an operation for him; he didn't want the day-to-day running of it any more. He wanted to keep the day-to-day running of the Beatles and Cilla and his initial arrangement was that Robert would run the rest of it. However, Brian tired very quickly of this arrangement, but certainly Robert wasn't given access to the Beatles in any way, shape or form.

Geoffrey still seemed to be fairly important in the running of NEMS in Argyll Street so people were confused and there was a certain loyalty to Brian that didn't transfer to Robert Stigwood. Robert was very different from Brian.

He had a different way of working, a different persona and certainly a different stature at that stage. I think Brian regretted it.

Paul McCartney: There was no question in our minds that if we were to be managed by anyone it would be by Brian. I think his father, Harry, had said to him this classic bit of business advice that I don't believe in. People always say, 'Don't put all your eggs in one basket.' They're always saying that. So Brian had us Beatles in one basket and this was it. So I think his dad said, 'You know, hang on, diversify a bit.'

And someone suggested, 'Why don't you sell them, the Beatles?' Well, we were horrified because this was a personal relationship we had with Brian after all those years. We were horrified by the idea that he might sell us and I think he was horrified with the whole idea, actually.

Well, we dealt with it very quickly. Brian said, 'Robert Stigwood wants to buy you.' And we said, 'Oh yes?' He said, 'And we're having a meeting with him and one of his business people.' And we said, 'Oh yes, well we're not very keen on this, Brian. You know that, don't you?' So we waited till the meeting and they said, 'We were just talking about the conditions, you know.' And we said, 'Well, let's just get this straight. We're not going to be sold to anyone. If you can do it, you can continue to manage us. We love you. We're not going to be sold. In fact, if you do, if you somehow manage to pull this off, we can promise you one thing. We will record "God Save the Queen" for every single record we make from now on and we'll sing it out of tune. That's a promise. So if this guy buys us that's what he's buying.'

Funnily enough the Sex Pistols did it years later. It was always a good idea.

Alistair Taylor: I personally am sure the Beatles would have stayed with him; maybe renegotiated, because he didn't have as much to do any more. We never talked about it, the boys or Brian, but basically they may have said, 'Well, look. Hang on. We're not paying 25 per cent when we're not touring any more. You're doing less for us.' It could conceivably have been something like that, but I personally do not believe that they would have left him. I really don't. Where could they go?

Nat Weiss: He was part of all these things that bind people together. It was the Beatles and Brian, a club. They got into every drug together and they got into every addiction together and he was always part of it. His relationship with the Beatles was excellent, as far as I can tell. They were not going to leave him, and if they were he wasn't aware of it. He certainly felt that they were going to stay with him.

Joanne Petersen: The Beatles just had to walk into a room and Brian would glow. He absolutely adored them. They were his whole life and he loved them like he'd love his own sons. I often thought over the years that they weren't there for him like he was there for them. They had their own lives and they were the centre of their own universe. I don't really think any of them really sat down to wonder if Brian was OK. They must have heard stories that perhaps Brian wasn't well or Brian was this or Brian was that. I don't think any of them really sat down with him and said, 'Hey, Brian. What's wrong? Can we help you?' I don't think that ever happened.

The irony of it all is that he protected the Beatles. He put himself at incredible risk to protect the Beatles. He might have courted danger but he didn't want danger for them in any way. He would have cancelled tours; he would have gone to any lengths to make sure that they were not physically or emotionally put in danger in any way. That was everything to him. So I don't think they were ever really aware of his own turmoil and his own anxieties and depressions until after he died.

Peter Brown: The Beatles started to take LSD in '66 and I think Brian and I took it in the winter of '66 and '67.

The first time Brian took LSD was a Saturday night. Brian and I were in Chapel Street when the delivery was made. I took it first while he was upstairs, somewhat to his irritation when he came down and found that I'd actually been indulging before he got to it. He took some and we had quite a pleasant time. We stayed in. We had dinner in. It was a controlled atmosphere so that there was no threat from this hallucinatory drug. Then late at night we had a call and Klaus Voorman and Gibson Kemp arrived. We were very friendly with them and they joined us and they took some and again it was a very relaxed situation and certainly not unpleasant.

I don't think there was any beneficial side to taking LSD for Brian. If there was, if people have said there was, it was Brian fooling himself. I think it was Brian clutching at straws and pretending or trying to be just cool with it and going with the trend, the ultra-trend of the time.

Joanne Petersen: He never threw tea at me again but he could get pretty irate at times, and other times he would have laughed it off or brushed it off, it just depended. Brian had a lot of mood swings and it was directly a result of the chemical imbalances in his body brought on by his reversing his days and nights. He would be up all night and out all night and then he would take sleeping pills to get to sleep. Then he'd take pills to wake him up and that stuff in his body would affect his moods.

Often I'd be getting ready to go home but he'd find a reason for me to stay. That usually meant that he was feeling lonely or that he wasn't doing anything that night. He'd say, 'Oh, let's work on something,' or 'Let's work on another,' or 'Why don't we have dinner and work on something else?' I always knew that he was keeping me there because he didn't want to be on his own. Then we talked, sometimes. Once he told me, 'I don't know, I'm no good with men and I'm no good with women. I just want to have a relationship with someone.' He was a very sad and lonely person at times, and I felt sorry for him. I thought it was sad that he had so much going and yet he felt insecure.

Brian was constantly searching, for love, for something to take his loneliness away, and in a way I think he went through a lot of self-punishment. He punished himself a lot.

Alistair Taylor: He was an extremely mercurial person. Over the years I had two phone calls from him saying, 'Alistair, I've had enough. I am saying goodbye.' And I've leapt into a taxi and shot round to his flat. Then all he'd do is just look at me and say, 'What are you doing here?' I'd say, 'Brian, you've just been on the phone half an hour ago.' 'Oh, don't be silly. Please go away. I don't want you here today.'

Joanne Petersen: I think it was obvious from his moods that he was taking drugs. I mean, he didn't stand there and shake out pills in front of me. I knew he was an insomniac. He took sleeping pills and then he was hung over and he'd take pills to wake up.

Alistair Taylor: I wouldn't say he was self-destructive ultimately, just a bit of a depressive. I mean he used to take pills to lift him up, pills to take him back down again and pills to put him to sleep. But I certainly wouldn't say he was self-destructive.

Geoffrey Ellis: The Seltaeb matter was eventually settled in January 1967. An accounting was struck between both sides, and my recollection is that NEMS did in fact pay Seltaeb a sum of something under $300,000, which was minuscule compared with the amount they originally claimed. It probably was barely enough for them to cover their legal expenses.

On our side, Brian insisted on paying our legal fees himself, out of his own pocket, not out of the company. He felt it was his responsibility and I think it was a very searing experience for him.

I think the effect of this unhappy experience on Brian was to depress him very considerably. At that time, it was well known that he was largely dependent on drugs: sleeping pills, uppers, downers and so forth. He retreated to his bed a lot of the time and became more and more difficult to deal with. He started appearing less and less in business and meetings. I have no doubt at all that this merchandising mess was a very important part of his depression.

The Beatles did know about it. Brian always made a point of telling them everything that was going on. A lot of the stuff they were not interested in, but they were certainly aware of these unfortunate lawsuits, not least because they were splashed in the headlines of the tabloid press at the time. As far as I knew, the Beatles did not hold it against Brian at the time. They knew he was in a difficult situation and I think they were sympathetic towards him.

Seltaeb was undoubtedly a notable failure so far as Brian was concerned. It wasn't the only failure at that time, I'm sorry to say. He'd had difficulties over the running of the Saville Theatre, which we'd all had high hopes for initially. There were problems concerning his direction of a play at the time and some of the artists that he represented and managed were not doing all that well. All these, of course, were counterbalanced by the continuing fantastic success of the Beatles and Cilla Black and Gerry and the Pacemakers, who continued to be very high earners.

George Martin: I don't think in order to be a successful manager of a number of people you have to be a good record person, you don't have to be a good publisher, you don't have to actually do those things. Brian couldn't go into a studio and produce a record but that didn't matter; there are very few business mangers who can. But he did have enough knowledge to handle the boys properly and handle all his acts properly. The big problem was he bit off more than he could chew. The big problem was he wanted to overextend, he wanted to do less with each artist, and you can't. When you have a successful artist you've got to do more. And he took on too much. Now, I don't think that this, in fact, led to his death. Obviously he was under great strain, but I don't think it did.

Nat Weiss: I remember one evening at the Waldorf Towers in February 1967. Before he was to give a radio interview with Murray the K, I came in the room to find Brian slurring his language. Obviously he had taken several Nembutals. He had this interview coming up and there were people in the waiting room waiting to see him, and he was like this. I found the bottle. I had to wrestle with him on the floor, throw the bottle out of the window of the hotel and just yell at him. Eventually, with coffee and things like that, we got him together and we took him to the interview.

Now, if anyone hears that interview you'll notice that the first ten minutes are sort of, 'Yes,' 'No,' 'No.' Brian is hardly vocal. As it goes on, as he gets more into himself, you have the old Brian Epstein talking about the future of the Beatles, and it becomes very positive when he's out of the influence of the drugs. Looking back at it now, I see that anyone taking barbiturates to that degree has got to be projected into a state of depression very easily. It didn't take much for Brian to get depressed, but with depression came a loss of self-confidence and it just got worse.

On this trip to New York, Brian held a press conference at Max's, Kansas City, a hang-out for Andy Warhol and his entourage. He was there to announce the new association between NEMS and the Robert Stigwood Organization and to promote Stigwood's three major signings – Cream, the Who and the Bee Gees.

Peter Brown: Immediately, Brian started to second-guess Robert, which really wasn't fair, but symptomatic of Brian's perfectionism. I was constantly telling him that he couldn't very well appoint this person and then expect him to run things exactly how Brian would have done it. He had to let him run things. But Robert handled it very well and was very patient about it. He signed the Bee Gees and brought Cream with him and this gave the whole operation a new impetus, a new force outside the Liverpool people.

Joanne Petersen: He was very good at conducting himself publicly in a way that no one would ever know that he was troubled. Often I would stay over at the house and work so that I could be there early next day. And a lot of the times he was fine. He ran his appointments. He ran his day. He was out or he was in on the phone; things were fine. Other days he didn't want to face the day.

13. All You Need Is Love

MIKE HENNESSEY: *What did you feel?*
BRIAN EPSTEIN: The feeling is too impressive and personal to convey in words. I know that I have sometimes had too much to drink and felt awful and unpleasant the morning after. But I have never had a hangover from smoking pot or taking LSD. I think LSD helped me to know myself better and I think it helped me to become less bad-tempered.

MELODY MAKER, MAY 1967

Marianne Faithfull: Six months before he died, he was actually undergoing a rather fascinating transformation. I don't know if he went to bed with John Lennon, although if he had, there would be a certain amount of contempt maybe coming from John. You know, going to bed with people can often destroy the respect you have for them. But whether or not he did, just the fact that he wanted to would have given John a bit of power that he probably shouldn't have had, or might have abused. I'm not saying he shouldn't have had that power, but he may not have known how to use it. But I think that was passing. I think it was changing.

I think he got on very well with Paul, and who knows what would have happened with his relationship with John? I can't help wondering about it, because I liked Brian so much and his spiritual strength was so important that I tend to think that everything would have been quite different if he hadn't died. It's overlooked a lot, but the sort of person who can interpret one person to another or interpret somebody to the rest of the world is more important than we know.

An amazing idea of Brian's was to have Joe Orton write the next screenplay for a Beatles film. It was a great idea, and it all kind of fell apart once Brian died.

All these wonderful connections. That was one of the connections I did know about because of my connection with the Royal Court. There was a lot riding on it for Joe Orton, and Brian was the only person that could have put it to the Fab Four. Brian would have been able to talk to John about doing the Orton script, and Paul would have seen the value of it. I don't think they would have recoiled in straight horror actually, but it was one of many, many, many dreams that fell the day that Brian Epstein died.

Peter Brown: Brian eventually bought a house in the country. I thought one of the solutions for Brian's problems was to get him out of London at weekends so he wouldn't be so vulnerable to late-night haunts and the temptations of the big city. I wanted this house I had seen near to John Pritchard. I told Brian about it and I thought I was rolling the dice, frankly, but he went to see it, immediately liked it and bought it.

Now he had a project in the country and he was actually quite happy about this for a little while. He furnished it. He set it up. He found staff for it and he had a project which he enjoyed doing and he was very good at that kind of thing. It was a lovely house and he furnished it very nicely.

Joanne Petersen: He'd have quiet weekends down at Kingsley Hill. He'd probably have some friends down to visit. I didn't go down there very often. In fact I only went down there a couple of times. But it was somewhere that he could go and retreat to on a weekend.

Peter Brown: The first thing would be to have all the Beatles down for the weekend for a house-warming. We invited them all with their wives and they all came. Brian was very happy about this because it was very unusual for Beatles and wives to assemble in one place for any length of time, and it was in his house that it was happening, and probably only in this house could it have happened.

Marianne Faithfull: The drugs that were there were already quite hard to handle. Being on acid almost all the time was not the easiest way to live, but we managed. The only clear memory I have is going down to see Brian in his house in the country in the afternoon one day.

We must have been coming back from West Wittering. I can't remember what we were doing but we stopped at Brian's for lunch or after lunch or something, and it was a lovely little group. It was some of the Beatles and their girlfriends and Brian, very happy. We all had a very, very nice time, which was quite a feat, because all of us didn't have that much in common, except that we happened to all be there at the time.

Joanne Petersen: Some days he was full of the joys of spring. He was effusive and he was warm. He was smiling and he was happy. Don't get the impression that Brian went through life in a total black hole. There were a lot of times where Brian enjoyed his life; he loved what was happening around him.

Peter Brown: The problem was boredom, and I think drugs made it worse. There were people who were invited back to the house that were a problem.

There was a couple of guys who came back who got stroppy and difficult and had to be thrown out. There were a few minor skirmishes like that, but I don't think they were anything terribly bad for his mental state. It probably rather excited him. Heavy drug-taking is not conducive to a very successful sex life. Part of it goes by the way and that's also not a very happy situation. It wasn't very easy living with Brian at that point of his life.

I would get up, go to the office, do the usual routine office hours and I would come home, which at that point was Chapel Street. I'd get there and find out whether he was up or whether he was around, what shape he was in and whether we were going go out to dinner or staying in for dinner. First I would have to see if he was coherent enough to do either. It was depressing and miserable.

I was sort of staying at Chapel Street most of the time. I don't know if I had been watching television or what, but I was in the house. Before going to bed, I suddenly realized that Brian had been missing for part of the evening and I found him in a very heavy state of unconsciousness and called his doctor. He took an overdose on purpose. We know that because we found a note. I called his driver and we carried him to the car because I was very nervous of calling the ambulance or police since it would have been a scandal.

Bryan Barrett: I got the call from Peter Brown. He couldn't handle it because of the weight of the man. Brian was a very heavy man, you know. I rushed round to the house. It was late at night and we broke the door down and rolled Brian up in a blanket.

Outside the house was the Bentley Continental, which is not conducive to carrying bodies around in. But I threw him over my shoulder and got him into the car and we rushed him up to Putney Heath. Peter Brown was very worried that someone might see him. I went, 'Who the hell's gonna see him that time in the morning wrapped up in the blanket?'

They pumped him out and he was moaning and crying on the table. I was watching them pump him out and he became conscious after a while. He was muttering and mumbling and you could hear what he was saying, but I don't want to go into that one.

He came back and said he was all right after that, but prior to that he had called me one night. I went up there and threw some salt water into him and he just threw up everything. He was conscious and he was mumbling and he was incoherent and he said, 'Don't tell anybody about this.'

Joanne Petersen: Brian did a lot of things that were dangerous. People did try to stop him but you'd have to follow him day into the night to really have been able to stop him. Bryan Barrett stopped him at times. I wasn't with him at night. He took risks that were dangerous when you consider his standing and who he was.

That last year his depressions got worse. Norman Cowan, his doctor, came to the house often, and I'd say, 'What's happening with Brian? Why's he like this?' He told me, 'Brian is on a collision course with himself. We all have an in-built ability if we're feeling depressed to try and rise above it or waylay it. But Brian heads straight towards it and collides with himself.'

Even when he went to the Priory [rehabilitation clinic] I don't think anyone said no to him. People just said yes to Brian and Brian could manipulate them. He could charm them. He could get what he wanted. So I think that people weren't strong enough around Brian.

He'd go to the Priory, be in there then for a while and then just check out. He'd come back and he'd be OK for a while. So, you know, I think those Priory visits were just Band-Aids.

Bryan Barrett: I used to worry about him at times. I tell you, I did worry about that man. As I say, I liked him. If I didn't like him I wouldn't have stayed, because the money was no damn good. I was at twenty-five pound a week and no overtime. But he did go away a lot so I'd get good stretches of freedom.

I used to see him when he was obviously either drunk or on drugs or whatever. He used to always seem to be depressed to me at those particular times. He'd come back and he'd be depressed, especially when he'd been left on his own. That's what he hated, I think: the loneliness.

He was a very moody man. Sometimes he would talk and talk and talk and chat and he'd ask me about my kids and say how lucky I was to have a family. That seemed to be one of his things. For all he's standing in a crowd, he was lonely and of course he was shy. He was very shy. I mean most of the blasé bit was acting. He was a very shy man and he'd go on and talk about different things. Then other times he'd be very morose and he wouldn't say a bloody word.

He wanted to be aloof and yet he didn't want to be aloof. He did put on airs and graces. I think he got upset about the way the Beatles went after he'd got them into their suits and all. They all went and reversed what he had done. They started doing their thing, painting their front doors in psychedelic colours, and I think he was sort of out of that scene. He thought it was all going downhill from there.

Gerry Marsden: He'd get very depressed at times just before he died and he would drink a little too much. The whole thing was getting to him. The Beatles were arguing about different things, which he never liked. I think he was losing control of the Beatles and they were the boys he loved. He'd brought them to what they were.

So Brian's last year was a bit sad. He was down and up. It was very hard for him. The boys had been taking their own path and each individual one of the Beatles was trying to go another way. I was doing different things and wanting more, like trying to get into the West End, like Brian had said.

Brian used to ring me up if I was in London staying in a hotel, and ask me to come round to have a little chat. I would go round to his place and ask him, 'Brian, what's your problems?' and he would tell me. He made a few mistakes. He seemed to choose bad company at the wrong time. I tried to explain to him that he had to be very careful. A man of his power and influence in the business had to be careful about who he picked as friends and who he would take back to his pad.

I used to speak to Brian a great deal. He would ring me when he was low at two in the morning and chat for an hour. Maybe I was a shoulder for Brian to cry on. I tried to help him and I hope in a way I did. But he still ended up dead. I just think the last year was a bit traumatic for him. Maybe it just got a little too heavy for him and he lost control of the situation.

Joanne Petersen: I think one of the most incredible times of the whole period of Brian's relationship with the Beatles was round the *Sgt Pepper* time. When he brought the test pressing back from the studio, I went down into the sitting room, and he sat me down and he said, 'I want to play you something,' and he put on 'Day in the Life' at volume 12.

It was so earth-shattering and I was literally pinned against the chair. I felt like the breath had been taken out of my body. I was so dumbstruck about the magnitude of this and so was he. It was just such a powerful experience to sit there and listen. He was full of joy and amazement that the Beatles could produce something that was so awesome. It was beyond his wildest dreams of what he always knew these boys could do. He was overwhelmed with it and just so happy and proud of them. He was thrilled and excited and he couldn't wait for the public to hear what he considered was the ultimate masterpiece.

Nat Weiss: When the Beatles went ahead and put all these pictures on the *Sgt Pepper* cover and had no releases from anybody, Brian found out. It was a nightmare to think of thirty or forty people suing the Beatles. Brian said, 'Look, as far as I'm concerned, put the album out in brown paper bags.' I had a note to that effect. But Paul McCartney had called me and said, 'Why is

Brian upset? We can do this. It's a fiesta.' Brian hit the roof and said, 'They must be on something,' because he knew the consequences of something like that.

Paul McCartney: I remember he liked *Sgt Pepper* so much and we were wondering about the cover and it was getting a little bit contentious. The record company thought we were spending millions on it, though I think it was maybe a thousand pounds, which was obviously not an awful lot. When Brian heard about all that he said, 'Put it in a brown paper bag.' He'd say these kind of things. We wouldn't necessarily go and put it in a brown paper bag but we knew what he meant. He meant it's good enough to go out in a brown paper bag. It was a vote of confidence.

Nat Weiss: I spoke to Brian at the end of May 1967. We had dinner and I can say candidly that there was no thought in his mind about the Beatles leaving him or of any termination of the relationship, even though he knew the contract expired that September. His own thought was to reduce the commission from 25 per cent to 15 per cent and remain with the Beatles and with Cilla and do what he was planning to do. He was actually in a very good mood about that.

Joanne Petersen: I think Kingsley Hill for me was the Kingsley Hill party, the *Sgt Pepper* party, where Brian decided that he was going to fly. He was going to have a wonderful party to celebrate the new album. He asked Derek Taylor and his wife to fly over from America. Nat Weiss came over and it was an incredible happening. It was an event.

I drove down with Lulu, who was my very close friend. I remember walking into the top room of the house and opening the door. There were the Beatles, sitting there crossed-legged in their *Sgt Pepper* costumes.

There were people everywhere. It was a fairly druggy party. I remember opening John's Rolls-Royce and Derek and Joan and Cynthia and John were in there. I looked in absolute amazement at all these people in the Rolls-Royce and then closed the door again.

Lulu and I did not take drugs. We had seen too many things happening around us and I just couldn't imagine doing things that would be so scary to my body. So Lulu spent the entire time making cups of tea and emptying ashtrays and saying, 'Och, I don't know why they do this to themselves,' and generally buzzing around.

Brian wandered around from guest to guest, from room to room. I think he really enjoyed this party. He really enjoyed the gathering of all his friends, people who were his nearest and dearest, people he cared about. I do remember seeing him on a number of occasions and he just looked really happy that night. He looked proud about what was happening and he was happy and he was pretty drunk.

Peter Brown: I was there with Kenny Everett, and we had the most wonderful weekend. A lot of acid and other drugs were taken, but it was a happy weekend. Kenny had a bit of a bad trip but I remember George Harrison looking after him rather nicely and affectionately.

Derek Taylor: Joan and I went to the *Sgt Pepper* party in Sussex, flown in by Brian and met by all the Beatles in their coloured Rolls-Royces and all their finery and taken to be given LSD. Brian was terribly happy that evening. All his friends were there: John Pritchard, Peter Brown, Nat Weiss and Terry Doran.

Nat Weiss: Towards the end of June, he was beginning to emerge from the depression. He had more positive moments than depressive moments. One night, at the end of the month, I was driving from New York City to Long Island. About three-quarters of the way out there, I called my apartment to see if there were any messages.

Brian had called from London and asked me to call right away. So I called him from a phone booth. He got on the phone. 'Nat,' he said, 'all you need is love. Love is all you need. Please call Capitol Records on Monday. Tell them that's the single. And goodbye.'

He'd arranged for the world-wide broadcast of 'All You Need Is Love'. Brian was always concerned about doing something bigger and better than anyone else had ever done. Just as Shea Stadium had been the biggest concert, this was to be the biggest TV show in history, and the Beatles would be seen live across the world. The net result of that live broadcast, the first ever of its kind, was that the Beatles were seen live by 400 million people around the world. It's another testament to Brian's creativity. He just saw no limits.

At that time, he really was in a creative mode, thinking about the Beatles' future and his own. We actually entered into an agreement where I would manage his own American career.

There was an offer from the CBC to host a programme and that's where I got involved with working with him. I was an attorney. I was familiar with the American scene and Brian was not the best businessman in the world. At this point he wanted someone to handle his business.

Many musicians who are very competent bring in an outside person to produce their record, even though they're capable of doing it themselves, only because they want to bounce things off someone's ear. It was the same mentality. He wanted someone to bring things to him and to talk it over with him. In that respect, we would have had an agent–client, manager–client relationship. I don't think Brian would have been an easy person to manage but I do think he certainly would have needed to seek advice. In what he was thinking of doing, he was really in uncharted waters because he was going to become the artist or the personality to be marketed.

George Martin: Brian was very excited about the idea of the broadcast which led to 'All You Need Is Love'. He came to me and said, 'Look, there's an international hook-up with all nations and the Beatles have been chosen to represent it. We'd be doing a live broadcast to 200, 300 million people in every part of the globe.' In those days that was unbelievable, because television was very limited. So he was enormously excited about it, and very proud of the fact that the Beatles were leading the way. It was very good that it was a very successful broadcast.

Of course, Brian was using it as an opportunity. He was offered the broadcast and he took it, but he could see that the Beatles were going to become important international artists without necessarily having to tour.

Brian wanted things to go on always the way they were: the head of an empire which had the Beatles and his beloved Gerry and Billy and Cilla, and have greater and greater success, and also, of course, he wanted to get involved in the theatre more.

Nat Weiss: We made these arrangements for him to come to the US on 2 September. We also signed a management agreement where I would handle his tours. It would have been me becoming the manager's manager. He was going to come to the United States for a month. He gave me a list of people he'd like to visit and his mood was very good. *Sgt Pepper* had been a very successful album and he was interested in pursuing the film thing with the Beatles, pursuing his own career while being relieved of the burden of the other things at NEMS. I would say that his mood was excellent.

He saw himself representing the counterculture. Being from Liverpool and being gay, he was outside the mainstream. I think that's one of the reasons that Lennon respected him. He was on the outside; he was an outsider.

Of course, when his father died in July, and he visited his family for a week, I saw some depression. He said he appreciated what they were going through but he felt very uncomfortable with it. Being from a traditional Jewish family background he couldn't wait to get out of there; he felt confined.

Liverpool, 25 July

My Dear Nat,

Thanks so much for the cable, it was nice of you and very comforting.

I'm coming to NY September 2nd. I'd have come earlier but my father's passing has given me the added responsibility of Mother.

The week of Shiva is up tonight and I feel a bit strange. Probably been good for me in a way. Time to think and note that at least I'm really needed by Mother. Also time to note that the unworldly Jewish circle of my parents' and brother's friends are not so bad. Provincial maybe, but warm, sincere and basic. But of course have not even looked at a possibility for eight days, I'm real hot for sex. I'm going back to London tomorrow Monday and returning Friday. I'll have to spend a lot of time with her. After all although my Father was sixty-three (a little young to die I think) she's only fifty-two and must find a new life. They were very devoted. She knew nothing else (married him at eighteen) and had nearly thirty-four years' happy marriage (must have been good). So you see I must do all I can.

Anyway I'll come in September for a couple of weeks or so. Should be able to fit in a trip to California (maybe Vegas en route).

The boys have gone to Greece to buy an island. I think it's a dotty idea but they're no longer children and must have their own sweet way. A few weeks ago they all (with wives, Neil and Mal) came to Sussex for a weekend. Mick and Marianne joined us on Sunday. It was a divine time. Poor Mick (he looked beautiful). I hope he gets off when the appeal comes up at the end of the month. Of course the whole thing, from the beginning, was stupidly handled. I'll tell you all when I see you.

Beatles maintaining number one here for some weeks. I'm very pleased. Should be OK in US. Hell, I'm hot for something good.

With love,

Brian

Rex Makin: The Saturday after his father died, I was sitting in the garden having tea and he came over. His appearance hadn't changed. Perhaps a little bit more pink but he always was quite pink: an English rose, delicate bone-china complexion.

He told me he was a bit world-weary, tired of jet-setting and problems with the boys. I said to him, 'Well, you've created a Frankenstein,' and he agreed he had. He was concerned about his mother and the future in general. He asked if he could go up to my children's nursery and look out next door over the garden that he'd grown up in. And he did that and I never saw him again.

Billy J. Kramer: There were times when I thought he was very happy. He came to see me at the Shakespeare in Liverpool. His father had died recently so he was bound to be unhappy. We hadn't been speaking for some time 'cause we had differences of opinion, but he said, 'I'm going back to the States, and when I come back I really want to work on your career because I think you've worked very hard and you deserve a break now. You're ripe for it.'

That was the early part of the week. Then on the Saturday I got a hand-delivered letter from Brian apologizing that he couldn't make the show because he didn't like to leave his mother alone. He said he'd see me when he came back from the States and he hadn't forgotten our conversation. That was the last time I saw Brian.

On this occasion he looked healthier than he had in years.

Nat Weiss: He wanted an apartment high up on the East Side facing the river. He loved to have a view of the river. In this case he wanted to have a view of the East River, which was the direction his suite of the Waldorf Towers faced. When we looked at that building, the St Tropez, that was the condition of any apartment he would take.

The plan was, when he came back to America in September, we would go through and work out a deal for buying the apartment.

Lionel Bart: The last time I saw Brian we were both really a bit out to lunch, I think. I was shopping. I was buying some strange clothes in some psychedelic shop in the Lower Kings Road called Granny Takes a Trip. Brian was in there looking very slovenly for him. He didn't have the tie, to start with. It was the first time I'd ever seen him without a tie in the city. That was shortly before he died. I believe a lot of things got to him by then that he couldn't handle, really. There was a lot of experimentation with drugs and to some degree he had to be involved with that to have any credibility. But somehow it didn't go with the suit and the tie of Brian, and I don't think Brian could really handle that.

Joanne Petersen: I think that he was worried a little about the Maharishi. The Maharishi was a fairly charismatic new phenomenon for the Beatles and they wanted to find out about it. Brian never talked to me about any anxieties he had. But I think, in the general state of mind that he was in at that time, the whole Maharishi thing wouldn't have been something that would have had enormous appeal for him.

Bryan Barrett: There were two strange expressions he used to me about three weeks prior to his death which on reflection did mean something. They were, 'Beware the ides of March,' and 'I feel as though I am Svengali that has created a monster.' These are very strange expressions and he asked me if I knew what the ides of March meant. I said, 'Yes, I do know.' He said, 'Well, we'll see,' or something very similar to that. I can't think why he'd say that other than the fact that he knew a lot was gonna happen to him and the ides of March was a threat.

In the finish, he didn't trust anybody. He just had this thing about people. I've never told anyone this before, but one day Brian asked me if I would kill Peter Brown. That's how trustworthy he got with Mr Brown. Would I kill him? What would it cost to kill Peter Brown? I thought, 'Christ.'

I told him there were ways of getting it done. 'There's money and money speaks, sir, but do you really want to do this?' He said he didn't want anybody else but me to do it. I thought, 'The state of mind he's in, he'd be round the police station.' He could build up this terrific hatred for a while. Then it seemed to fade and fade.

Paul McCartney: I can't remember the last time I saw Brian. It would have been a few weeks before he died, I think. I saw him at Chapel Street. We would stop round there a lot just out of friendship, have a cup of tea or a drink.

Simon Napier-Bell: I met Brian at Robert Stigwood's. I had gone round to have a drink or dinner and Brian was just sitting there having a drink with Robert. What was so strange was that it was almost as if I knew him. And anyone in the music business at that time would have known Brian Epstein, not just of him but almost intimately because the talk in every newspaper was about Brian Epstein and the Beatles, these five people. So having been a manager myself for almost a year it was as if Brian was someone I knew well already.

Nat Weiss: Near the end of his life he told me, 'If you're going to go to an affair with a boy make sure he's very good-looking, because it's far worse to be accused of bad taste than being gay.' I've never forgotten that.

Simon Napier-Bell: That first time I met Brian at Robert Stigwood's house, he was very friendly, very easy-going, but he was refined. He wasn't camp, or gay in that sense of the word. Some people might have called him fussy but I would have just said he was what you would expect him to be, a middle-class, well-brought-up Jewish boy who had begun to find out there was another world, which was both show business and working class.

That night we were very friendly immediately, and Robert said, 'Let's go to the Battersea Fun Fair.' Maybe Robert thought he'd meet some boys there or something. So there was Eppie and me and Robert and we went round the fun-fair and did all the rides. We egged Brian on to get up on the stage where there were three mirrors that said TURN A MAN INTO A WOMAN. So he stood in front of the mirror and he was turned into a woman.

Then we went out and had drinks. The next morning Brian phoned up and asked me to have dinner with him. I did and it was fascinating because anyone who'd been in my position, a manager of a top group, or who wanted to be a manager, aspired to being what Brian was – the manager of the biggest, most enormous success in history.

There was this innate jealousy of not being as big as he was or not having experienced what he had. Therefore, to have dinner with him and get second-hand all the experiences he'd gone through and get to ask all the things you've ever wanted to ask, I would imagine that everyone in the country would want to do that. There were a thousand things I wanted to ask. At about one o'clock in the morning he kept saying how much he liked me. It was quite obvious it was a good time to leave because there was not much more I was going to find out that would interest me and he was after something else.

So I left. Just as I was leaving he asked if I would come down to the country at the weekend with him because he had a house in the country where he took lots of people every weekend. I said no, because I was actually going to Ireland for the weekend with Nick Cohn, a journalist. I said, 'Oh, there's lots of other weekends. I'll come another time.' But he asked three or four times. After I got home, I think it was the next morning, he called again and asked me to come and I said no, and went off to Ireland.

14. Death

CLIFF MICHELMORE: *Do you envy the Beatles?*
EPSTEIN: No.

MICHELMORE: *Why not?*
EPSTEIN: Well, I couldn't do what they do. It's not my job.

TONIGHT, BBC TV, 1 OCTOBER 1964

LETTER TO NAT WEISS

24 Chapel Street, London SW1

August 23, 1967

Dear Nat,

Just got yours of the 21st, we have since conversed on the telephone when I told you that Sunday and Monday I'd quite like to take yacht trip on similar lines to that which we took last year when I came to the States in connection with Jesus Christ. Maybe on Sunday we could have all manner of lovely pretty mortal persons aboard and then on Monday we could mix the company a bit with the likes of Eric Anderson [singer], etc.

I hope I'm not asking for too many things but I'm anxious for this to be a good trip for us both, anyway, say I indignantly, you are my manager.

Eric's album makes lovely, happy contented dreamy listening. I am very addicted to Anderson.

Till the second, love, flowers, bells, be happy and look forward to the future.

With love,

Brian

Peter Brown: A few weeks after Harry had died, Queenie stayed with Brian at Chapel Street for about ten days. He adored his mother and she adored him. It was a great relationship between them and I think she was very aware of all of his problems. I don't know how vocal they were about it to each other.

Probably not very much, but she was very savvy and she was very understanding.

However, I think her visit was very restricting on his activities. He made a great effort to look after his mother and take her places she'd like and to spend as much time with her as possible. He wanted to look after her and nurture her, since it wasn't long after Harry died. But after she left, he felt like playing. But all that was on offer was a weekend in the country.

Joanne Petersen: The last time I saw Brian was on the Friday of the August Bank Holiday long weekend. It was a beautiful sunny day. He'd asked me about a day or so before what I was doing that weekend and whether Lulu and I wanted to come down to Kingsley Hill for the weekend. I said I didn't, because I hadn't seen my mother very much at all and I wanted to spend the weekend with her. Lulu had some other plans that weekend. At about four o'clock that afternoon we walked down the stairs of Chapel Street together. He was in a very relaxed, very happy mood; he seemed very sunny. He was like the weather, very sunny. I walked him to the car. The Bentley was parked outside with the roof down. He told me to have a nice weekend and I told him the same. Then he got in the car. And just as he pulled away he turned and he waved to me and he smiled at me. That was the last time I saw Brian alive.

Geoffrey Ellis: At the time of the August Bank Holiday in 1967, Brian invited Peter Brown and myself to stay with him at his house in Kingsley Hill in Sussex. Brian had also invited a friend of his whom he wanted to get to know better but who was unable to join us, and Brian was rather disappointed.

He'd had a difficult few weeks. His father had died six weeks earlier, his mother had been staying with him in London. He really wanted to relax with a few old friends in the country. Peter and I were very happy to be there. It was a lovely house to stay in.

Peter Brown: Geoffrey Ellis and I drove down together, but it wasn't soon enough for Brian. He'd already been down there for a day or so and was already bored.

We had invited people down later who subsequently didn't turn up. Brian, in his agitated state, was suddenly confronted with the fact that there was this long holiday weekend yawning ahead with no apparent entertainment arriving. All he was stuck with was two of his oldest friends, which was not very exciting.

Geoffrey Ellis: These people didn't appear after dinner, and so Brian suddenly decided that he would go up to London and spend the night in London. Peter

Brown and I tried to dissuade him because he'd had a fair amount to drink and we felt that he ought to keep to his own plan of spending a quiet week in the country. But he was determined, and so he drove off in the car which was a large Bentley convertible – open, at the time – and drove off up to London leaving Peter and myself there.

Peter Brown: I was concerned because I didn't think he was in a fit state to drive. He went off assuring me that he was going to be all right. He said I should go to bed and that we would all be together the next morning for breakfast.

I had no belief in that at all. I hadn't seen Brian for breakfast for years.

Geoffrey Ellis: After a short time a London taxi drew up with about four people in it, who were the friends and friends of friends that Brian had telephoned and suggested to come down for the evening, possibly the night. I think they were a little surprised to find that their host had left, but they stayed. We all had a few drinks and just spent the night there.

On the Saturday morning Peter Brown and I, who were the only ones left, spent the day. We had lunch and tried to telephone Brian in London. Eventually he called back and said that he was going to stay in London for another night. He wasn't feeling terribly strong and so he was relaxing at home in bed. So Peter Brown and I were left again to our own devices in the house.

Peter Brown: He called late in the afternoon and was speaking in a woozy voice. He apologized for not coming back and maybe letting us worry. I suspect that when he went back to London he did go out, cruised the West End for a bit and then went home.

I urged him to come back to the country. But there was no way he could drive back because he sounded pretty awful, and I suggested him coming on the train. It was an unlikely thing for him to do but it was the only thing I could think of at the time.

Geoffrey Ellis: On the Sunday morning Peter and I were feeling a bit shifty at enjoying Brian's hospitality without him being present, and we telephoned again and spoke to Brian's butler, Antonio, who said that Mr Epstein was in the house. They had not seen him the night before but his car was outside and his bedroom door was locked. So we said, 'Well, please, as soon as he wakes, let us know, because we'd like to speak to him,' to see if he was coming down for the rest of the weekend.

Peter Brown: We went to the local pub for lunch. I think the housekeeper at the house in the country called me at the pub and said that the houseman in Chapel Street was concerned about Brian.

Joanne Petersen: On Sunday lunchtime I got a call from the couple that lived in the house, Antonio and Maria. Antonio said that he was very concerned that Brian had come back from Kingsley Hill on Friday, his car hadn't moved since Saturday and it was now Sunday lunchtime. I asked him why was he concerned, because it wasn't unusual for Brian to go in his room and stay there, take some pills, go to sleep and check out for twenty-four hours. I told him not to worry, that I was sure that everything was all right and thanked him for the call. And then I put the phone down and went back inside to have my lunch. But I said to my mother, 'You know, I just think I might drive over to Chapel Street and make sure that all is OK.' I was just a little concerned by then.

So I got in my car. Since it was Sunday, there was no one around and it was a very quick trip across town. I got to Chapel Street, let myself in, found Antonio and went up to Brian's door and knocked on it. There were double doors leading into a dressing room and then there was a single door leading into a bedroom, so there was quite a bit of a distance between the hallway and Brian's room.

I knocked on the door and I called out his name. I called, 'Answer the door. Are you there?' And then I went up to my room and I tried the intercom, and there was no reply. So then I went down to the kitchen, and I called down to Kingsley Hill and spoke to Peter Brown. I asked, 'Why did Brian come back? Why is he here? He's meant to have been there with you.' He gave me some reason that Brian was bored and came back into town. I said, 'Well, I'm very concerned. Brian's in his room. He hasn't been out of it since Saturday. I'm going to have them break the doors down.' Peter said, 'No, don't do that. You've done that before, and Brian gets furious.' I told him I was going to do it anyway.

I hung up and tried Norman Cowan, Brian's doctor, who was away. I knew I didn't want to be there on my own. Antonio and Maria couldn't speak very good English and they were a very shy couple. I needed someone nearer, that could be a support system. So I called Peter back and I told him that Dr Cowan wasn't there and Peter suggested I call his doctor, John Galway. He was there so I told him that I was concerned about Brian and asked if he could come over to the house. He would. And in the meantime I also called a few other people but I couldn't find them. Then I found Alistair and asked him to come to the house.

Alistair Taylor: I'd literally just got back from San Francisco, having called in at Los Angeles on Brian's request, and I got a phone call. I was giving my wife her presents and we were just chatting. I always remember I was in bare feet and sandals and jeans and a denim shirt for travelling. And Joanne rang and she said, 'Brian's not answering his door and I don't really want to be at the house by myself. Could you possibly meet me there?' And I knew Joanne wouldn't have asked me that unless she felt something was wrong. My immediate reaction was to say, 'Look, Joanne, forget it. I've been through this before.' Lesley went spare. I'd just got back off a trip that I shouldn't have been on anyway, and I just said, 'Lesley, I've got to go. Don't ask me why. I've got a feeling.' I said, 'I'll be home in half an hour or I may be a long time.' I was a long time.

Joanne Petersen: Then John Galway arrived and we went up to Brian's room, up to the outside doors. Antonio and John Galway broke the doors down. I think in the meantime I'd called Peter back and left the line hanging. Then I went up as they broke the doors down.

Antonio and John Galway went in and I followed them. Maria was staying behind. The curtains were drawn and John Galway was directly ahead of me. I could just see part of Brian in the bed and I was just totally stunned. I knew that something really bad had happened. Then I think John Galway told me, 'Just wait outside.' I stood in the doorway. A few minutes later John Galway came out. I've never seen a doctor so white. We were all white and we knew that Brian had died.

Peter Brown: I held on the phone while the doctor went in and found out what had happened. Then he told me that Brian was indeed dead. The first thing I did was call David Jacobs, Brian's friend and lawyer who lived in Brighton.

Geoffrey Ellis: Peter Brown and I left for London immediately.

Alistair Taylor: I arrived at the house. Joanne opened the door and she just pointed upstairs. I don't think she said a word and I went running up the stairs. Brian was lying there looking as if he was asleep. And the doctor just said, 'I'm sorry but he's dead.' The room was looking so normal. There was a plate of chocolate digestive biscuits on the bed, some correspondence, which was typical of Brian, and a half-empty bottle of bitter lemon. No sign of any alcohol around, just one joint I found in a drawer.

Joanne Petersen: We all went down in the study and had a brandy each. We were all totally shocked. By this time Alistair had arrived. Maria was crying, and repeating, 'Why this happen? Why this happen?' Then it was some time before we called the police because we wanted to make sure that things were OK in the house, that there were no substances for them to find. So we actually went all through Brian's things before we called the police.

Alistair Taylor: Within literally very few minutes of the police being informed, there's a ring on the doorbell and it's a reporter I knew. He just looked at me and said, 'What are you doing here? I hear Brian's ill.' And I said, 'No, he's fine. He's gone out. He just called me over, actually. You know what he's like, you know, typical Brian. I've come over specially on a Sunday morning and he's gone out in the car.' Then I wondered if the garage door was closed because if the car's sitting there the reporter's going to say, 'Which car?' I was concerned that, before this news broke, somehow we had to get hold of Queenie, and we couldn't find her.

Then I was trying to get hold of Clive so that he could look after Queenie. Finally I got hold of him. When he answered the phone, there was already a crowd outside the house. He just said, 'Did you have a great trip?' I just said, 'Right, it's Brian. He's had an accident.' So he said, 'Oh, is he all right?' And I said, 'No.' And I didn't know, to this day I don't know what else I could have said. I just said, 'No, Clive, I'm afraid he's dead.' And he just let out the most horrendous scream and the next second Barbara, his wife, was on the phone. She said, 'Alistair, what is it?' So I told her. She said, 'Don't worry.' I said, 'We've got to get hold of Queenie.' And she just said, 'Don't worry, I'll see to it. Relax.' That's it.

Joanne Petersen: Geoffrey and Peter arrived back from Sussex some time later. Peter and I were good friends, and I was really wanting him to get back. I remember the first thing I asked was why did Brian come back from Kingsley Hill? Neither of them answered. They just started to go up the stairs. And I remember thinking that they seemed weird and I knew there was something wrong.

They appeared distant when I expected them to be grief-stricken. I expected that Peter would give me a hug, but he didn't. He was just cool and I'm not sure that it was shock. I've asked myself many times what happened in Kingsley Hill. It's just one of the question marks I have about Brian's death.

Peter Brown: When we got to Chapel Street, David Jacobs was already there because he had got the train from Brighton to Victoria and he was sort of in charge by that time. The news was already out, somehow or other, and the street was already filling with the press.

Death

Geoffrey Ellis: We stayed in the house for the evening, not knowing quite what to do. David Jacobs had contacted the authorities because there had to be an inquest. Unfortunately, the next day was Bank Holiday Monday when everything was closed and no inquest could be held. This was distressing for Brian's family. Being Orthodox Jews, they wished him to be buried within twenty-four hours of his death. Unfortunately, this was not possible.

I had the curious experience of being inside the house in Chapel Street and watching the TV news. There was a reporter outside Brian's house, reporting on what had happened and showing a picture of the house. That was happening as we were inside the house looking at the television at what was happening outside.

Joanne Petersen: I remember them taking Brian out in this black coffin and a photographer photographing the coffin. I got really distressed about this and I didn't want him to be photographed like that in a coffin.

Queenie came up from Liverpool on the train that night with Clive.

Paul McCartney: We got a phone call. It was just like one of those phone calls. Brian's dead. Oh my God. You just sort of went pale and immediately sort of traipsed off to the Maharishi. We said, 'Our friend's dead. How do we handle this?' And he gave us practical advice, 'Nothing you can do. Bless him, wish him well, get on with life,' kind of thing. But we were very shocked and what added to it, as it always does with celebrities, the media want to know how you feel and it's always too quick. It's always too soon. You've got to try and put it into words after a lifetime's relationship with this guy. I always find that impossible. It's like music. You just can't talk about it. It's just too shocking.

We were all horrified and frightened by his death. It was a shock. We'd gone to Bangor with the Maharishi. This was the start of that phase for us and I think Brian was going to come along at some point. He was going to join us there.

I think John got particularly frightened. I remember sort of thinking that, well, we'll just have to carry on and we'll do it ourselves because that's how we were behaving in the studio. That was the technique to carry on.

Reading through some things that John felt and hearing some stuff, I think he thought, 'Right, this is it. This is the end. This is the end of the Beatles,' and it kind of was. We made a few more albums but we were sort of winding up. We always felt we'd come full circle and Brian's death was part of that.

Marianne Faithfull: It was agony to be with the Beatles with nobody else there. This was very unusual. Normally the Beatles had thousands of minders and Mal and Neil and Derek Taylor and everybody . But then it was simply John and Cynthia, Paul and Jane, Patti and George, Ringo and me and Mick. That was it. Of course, the Maharishi had millions of minders.

The minute the news came through that Brian had died, it was shameful the way the Maharishi exploited it. The Beatles were shattered. I can hardly bear to remember it. I think he actually said, 'Brian Epstein is dead. He was taking care of you. He was protecting you. He was like your father. I will be your father now.' These poor bastards just didn't know. It was the most terrible thing.

Gerry Marsden: I was actually at Anglesey, which is a little island off the coast of Wales. We didn't have a phone there. The farmer got a message, came to my place and said, 'Gerry, I have a message. Mr Brian Epstein's dead.' I said, 'What?' He said, 'Yes.' I said, 'No, you mean he's sick?' He said, 'No, Epstein is dead.' So I run to the phone and there was his doctor, Norman Cowan, who had rung me to tell me, and I was very shocked. The strange thing was that the Beatles were up there at Bangor, which was only ten miles from where I was, having toured the world and everything in between. But the day that Brian died, I was in Anglesey and they were in Bangor. Very strange. It was a very, very sad time.

Lonnie Trimble: It was a Sunday, Sunday, 27 August 1967. I had some theatre acquaintances to lunch and we were sitting drinking after lunch. A lodger was downstairs watching the news. Suddenly he rushes upstairs and says, 'Lonnie, switch on the television.' And of course my eyes popped out because I couldn't believe it. So I switched the television on and of course he was dead. And I cried, like other people that I knew had cried. And it was awful because I loved him, not sexually though.

Simon Napier-Bell: I think I arrived in Ireland on a Saturday or Sunday morning. I got a call from a friend saying that Brian had been found dead. I knew instinctively, immediately, that there would be a message on my answerphone. I just knew that he would have called me. And I went back to London and sure enough there were about four messages that were just sort of ordinary. They were like, 'I'm in the country. I'm bored and I wondered if you really had gone away.' Then there was a later one where his voice was a bit slurred as if he was sleepy or was drinking, and then another later one, but only that, nothing more than that. I had a feeling he'd got bored in the country and just come back to London and sat around and got drunk and wondered what to do. I'm sure he called other people too.

I don't remember what he said; he just rambled on about being affectionate and wanting somebody. It didn't have anything to do with me. It might have done in the sense he had an infatuation with me in his mind, but what he expressed in that infatuation probably related to somebody else who he'd had a much more serious involvement with at some previous time.

I know when I first heard the news I remember that it had something to do with me or that there was something connected between his death and the fact that he'd been calling me and saying please come down to the country. My first thought was he almost sort of did it deliberately, to show me that he meant it when he said come down to the country. But he was into playing games to such a degree that it could be the case that it was something to do with me. I didn't feel guilty. If he's living his life in that sort of silly way it would be up to him, but I felt it was to do with me and when I got back home and heard the messages I knew it was in some way to do with me.

I remember at the time having the classic symptoms of anyone who has a friend die of being incredibly angry. I was really pissed off with him. I was really angry because I'd had this dinner with him, which was fascinating, and I had a million more questions I wanted to ask him and there were a million things I was really interested in and so I was angry. I thought, 'Stupid sod, he's playing this silly game and now he's not around to talk to.' But I think that's quite a common reaction of anyone who has someone who dies.

I thought, 'What a selfish trick. Fancy doing that just to prove a point.' I felt like I'd opened up a newspaper, seen a riveting headline and had it snatched out of my hands before I could read the details. I wanted to spend more time with him. There was the whole story of the Beatles in his head and now he'd deprived me of it. I couldn't really believe he'd gone. He'd only met me last week.

Bryan Barrett: I was with an ex-army pal of mine in the New Forest. Suddenly he started flashing his headlights as we were getting towards Ringwood and he said, 'Epstein's dead, but I'm not sure whether they mean the sculptor.' I just caught the back end of this. I think he got it from a Bournemouth radio station or something.

I said, 'You're kidding.' He said, 'It might not be your boss,' and he was killing himself laughing. He actually thought it was funny. He thought he was winding me up. He didn't dream it'd be Brian Epstein 'cause he knew how young Brian Epstein was. I said, 'No, I'm going to check this out,' and I stopped at a couple of telephone boxes and finally got somebody. I can't remember who. I got someone who said, 'Brian's dead.' I just immediately spun around, packed up, and left.

I think I left two of the kids with my pal to bring back to London. Then I shot back as fast as I could and when I got to the house there was nobody there. I had keys and I wandered round the house. I couldn't believe it. I went upstairs and the bed was still unmade where he'd died. I suddenly started looking around and I realized the place had been hoovered. All his stuff was missing, small stuff, small items that usually hung around the house. I thought, 'Where the hell's all this gone?' So I thought I'd better ring Clive in case he thought I had it. It's just one of those situations where you think along the lines: protect your own backside.

Clive came down to London. I explained the situation to him and he didn't want to know. He didn't want any sort of fuss about it but it's damned annoying to think the old butler and his wife that were in the house were panicking like mad. They were staunch Catholics, I believe, and they had this thing about the spirit and suicide, which they said Brian's death was. They said, 'He's here.' I said, 'Well, were you in the house all night with him. What happened?' Antonio said the next night Peter Brown came and was wandering around all over the house. He said he and Maria never got a wink of sleep because Peter Brown was going through things, wandering around and round the house. It kept them up all night.

Nat Weiss: I got a call from Geoffrey Ellis saying I'm the first to know that Brian is dead, and I flew to London that night. The next day I met with his mother and the Beatles came over. They'd just returned from their visit to the Maharishi and were going into detail about Hindu philosophy. They were saying that Brian was really in a transitory stage at the time and wasn't dead. I don't know whether Mrs Epstein took to it too well, because she was still in a state of shock.

Joanne Petersen: Queenie was sitting in the drawing room and the Beatles came in and I think Cynthia went up and gave her a red rose. Nat was there, walking around, looking pretty distraught. Peter was there and I was there. And I remember thinking, 'These are all the people that Brian really loves and he's not here.' I got really tearful and started to cry.

George came and sat down next to me, sort of patted me, and said in his enigmatic way, 'He's OK. Nothing can hurt him now. You're just grieving for your own loss.' He'd just come back from the Maharishi and he was being very spiritual. The Beatles all sat with Queenie and it was a very moving time. I just felt so sad for Queenie and I felt so sad for the Beatles and I felt so sad for all of us. Most of all I felt so, so sad for Brian, because I really think he should have been there.

Rex Makin: On the Monday morning after the death was discovered on the Sunday, Clive rang me from London in a very disconsolate state and asked me could I come down and assist him. So I jumped on a plane from Speke, was met by the NEMS limousine at Heathrow, whisked to the house in Belgravia, which Brian had asked me to come and have a look at when I last saw him. There were his uncle and his cousins and they were in a terrible state of shock and disbelief. I made the necessary arrangements with the coroner's office. I made the necessary arrangements with Rabbi Nemeth of the new West End Synagogue because Rabbi Nemeth had been the minister at Green Bank Drive, where the Epsteins were connected. And we made the necessary arrangements for the body to be brought back in due course to Liverpool for burial.

Geoffrey Ellis: The inquest was held on Tuesday. I believe David Jacobs, the lawyer, had pulled a few strings and managed to get it brought forward as early as possible. The evidence given at the inquest, medical and otherwise, was given as to Brian's health, both physical and mental. The coroner gave his verdict of accidental death, which was a great relief, of course, to Brian's family, and indeed to all his friends. The coroner then released Brian's body for the funeral.

Lonnie Trimble: I went to the inquest afterwards and there were a hell of a lot of lies told at that inquest. I thought, 'Right, you better leave this alone.'

Geoffrey Ellis: After the inquest, a lot of us went up to Liverpool by train while Brian's body went in a hearse by road up to Liverpool. We went to Brian's family's house where his mother was, needless to say, distraught. The hearse was delayed on the road. Inevitably people tried to lighten the atmosphere by saying, 'Brian's even late for his own funeral,' because he did have a reputation for being late for meetings and business matters in the past. When it arrived we all set off for the Epstein's local synagogue, where the rabbi pronounced a blessing. Then all the women went back home and only the men went to the burial.

Gerry Marsden: I was invited to the funeral. It was very sad because his father Harry had just died and I had gone to Harry's funeral. I was losing a very, very dear friend and so was my wife Pauline. I was losing a man who had given me the career that I'd always wanted and still have because Brian Epstein got me records. Oh yes, the funeral was sad for me.

Geoffrey Ellis: I happened to be travelling in the car which belonged to NEMS, which was a black-windowed limousine which the Beatles had often used to travel to their performances. When we got to the gates of the cemetery, we had to stop while the gates were opened.

There was a factory opposite. People were looking out of the windows of the factory at the cortège arriving and they saw this black-windowed limousine. A lot of them imagined that the Beatles were in it, since it was known that this was the car the Beatles often used. They rushed out and surrounded the car.

Those of us in the car had to get out of the car to show them we were not the Beatles, and we walked into the cemetery. I should say that the Beatles themselves were not present. They had wishes to be present but Brian's mother and brother asked that they not come. It's obvious from our own experience of the black-windowed car that their presence would have provoked a sort of riot.

After the burial, prayers were said in the small Jewish chapel by a rabbi, who distressed all of us present by referring to Brian and his death as being symptomatic of the worst aspects of the 1960s youth revolution – drugs, excess. It was a very unhappy and unnecessary oration to have made. After that we travelled back to London.

Nat Weiss: The rabbi hardly knew Brian but he said something about him being a symbol of the malaise of his generation, which was amazing. How can a man who filled stadiums, who literally was the catalyst for the greatest musical event of the twentieth century, be treated as a malaise of his generation? It was such an unjust epitaph.

I think it was George Harrison, who couldn't go to the funeral because they didn't want any Beatles at the funeral, who gave me a sunflower. When everyone walked away from the grave, George wanted me to put the sunflower on his coffin, which I did do. And that was the end.

Paul McCartney: I think he went back to London looking for a bit of action, maybe found a bit, I don't know. Then went back to his house after having drunk a bit that evening, I would think, and took sleeping pills. My feeling is that he would wake up in the middle of the night – it's so easy to do – and think, 'Why am I not sleeping? I haven't had my sleeping pill.' Then in a drowsy state he thought he better take some more. That's my feeling as to what happened. That was certainly the feeling around the time. Since then it's become legendary and there's millions of rumours that he killed himself or he was killed.

Nat Weiss: There are many people who feel that he committed suicide. I believe that was certainly not true. Brian's death was accidental. It was accidental in the sense that he had taken Seconals in conjunction with alcohol unaware of the fact that he had taken the Seconals earlier that evening. In the end, that's fatal.

He certainly was in a very positive state of mind. I had spoken to him two days before and he was anything but suicidal. Unfortunately, he suffered an accidental death at the early age of thirty-two.

Alistair Taylor: I know that Brian didn't commit suicide and my proof is what was on that bedside table when I first walked into Brian's room after he died. There were about eight bottles of prescribed drugs with chemists' labels on. They were all half full and all the lids were screwed back on.

Now if you were going to commit suicide you don't just half do the job and screw the lids back on the bottles. That's why I have fought all these years with the argument that Brian didn't commit suicide. It was an accidental overdose. It's what the inquest said. Everything points to it being accidental. You know, his father had only died six weeks before. He's just had his mother down with him. And all this business of the pill bottles. That's not suicide.

It was a build-up of what he had been taking all along. That night I think he took one or two tablets more than he should have done. Basically it was the two substances in the particular pill – one was going through his system OK and one was building up. And just those couple too many did the trick.

George Martin: I don't believe he committed suicide. I know he was into a pattern of taking uppers and downers. He drank quite a bit and took further drugs in the middle of the night, four more sleeping pills but too many. I think it was just carelessness, to be honest.

Joanne Petersen: It's a very curious point. Harry had died six weeks before. Queenie came to London and stayed with Brian. He was very attentive and he cared a lot about her grief after losing Harry. So the idea that he would kill himself six weeks after Harry died, that he would do that to Queenie, just didn't seem possible. It didn't seem true to me. If it was suicide I can't imagine why he would have done that at that stage. After all, Queenie lost her son and her husband within six weeks.

Derek Taylor: It was an accidental death, as I insist on telling people. His social arrangements had gone wrong, people hadn't turned up. By the time he got to London, anyone who was anyone in London had fled to go to the country and in that muddle he died.

He died on a bad night, not a bad weekend.

Joanne Petersen: Some weeks after Brian died Clive asked me if I would go over to the house and maybe clear out some of the papers and stuff. I didn't want to go back to the house. The staff had gone by then and the house was empty. I walked in and I was in Brian's room. I was really spooked out about being in Brian's room. It was eerie. I felt Brian's presence.

All I wanted to do was get everything, put them in bags, get rid of it and just get out of the house. Then I found a book that I used to leave letters in for Brian to sign or he'd leave things in for me to sign. I opened the book and to my absolute horror I found the suicide notes, one to Queenie and one to Clive. Only they were dated some time much earlier, maybe six, seven, eight weeks before he died.

They were just one-page notes and I was really shocked about finding these. They said something to the effect of, 'Don't be sad. Don't be unhappy. I'm OK. Take good care of yourself. I love you.' They were very short.

It was much the same to both Queenie and Clive, just one-page notes in his very large, distinctive handwriting. They were brief and reassuring them that he was all right and for them not to be sad. Maybe he'd put them in there and forgotten, I don't know. It was odd that they were there. Maybe they'd been there ever since he had written them and then he never looked in that book again, never gone back to them.

So I think what had happened was that Brian had obviously been contemplating suicide. Then Harry died and he changed his mind. He couldn't do that to his mother.

I don't know that it was suicide when he died. But clearly it had been on his mind some time earlier than that. I called Peter and I was hysterical. I was really upset and I said, 'Something awful has happened. Please come to the house.' Peter came to the house and I gave him the notes.

Some years later I was up in Liverpool. Clive picked me up to go and see his mother. I asked, 'Did you ever get those notes?' He said he had but it was obvious from his reply that this was such a sensitive subject he didn't want to discuss it any more. I was relieved to know that Peter had passed them on.

Alistair Taylor: I sometimes feel – and it's a weird thing for me to say – that I would have been happier in one way if he had committed suicide. I'd have still been as upset but I think I would probably have said, 'Well, we knew he was going to do it one day.'

HM CORONER'S COURT

1	Name of deceased:	Brian Samuel EPSTEIN
2	Injury or disease causing death	Carbrital poisoning
3	Time, place and circumstances at or in which the injury was sustained:	At 3pm on Sunday 27th August 1967 at 24 Chapel Street, Westminster, sw1 was found dead in bed.
4	Conclusion of the coroner as to the death:	Unconscious self-overdosage. Accidental

15. Aftermath

Joanne Petersen: Things started to unhinge pretty quickly, almost immediately. It seemed to me that things became unstable very quickly. Brian was the glue. He held it all together and the moment he wasn't there it was like a rudderless ship. There was no one steering the ship.

Peter Brown: The balance had gone at NEMS. Although Brian hadn't been there on a day-to-day basis, his personality was there. So you had a situation where you had Clive, who was the heir and had never been inclined to be involved, and you had Robert Stigwood operating the company on a day-to-day basis, but who had never been involved in the management on a day-to-day basis of the Beatles or Cilla. It was a terrible problem about whether one should go.

Joan Peterson: Some days later there was a meeting at Hille House. I went there and Robert Stigwood arrived with his associates David Shaw and I think Vic Lewis. Clive was there. Peter Brown was there. Geoffrey was there. I remember they all arrived in very dark suits. It was like: the king is dead, who was going to take over? It was very much a meeting to see what was going to happen from now on, and I was horrified. Brian had just been buried and they were all there for the rich pickings called the Beatles. I thought it was a very sinister meeting.

The problem, of course, with that whole meeting was that the Beatles didn't want anyone else to run them. I mean, I don't think it was ever a consideration. I think it was always very evident from the moment Brian died that they would run themselves, certainly for the foreseeable future. So any ideas that those present at the meeting had that they would take over the Beatles I think were completely unfounded.

Geoffrey Ellis: After Brian died, Robert Stigwood quite naturally felt that he should make a pitch for managing the Beatles in Brian's stead. A week or two perhaps after Brian died, Stigwood asked for a meeting with the Beatles, which was arranged.

It was held in Brian's old private offices. There were present the four Beatles, Robert Stigwood, his associate David Shaw, Clive Epstein and myself.

Robert Stigwood spoke and said how fond he had been of Brian and how much he respected what Brian had done for the Beatles, how much he admired the Beatles themselves and that he believed that he could continue to guide their career in much the same way that Brian had done, that he would very much welcome the opportunity of doing so.

He probably spoke for about ten minutes or so, and at the end of Robert Stigwood's speech John Lennon and Paul McCartney both said, 'Well, no, I'm afraid not, Robert,' and that was the end of the meeting.

Robert Stigwood: Well, we were all in a state of shock. It wasn't the time to talk business. I can't remember who actually said, 'Let's meet in a few days and sit down.'

It was a really amazing meeting but we were all united to move forward. The proposal was that NEMS and Apple merge and a joint company be set up between us all. The Beatles would have 51 per cent and I would have 49 per cent. And we could not resolve that.

I think a week went by. I was very nervous with Apple. There was Paul's publishing and the clothes-shop money was really flowing out. I thought a joint company won't work unless I can control it. There's not £100,000 to spend every week. So I think we met every second day for a week or ten days and then decided to separate. Cream, the Bee Gees and other assets came with me. NEMS kept their artists. And we shook hands and I don't think we've ever had a cross word about it.

Peter Brown: It was a very peculiar time for the Beatles because they'd just got into the Maharishi situation and they were up to their eyes in this meditation stuff. I think John and George had completely believed it and I think Paul and Ringo to a much lesser degree did, but they were making an effort to believe it and I think that to some degree it cushioned them from the horror and the shock. They were able to fall back on what the Maharishi would advise but it was a terrible shock. Paul reacted in a predictable way of 'We must go on with business,' and he immediately went into structuring the *Magical Mystery Tour*.

George Martin: Brian's death was dreadful to everybody. I mean, it was actually shattering. No one could conceive that it would happen, and the boys were completely broken up by it. They were like a ship without a rudder for a while, and *Magical Mystery Tour*, which followed, was Paul's attempt to try and pull everybody together. It was a really tough time.

Alan Livingston: I was sad. I mean I felt badly. He was not a man that I felt had troubles or had any reason not to live and there were rumours about how he died. I didn't know what to believe and I thought it was just sad. And I missed dealing with him thereafter.

Peter Brown: After Brian died I looked after the Beatles on a day-to-day basis as I had been for quite a long time while Brian had not been active. I continued to do that until we restructured everything and Apple was formed and Neil [Aspinall] and I started to operate the Apple Companies.

With Brian no longer there, Paul started taking an active part in the continuation of the Beatles – and great that he did. John wasn't in good shape at that time. He was doing a lot of acid and was out of it a great deal.

When Apple was formed, it was formed to a large degree in Paul's likeness. Paul was the one who turned up every day. Paul was the one that helped to make the decisions. Paul was the one who formed the structure with Neil and myself kind of doing the work. At that point Derek Taylor was brought back from the US. So the whole thing was done in Paul's likeness. When John came back and wanted it changed, it did, but Paul took the lead in Brian's absence.

One of the most notorious figures in the American music business was a short, energetic accountant named Allen Klein. He was famous for his creative accounting skills that helped many bands, including the Rolling Stones, find hundreds of thousands of previously hidden dollars. He had been making overtures towards the Beatles for several years before Brian's death, letting them know their record deals could be a lot more lucrative. Brian knew about this and it caused him some anxiety.

George Martin: If Brian had lived there wouldn't have been the complications of management where you had two camps, you had the Allen Klein camp and you had Paul's camp. But the Beatles would have split up after a while anyway. It was quite remarkable that they lasted a decade together. It's pretty tough staying together when you have that kind of degree of success and you want your own life.

Gerry Marsden: When Brian died we split because Brian held us together. We missed him.

It affected a lot of us. NEMS didn't become anything. The guys who tried to look after us, we just didn't have the same love for them as we did for Brian.

Derek Taylor: Had he lived, Brian might have been more decisive and more tenacious and seen the Beatles through a lot of the things that no one else could. John has a famous quote, 'We've fucking had it now,' and, to the extent that they did break up, that's true.

Marianne Faithfull: I was absolutely fucking flabbergasted. To me that was the beginning of the end. It went on and on and on, the horror, the horror, the horror. It didn't stop.

That was just the beginning, and it ended for me in the overdose in Australia, which was the ultimate nightmare. I'm pretty unscathed but not as unscathed as I seem. One of the things that has happened is that I've actually completely obliterated nearly all the happiness and the hope that was connected with Brian and with those times.

The whole thing just changed us and it began with Brian's death, and nobody meant that to happen. The Beatles were just fucking around, really, with the Maharishi, that's all. Brian was much more than a brilliant businessman. He was a spiritual centre. So I think what happened with the Maharishi was a betrayal of spiritual values, or that's how it must have appeared to Brian. If he had met the Maharishi, he would have seen immediately that this idiotic little guy wasn't going to be able to take his place. I think everybody realized that from the minute they met him.

Brian would have had no problem talking to the Beatles about the Maharishi. Here's what would have happened if he hadn't taken the overdose: they would come back to London and Brian would have said, 'How was it?' and they would have all cracked up laughing as if it was the most ridiculous thing. The trouble with him dying at that moment was that it actually pushed them into the arms of the Maharishi, whereas if he hadn't died, it would have blown over. The Maharishi was the most ludicrous little man you could imagine. Everybody realized this and we were all embarrassed.

Brian might have teased them later, but he would have realized this. He had an incredible antenna for sensing things. If he had been there in London when they got back from Wales and answered the phone in his silk dressing gown when John or Paul rang, the Beatles would not have gone to India and all these things would not have happened.

Lionel Bart: For a year after he died, whenever I came back to the West End, I always stopped by Brian's house. I'd automatically stop there for a long time and I'd have to tell myself, 'No, he's not there any more.'

For a long time his house was a port of call. The sixties was kind of an open house for most people but there were a few people you could really drop in on day and night. Brian was one of those people. Brian was one of the routes home.

Paul McCartney: Brian's death kind of opened the floodgates. It gave other people the possibility to come in whereas there had been no possibility before. The gates had been firmly shut and it was only Brian you ever dealt with. So other people started to arrive and say, 'Hey, I'll manage you.'

I think one of two of the other guys were quite enamoured of some of these other people, particularly Allen Klein.

I'd never liked the idea, partly because I'd seen how Brian did it and no one else was going to stack up against Brian in my mind. No one would ever be able to do it as good because you couldn't have the flare, the panache, the wit, the intelligence Brian had. Anyone else would just merely be a money manager.

Brian was far more than that. So people did get an opportunity to come in and make approaches but they were destined not to work because Brian was just too good.

Index

Index

Index